Living Through the Generations

Living Through the Generations

Continuity and Change in Navajo Women's Lives

Joanne McCloskey

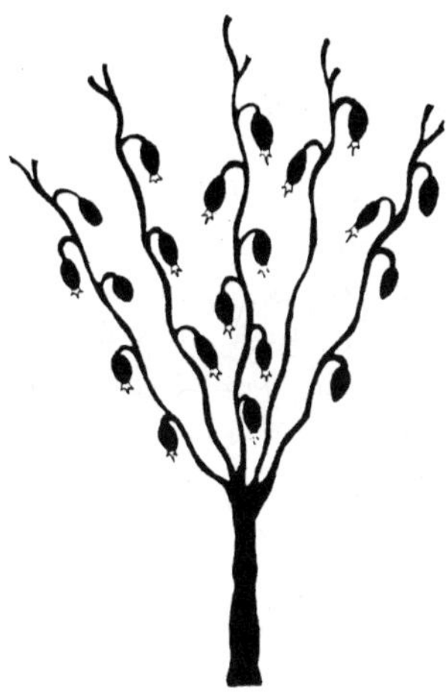

The University of Arizona Press

Tucson

The University of Arizona Press

Library of Congress Cataloging-in-Publication Data
McCloskey, Joanne
Living through the generations : continuity and change in Navajo women's lives / Joanne McCloskey.
p. cm.
Includes bibliographical references and index.
ISBN-13: 978-0-8165-2578-2 (hardcover : alk. paper)
ISBN-10: 0-8165-2578-1 (hardcover : alk. paper)
ISBN-13: 978-0-8165-2631-4 (pbk. : alk. paper)
ISBN-10: 0-8165-2631-1 (pbk. : alk. paper)
1. Navajo women—New Mexico—Crownpoint—Kinship. 2. Navajo women—New Mexico—Crownpoint—Social conditions. 3. Navajo women—New Mexico—Crownpoint—Economic conditions. 4. Crownpoint (N.M.)—History. 5. Crownpoint (N.M.)—Social life and customs. I. Title.
E99.N3D555 2007
305.48'89726078983—dc22
2006023546

Publication of this book is made possible in part by the proceeds of a permanent endowment created with the assistance of a Challenge Grant from the National Endowment for the Humanities, a federal agency.

Manufactured in the United States of America on acid-free, archival-quality paper containing a minimum of 50% post-consumer waste and processed chlorine free.

12 11 10 09 08 07 6 5 4 3 2 1

If you have children, never say that you are poor.
Children will give you children, grandchildren.
You live through the generations—that's what they tell us.
—Ellen Mitchell (pseudonym)

To the women of Crownpoint,

who taught me not only about

Navajo cultural traditions and values

but also about

living life with dignity, strength,

and purpose.

Contents

Illustrations

Living Through the Generations

I

Introduction

On a cold November day, I accompanied ninety-four-year-old Jane Jim; her son, Raymond; and Bonnie Yazzie, to the Jims' land and former home in the Whitehorse area east of Crownpoint. To the north was what my guides referred to as White Face Mesa (Chaco Mesa on the map), and to the south were hills that stair step up to Mount Taylor, one of the four sacred mountains that borders Navajo land. Jane Jim lived here as a child and later moved back with her children after her husband left for World War II.

On this land, Jane, her mother, and stepfather herded sheep, wove rugs, and raised crops: squash, corn, pumpkins, watermelon, cantaloupe, green beans, and pinto beans. They irrigated the crops with rainwater and stored much of the harvest for winter. The pumpkins, watermelon, squash, and cantaloupe were stored in a hole in the ground, whereas the pinto beans and some corn were stored in bags. Corn, the mainstay of the diet, was also dried on racks or ground up to cook in numerous dishes. For a second income, Jane periodically worked for the German trader and his wife who operated the trading post in Whitehorse, a few miles to the east. Even in snowstorms, she rode her horse to the trading post to do domestic work for the couple.

Jane described how she cared for the sheep.

> I had quite a big herd, probably about three hundred at times. You have to find the right ram so that the lambs will grow up fast. When they were having trouble giving birth, I would help by pulling out the forelegs and then gently pull out the head. Then

> sometimes they would abandon the lambs, and I would have to tie them up and be sure the abandoned ones got fed.
>
> When the lambs got a little bigger, then it's shearing time. I used to go ask my relatives to help. I would get four big bags full. I would take them to the trader and sell them. (11/8/96)

Jane showed us her weaving tools, a batten and comb that were made from a hard cottonwood that grows nearby. "I got it against the mesas," she told me. "It takes root in rocky areas, and the wood gets extra hard." Jane wove rugs throughout the year. "It doesn't matter whether it was cold or hot. It was my second income. Even though I had a job, I would let it [the loom] stand there and come home and weave." I did most of my weaving during the summer," Jane explained, "because the sheep were not as difficult to herd because they had grass and water. In between my weaving I went to the fields" (11/8/96).

In the storage room adjacent to their frame house, which was built in 1952, Raymond found remnants of two saddle blankets that Jane had woven. Excitedly, she examined the designs in order to remember how they were woven. After analyzing the structure of the weave in one of the old blankets, she planned how to set up a warp to weave a double-sided saddle blanket.

Later in the afternoon, we drove across the former agricultural field, a slightly depressed basin the size of a football field, to a hogan built out of yellow stone from a nearby mesa. As the sun started to set, I imagined their lifestyle in this beautiful spot. Jane remembered the hard work involved.

> Hard work is what made me have a lot of good sheep. I had to work hard to raise my family. I worked at the trading post. I worked hard to buy food. I rode to work on a horse, and I herded sheep on a horse. They were trained to round them up, feed them, and water them.
>
> Even when it was snowing very badly, I still managed to work. With my three children, I struggled. I considered myself poor, and the man I was with was poor. He had to go far away to find

> work. I used to do a lot of hard physical labor, like chopping wood. (11/8/96)

While Jane labored at home and supplemented her income by working for the nearby trader, her husband sought wage-earning opportunities off-reservation. Still weaving and spinning wool at ninety-four, Jane wove rugs almost until the time of her death less than a year after I interviewed her.

In their life histories, Navajo women reveal the multiple factors shaping their lives that lead to both continuity and change. Navajo women respond to historical, social, cultural, and economic factors in their lives, but not passively. In their histories of education, work, and relationships with men, and in their family lives, they document their ability to develop strategies beneficial to themselves and their families. Women actively strategize to shape their lives, negotiating among complex realities to find new solutions while preserving their cultural identity.

As Peter Iverson (2002) emphasizes for all Navajos, the response to harmful policies and actions of outsiders from the time of early contact to the present has been to incorporate new elements in innovative, productive ways. Navajo women repeatedly demonstrate this pattern by building on strengths drawn from Navajo culture and society and creating new cultural strategies. In spite of federal policies that often targeted Navajo men and ignored women's egalitarian position in Navajo society and their contribution to the family economy, Navajo women seized opportunities in education, employment in the cash economy, and entrepreneurship in the informal economy to contribute to the support of their families.

Two recent ethnographies about Native American women demonstrate that Navajo women were not alone in being subjected to profound change in the twentieth century or in their resilience and determination to maintain their identity and culture. Lillian Ackerman (2003), in her study of gender equality on the Colville Reservation in Washington state, outlines the history of land loss and loss of food resources when Plateau people were restricted to reservations. When Colville Reservation people became poor compared to both their white neighbors and their own former well-being in their traditional economy, they were taught by mothers and grandmothers to endure in the face of poverty. Ackerman asserts that "Women's economic activities were critical to survival in the early reservation years, especially as the men were prevented from hunting and fishing in quantity due to control by the State of Washington. I believe it was because of their key role in survival that Plateau women never lost egalitarian status in their own society" (2003, 32).

Ackerman insists that gender equality is only one indication of cultural persistence despite the pressure for acculturation. Another persistent trait, often cited for the Navajo, is the Colville people's readiness to incorporate innovations that enhance the culture.

Tressa Berman (2003) emphasizes the centrality of Mandan, Hidatsa, and Arikara women living on the Fort Berthold Reservation in North Dakota. When the Garrison Dam was built on the Missouri River, the Mandan, Hidatsa, and Arikara lost their fertile bottomlands and their traditional horticulture-based way of life. In resettled communities, Fort Berthold women retain kin networks. "Women's kin networks serve as the vehicle for reconstructing 'old time' family arrangements that have continuing, if tenuous, ties to their common land-based community" (Berman 2003, 19). Fort Berthold women participate in wage work and social and ceremonial life through their sewing, beading, and cooking in preparation for ceremonies and feasts. In addition, they transmit traditional knowledge to children in their roles as mothers.

These two studies highlight the strengths of Native American women who daily confront the aftermath of imposed change and the loss of traditional lifestyles. These women must deal with contemporary issues such as discrimination, poverty, and alcoholism. Meanwhile, they seek the benefits of education, wage work, and modern technology. In such situations, these women respond with individual agency and cultural strategies to merge elements of mainstream culture and valued cultural traditions.

In discussions of various aspects of Navajo women's lives, I will explore their agency, purposeful actions of theirs designed to adapt to and alter both limiting constraints and promising opportunities. Their life-course experiences reveal "people both gripped by circumstances and transforming them" (Ortner 1999, 11). An emphasis on women's agency will illuminate "the complex motives and complex debates that are the stuff of real lives and struggles" (Ortner 1999, 11). Navajo women's decisions and choices reflect personal initiative mediated by the progressively more influential presence of Western goods, institutions, and programs.

Western influences constitute undeniably powerful factors that shape Navajo women's lives. Nevertheless, despite their disparity in age, the three generations of Navajo women—grandmothers, midlife mothers, and young mothers—often share common cultural strategies that have withstood the changes brought about by definitive twentieth-century historical events. The differences in life history experiences among the three generations of women in large part arise from the inescapable influence of the historical period in which they grew up and reached adulthood, whereas similarities arise from tenacious cultural values and attitudes. In the context of historical change, Navajo women's lives display patterns of both cultural continuity and cultural change.

Research in Crownpoint, New Mexico

Crownpoint, New Mexico, offers an ideal location for studying the effects of twentieth-century change on Navajo women's lives. Crownpoint lies in the northwest corner of New Mexico, 135 miles northwest of Albuquerque. Crownpoint is a transitional community in which families may live either in town or in rural areas but divide their time and allegiance between rural family relatives, home, land, and livestock, and services, agencies, and jobs in town. As an administrative center, Crownpoint served a population of 10,000 in 1990 (Etsitty 1994). Crownpoint's population grew from 1,134 in 1980, to 2,108 in 1990 (Technical Support Department, Navajo Nation 1988; Etsitty 1994), to 2,906 in 2000 (Choudhary 2003).

Crownpoint, the headquarters of the Eastern Navajo Agency, is one of five administrative centers in the Navajo Nation. Navajos living in the area work in administrative centers at "jobs with the BIA [Bureau of Indian Affairs] or the Navajo Tribe and with private retail establishments such as trading posts, garages, etc. On the whole these jobs were stable and full-time. On average, people in administrative centers could reach the homes of their rural relatives more easily than could people in towns, both to help

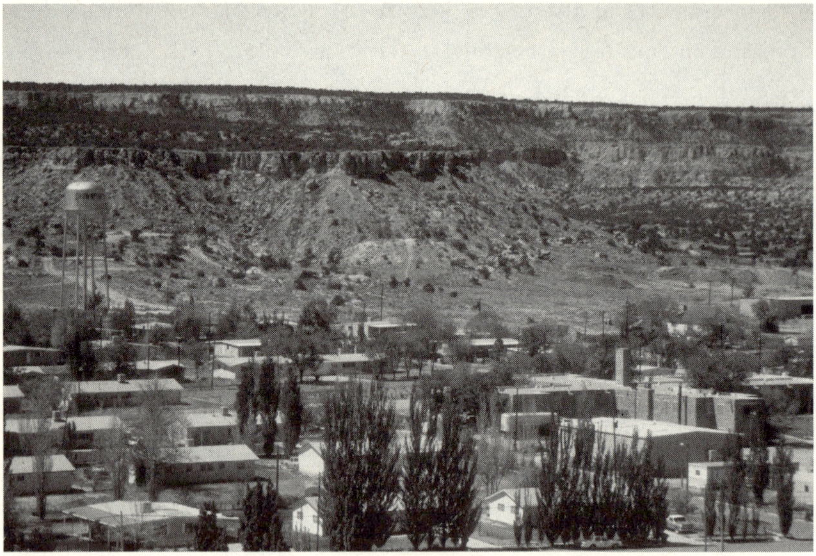

A view of Crownpoint from a mesa east of town.

them and to receive help in such matters as ceremonies" (Aberle 1989, 409). Besides job accessibility, residence in Crownpoint offers convenient access to children's schools, health care, modern housing, and limited shopping.

Situated 8.5 miles east of the official boundary of the Navajo Reservation, Crownpoint, New Mexico, is located in the Checkerboard Area, where Navajos own individually allotted land issued in the early twentieth century (Iverson 2002; Young 1961). Interspersed with Navajo land is privately owned and federal land, such as that administered by the Bureau of Land Management and the National Park Service. The entire Eastern Navajo Agency consists of six land management districts further divided into thirty-one chapters, each of which has elected officials. Crownpoint is located in Land Management District 15, which consists of ten chapters.

Beginning as the site of the original BIA boarding school and hospital, Crownpoint became the headquarters for BIA administrative offices and tribal agencies such as the district court and jail. Among other tribal agencies present in Crownpoint are the Senior Citizens Center, the Navajo Preschool, the Youth Crisis Center, Elderly Home Care Services, and the

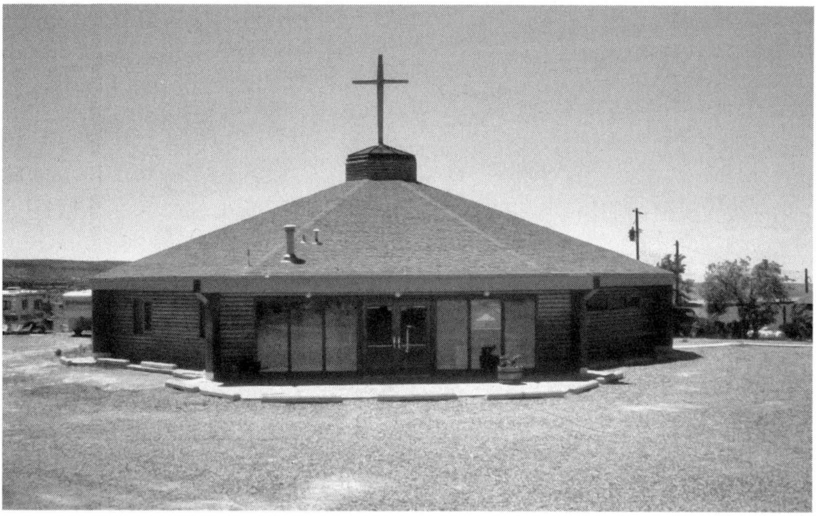

The Catholic Church in Crownpoint. The church is built like a hogan with door facing to the east and with four stained glass windows in the cardinal directions depicting the four sacred Navajo mountains.

chapter's Public Employment Program, which offers ten- and twenty-day jobs. Schools located in Crownpoint are the BIA Crownpoint Community School and Gallup–McKinley County public elementary, middle, and high schools. The Crownpoint Institute of Technology is a vocational school that serves the entire Navajo Reservation. The Crownpoint campus of Diné College (formerly Navajo Community College) offers a curriculum for students working toward associate degrees.

Christian denominations represented in Crownpoint include Assembly of God, Christian Reformed, Mormon, Baptist, and Roman Catholic. Some Christian churches in the Crownpoint area have gained adherents by adapting to Navajo culture. Among those who attend the Crownpoint Catholic Church are local medicine men. The church is constructed in the shape of a large hogan, with the entrance facing east. Stained glass windows aligned with the four directions depict each of the Navajo sacred mountains. On a platform to the west, a table supported by legs of rocks from the sacred mountain faces the pews. Consistent with the church itself, the priests and sisters in Crownpoint respect Navajo traditions and ceremonies. According to a former priest, Father Tom Manion, "The Catholic Church has never demanded that they have to give up their customs" (1/5/96). Besides having a shape like a hogan, which makes parishioners feel at home, the church has stations-of-the-cross in the form of sand paintings. Father Tom read the Scriptures in Navajo and burned cedar instead of incense at funerals.

In contrast to the tolerant views of the Catholics, "the new Protestantism movement," in the fundamental and evangelical tradition, fiercely opposes Navajo ceremonial traditions. Yet these evangelical groups emphasize healing, as do Navajo ceremonies. Many of these Pentecostal churches have Navajo pastors, charismatic individuals with little or no formal training (Pavlik 1997). Thus, in spite of the demand that Navajo adherents forego attendance at traditional ceremonies and do away with their medicine bundles, the presence of Navajo pastors and emphasis on healing contribute to the growing number of adherents.

Crownpoint residents do much of their shopping in the closest urban areas, Gallup and Grants, both of which are an hour's drive away. With the opening of the Crownpoint Shopping Center in February 1989, residents now have a full-service grocery store. Also in town are a gas station, two laundromats, a movie rental store, and two convenience stores.

Many visitors to Crownpoint come for the rug auction, a regular event since 1968. Now a monthly event at Crownpoint Elementary School that draws weavers from throughout the reservation and buyers from throughout the United States and beyond, the auction offers hundreds of rugs sold at prices that the weavers rate as poor to fair.

Introduction to the Crownpoint Community

At the invitation of a supervisor in a local office, I began interviewing his female staff in February 1988. The supervisor assured me that "Navajo culture is alive and well." I soon realized that the Navajo women in this office were privileged to have stable jobs with benefits and opportunities for training and advancement in a community with a high unemployment rate. Overwhelmingly, the staff consisted of midlife women who

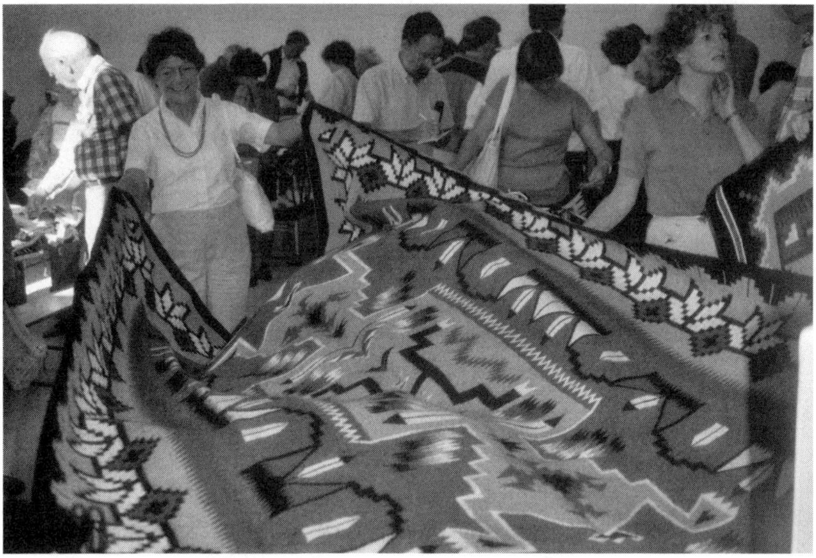

Previewing rugs at the Crownpoint Rug Auction, a monthly event held at the Crownpoint Elementary School.

reached adulthood in the 1960s and 1970s, when education, training, and jobs first became available for Navajo women. After graduating from high school, they took advantage of opportunities to obtain training in a business school in a distant urban center before returning to the reservation to find a job. Because they held their jobs throughout the years they were raising their children, these women had long work histories.

As I got to know the women in the office, I asked if their mothers, grandmothers, sisters, and friends would be interested in participating in my study of three generations of Navajo women, which emphasized motherhood, family, and childbearing patterns. Through these contacts, I began interviewing grandmothers, unemployed midlife mothers, and young mothers, as well as other employed midlife women. Two bilingual women in the office acted as interpreters during interviews with Navajo speakers, one for her mother and one for her grandmother. In the pages that follow, I quote from the resulting interviews and indicate their dates within parentheses.

After unsuccessfully trying to find a place to live in Crownpoint, in September I moved a small, twenty-three-foot trailer into a local trailer park, where I spent part of each week for the next fifteen months. Since my son Eric, eleven, and my daughter Laurel, seven, were resistant to moving to Crownpoint because both were involved in school and other activities at home in Albuquerque, we decided that they would stay at home with their father. I was close enough to respond to any emergency. Toward the end of the school year in 1989, my husband called to say, "Eric broke his arm." With that startling news, I immediately left for home and cancelled some appointments for interviews the next day. The trailer, a convenient and private setting, proved to be a preferred location for interviews. Living in Crownpoint gave me the opportunity to visit with women in the community as well as participate in local activities such as eating lunch at the Senior Citizen's Center, attending Foster Grandparents' workshops, and watching Headstart performances with children dressed in traditional outfits.

Bonnie Yazzie, a thirty-two-year-old mother I interviewed, agreed to be my interpreter for monolingual Navajo women or women who spoke English but preferred to have certain questions explained in Navajo. A lifelong resident of the Crownpoint area, Bonnie knew many members of the community. She was also a skilled, tactful interpreter, able to use good judgment and exercise diplomatic caution in dealing with sensitive topics. For instance, to gather part of a woman's reproductive history, I asked about miscarriages, abortions, stillbirths, and deceased infants. Because Navajo beliefs prohibit talking about the dead or speaking the names of the deceased, women hesitated to voice the names of infants or children who had died. To avoid asking for such names, Bonnie asked in Navajo, "Were there any infants who were conceived and did not live long?" If so, she asked if they were male or female and what their birth order was.

Through Bonnie, I met her mother, Loretta C. Benally, whose wealth of traditional knowledge guided discussions and wording of questions. For example, she referred to the meaning of stillborn in Navajo as "the one who has not spoken yet" and warned that one must be very careful when talking about stillborns because they have very powerful spirits. Initially, Loretta was hesitant to talk to me, suspicious that I was in some way connected to the Hopi and involved in the relocation of Navajos from Navajo-Hopi partitioned land. Loretta turned out to be a staunch ally not only in sharing the story of her life and detailed information about Navajo childbirth, traditional weddings, and the Kinaaldá, the girls' puberty ceremony but also for recruiting women for me to interview.

Through Loretta and Bonnie, I met the majority of grandmothers and midlife mothers who worked in the informal economy. Loretta called me *schich'é'é nez*, my tall daughter, and became indignant when consultants were not as forthcoming as she thought they should be. When a grandmother did not reveal that she had carried a stillborn whose father was not the man she later married, Loretta said, "If they are being interviewed, they should tell everything."

Four Groups of Navajo Women

My sample included four groups of Navajo women: (1) thirty grandmothers beyond childbearing age, (2) fifteen midlife mothers in their thirties and forties who worked in the labor force, (3) sixteen midlife mothers in their thirties and forties who worked in the informal economy, and (4) sixteen young mothers in their teens and twenties. Embedded in the sample are two extended family clusters, whose members I got to know well. By participating in extended family activities such as births, weddings, funerals, graduations, and Navajo ceremonies, I gained insights unavailable from life history interviews. I learned about family plans and conflicts, and about extended family members' cooperative networks. When one sister's home smelled of gas from an old stove, for example, another sister bought her a new stove, expecting to be repaid in installments. I participated in these extended family networks by providing rides, passing on outgrown children's clothes and books, and contributing cash and food to ceremonies and funerals.

Because I interviewed women who met the criteria for each of the four groups, the sample constitutes a purposeful one designed to find information-rich cases (Patton 2002). The seventy-seven Navajo women ranged in age from eighteen years to approximately ninety-three years at the time of the interviews. Most women were articulate and open when talking about their lives, attitudes, and values, with the exception of some young mothers, who were more hesitant and shy.

The women in the sample came from all District 15 chapters in the Eastern Navajo Agency, plus additional areas in the Eastern Agency. District 15 includes the following chapters: Becenti, Crownpoint, Nahodishgish, Lake Valley, Little Water, Standing Rock, Torreon/Star Lake, Pueblo Pintado, Whitehorse Lake, and White Rock. Many of the women who now live in Crownpoint grew up in surrounding areas and often visit relatives still living in the rural chapters. Women who do not live in town need to go to Crownpoint, where they may have a post office box, keep clinic appointments at the Crownpoint Indian Health Service (IHS), do business with various agencies, shop at the Crownpoint Shopping Center, or wash their laundry. Also, employed women may commute to town daily from a rural area.

Among the most gratifying experiences I have had in Crownpoint has been teaching at Diné College between 1998 and 2000, and again in 2005, as a social science instructor. I have taught classes in anthropology, sociology, political science, Indians of North America, and Navajo history. The Diné College program requires courses in Navajo culture, language, and history, as well as basic classes to prepare students to earn a bachelor's degree in a four-year institution. At this small branch campus, a nucleus of earnest, involved students set the tone for an enthusiastic learning atmosphere. Two women, whom I interviewed in 1988 and 1989, were outstanding students pursuing their associate degrees and planning to continue their educations. Both women typify the norm for many Navajo students in that they are older and have returned to school after marrying and having children.

Following the ethnographic practice of protecting the anonymity of consultants, I gave each of the women I interviewed a pseudonym. However, I later learned that many grandmothers preferred to be identified by their real names, in recognition of their knowledge of Navajo culture. They are proud of their roles as guardians of cultural traditions and have a strong desire to educate young people about "the Navajo Way." When I then asked several of the midlife women if they wanted to have their names used, they told me they did not. Thus, based on the original understanding that names would not be used, the remainder of the women, with few exceptions, are identified with pseudonyms.

According to the research protocol in existence at the time I conducted the study, I received approval from the University of New Mexico Arts and Sciences Institutional Review Board and conferred with the Crownpoint Chapter president, Charles Long, about the research project.

The average number of interviews was two for each woman, but the overall number ranged from one to four. The majority in the initial group of women were interviewed in a local office three times, twice in the spring of 1988 and once for a follow-up interview in the spring of 1990. At the beginning of an initial interview, I stated that I could either tape-record or take notes. About one-half of the women agreed to be tape-recorded, whereas the other half preferred that I take notes. The grandmothers asked not to be tape-recorded more often than the midlife mothers and young mothers. One woman explained why some individuals object to being tape-recorded. "In the Navajo way, they say that if your voice is recorded, they can take it to another country. It can be written down. It is taboo. My mother was talking about it yesterday. I would be more comfortable with notes" (5/24/88).

Besides the three generations of Navajo women that fulfilled the research design, I also interviewed women who worked in agencies that offered services to women and children. These community interviews added valuable insights on the needs and issues that confront Navajo women. Among the IHS personnel in Crownpoint, I interviewed a doctor, a social worker, and two nurses. Among the personnel in local tribal agencies, I interviewed the Eastern Navajo Agency district judge, the children's court judge, the director of the Women, Infants, and Children's program, and a counselor for the Navajo Nation Family Planning Program. In Window Rock, headquarters for the Navajo Nation, I interviewed the director of the Office of Navajo Women and Families. Also, I interviewed the district representative to the New Mexico State Legislature, who lived and worked in Crownpoint. She identified as issues of concern teenage pregnancy, the need for child care facilities, and child abuse and neglect.

Motherhood in a Matrilineal Society

The centrality of motherhood in Navajo thought and belief systems arises from three major cultural domains: relationships defined by matrilineal social organization, gender ideology modeled on revered female deities, and women's significant economic contribution to the family. As a powerful symbol, Navajo motherhood is culturally constructed by interlocking, reinforcing concepts shared by all members of society. Through the act of giving birth, Navajo women bestow membership in a matrilineal clan. And just as the beloved and honored Navajo deity, Changing Woman ('Asdzą́ą́ Nádleehé), nurtured, protected, and guided her sons, the Hero Twins, Navajo mothers devote themselves to the well-being of their children. Women as well as men expect to work in order to support their families.

Motherhood, the central symbol of Navajo social organization (Witherspoon 1975), directly links matrilineal clan members through the act of giving birth. Clan membership is transmitted through mothers, creating a multigenerational clan segment headed by the senior living female. Thus, a matrilineal clan segment may include a great-grandmother, her children, her daughters' children, and her granddaughters' children. An individual also identifies with his or her father's clan, the "born for" clan, but membership in the mother's clan is the one passed on through the generations. When grandmothers were asked, "How many grandchildren do you have?" they responded by distinguishing between those grandchildren born to their daughters and those born to their sons. Referred to as maternal grandchildren, children of their daughters represent the perpetuation of their clan, whereas paternal grandchildren, children of their sons, have the primary clan affiliation of their sons' wives. The continuity of the extended family depends on mothers whose fecundity generates new clan members.

Not only does a matrilineal society modify the parenting roles of mothers and fathers, it also has implications for single mothers who raise children. Replacing the Western conception of the female-headed family as weak and dysfunctional is the perception of the single mother in a matrilineal society as strong and capable (Fast 2002; Watson-Franke 1993).

In the traditional, matrilineal, matrilocal extended family, the absence of a Navajo father promoted the development of strong bonds between children and other male family members. In multigenerational residence groups, grandfathers and uncles nurtured and guided children who did not have fathers. In contemporary Navajo families, grandfathers and uncles are less likely to be coresident, but strong extended family ties still ease the effect of a divorce or separation. Even in nuclear families, single mothers raise their children in strong, functional family units. Resourceful Navajo mothers carry on the examples of mothers, grandmothers, and aunts, women empowered by a matrilineal ideology of independence and autonomy.

Associated with the concrete social system of matrilineal clan relationships is the Navajo cosmological system, which originates in the Navajo creation story. In societies with prominent female deities, women have high levels of status and power and their creative abilities are respected (Sanday 1981). Knowledge of Changing Woman is essential to an understanding of Navajo motherhood. Raised by First Man and First Woman, Changing Woman had the first Kinaaldá performed for her by the Holy People at the time of her first menstrual period. The Kinaaldá ceremony celebrated her ability to bear children. Fathered by the Sun, her sons, Monster Slayer and Born-for-Water, made the earth safe for humans when they killed the monsters that roamed the earth. Changing Woman, the Sun, and their twin sons "form a sort of 'holy family' " (Wyman 1983, 539).

Changing Woman is further associated with the earth, the seasonal cycle of life, and the power of the earth to provide food for her children. She sustains vegetation with female rain, the gentle steady rain that nourishes crops. As an encompassing symbol of motherhood, Changing Woman is identified with reproduction, sustenance, and nurturance. Witherspoon states, "Changing woman or Earth woman is called mother. Agricultural fields are called mother. Livestock are called mother. Changing woman is in charge of female rain and all vegetation" (1975, 60). Changing Woman acts as a role model for all Navajo women and as the central symbol of motherhood.

Ruth Roessel, in *Women in Navajo Society* (1981), identified principles from stories and ceremonies about Changing Woman that apply to motherhood and mothering. "Changing Woman kept a good and happy home, with adequate food which sometimes was supplied by others" (1981, 41). Changing Woman, a "single mother," counseled with her children, Monster Slayer and Born-for-Water, and taught them many skills such as "how to race, how to shoot the bow and arrow, how to approach danger, how to get help" (1981, 41). When they were in a dangerous situation, she helped them or got help for them. She provided protection and security for them while they were growing up and passed on the teachings that the Holy People had taught her. Her sons, in turn, learned to take responsibility, maintained a strong sense of identity, and grew up to be independent, resourceful adults. Changing Woman personifies the ideal Navajo woman by her steadfast, purposeful behavior in maintaining a home and in her compassion and care for her sons.

Changing Woman embodies the Navajo cultural construct of motherhood. By having a Kinaaldá at menarche, Navajo girls follow in the footsteps of Changing Woman when she celebrated her future potential as a mother. By giving birth to and raising her sons, Changing Woman demonstrated the ideal relationship of a mother to her children. "The relationship of Changing Woman to her children provides the major conceptual framework for the Navajo cultural definition of motherhood" (Witherspoon 1975, 15). Motherhood is defined by the acts of giving and sustaining life to create strong bonds of solidarity. The strong and close mother-child bond serves as a model for the enduring relations of kinship.

Early Indicators of Factors That Shape Navajo Women's Lives

Early on, I became aware of pieces to the puzzle that would later begin to answer some of my questions about women's roles in Navajo society. Immediately apparent among virtually all persons with whom I came in contact was their strong identity with Navajo culture. Whether they considered themselves traditional, modern, or somewhere in-between, their cultural identity was firmly rooted in Navajo history, land, language, clan, extended family, and various traditional practices. Traditional subsistence patterns relied on livestock and agriculture while living in hogans, traveling in wagons, and eating a diet of corn dishes, wild plant foods, and mutton. The new wage labor economy accompanied by living in frame houses, driving cars and trucks, and eating foods purchased in grocery stores and fast-food restaurants has dramatically altered the Navajo lifestyle but not core Navajo values and beliefs.

Even education, employment in professional positions, or membership in a Christian church leaves room for cultural beliefs, values, and practices. In fact, a dichotomy or even a continuum between traditional and modern failed to be useful for categorizing women's cultural orientation. For instance, women who did not have a Kinaaldá at puberty, a frequent indicator of traditionality, now arrange to have the ceremony for their daughters or granddaughters. One midlife mother, who did not have a Kinaaldá as a girl, later had one for her own daughter and was planning a ceremony for her granddaughter. She explained, "When I was growing up, I went to a Protestant church. It was a must. I don't go to church now. I have a lot of respect for Navajo religion and the Blessing Way sings. When I was young, I didn't have a Kinaaldá because at that time my parents didn't participate in traditional religion. When my dad was sick, I got into ceremonies before he died, about 1961. Now I use medicine men" (2/26/88). This mother's participation in traditional ceremonies and activities as an adult illustrates the mixture of practices engaged in by individuals, making it difficult if not meaningless to categorize them as traditional or modern.

In addition to maintaining their cultural identity, Navajo women's employment patterns offered a clue to Navajo women's confidence and high stature in Navajo society. At lunch one day, Bonnie and I talked with her cousin, who worked for the Headstart program in Crownpoint. She observed that she saw a lot of role reversal among Headstart employees, in the sense that often women worked while their husbands stayed home. Ruth Roessel, the respected Navajo educator, made a similar observation in her keynote address at the Eastern Navajo Agency Women's Conference when she stated, "The mother may be the only breadwinner. We got a job; we went to school for it, and we got it" (Ruth Roessel 1991).

Employment statistics confirm this observation of gender-biased employment opportunities in Crownpoint. In 1991, the total number of Navajo females employed in the Crownpoint community was 1,363, whereas the total number of employed males was 845 (Etsitty 1994). Because there are fewer local job opportunities for men, they must seek employment away from the reservation. For instance, one midlife mother worked in a permanent position with the BIA while her husband, a union member, worked intermittently, often at out-of-state jobs.

The Navajo women who were employed and in their thirties and forties at the time I interviewed them benefited from job opportunities resulting from Crownpoint's growth as an administrative center. They all graduated from high school, an opportunity made possible in the late 1950s and 1960s by the major expansion of school facilities for Navajo students both on and off the reservation (Robert Roessel 1979; Thompson 1975). After graduation, they took advantage of career training or higher education programs offered by the BIA or Navajo Tribe. This training or education qualified them for newly created jobs in schools, administrative offices, and agencies as Crownpoint expanded. After they married and started their families, they found opportunities for child care, often among relatives who lived in Crownpoint.

By 1988, employment opportunities for both women and men became more limited, but young women often took steps to complete their high school educations and to pursue higher education. At the Diné College, Crownpoint campus, female students far outnumbered male students. At the three largest Diné College campuses—in Shiprock, Tsaile, and Crownpoint—72 percent of the students were female (Litson 2001). In turn, the fact that a larger percentage of women pursue a higher education qualifies more women for some of the best jobs on the reservation.

A third reoccurring theme that I encountered when talking with Navajo women was the venerable position of grandmothers in their families and in the community. Crownpoint women often acknowledged their grandmothers as their source of information about Navajo beliefs and traditions. Referring to grandmothers' strong opinions about what is appropriate or traditional, one woman noted, "They are always telling us what to do and what not to do." A powerful presence in their families, Navajo elders act as culture bearers by participating in traditional practices and recalling experiences that vividly typify their cultural heritage. Grandmothers' influence is magnified in Navajo matrilineal society, where they hold the position of the senior female in their family's matrilineal clan segment. Also, grandmothers outnumber grandfathers not only because of the biological tendency for women to outlive men but also because Navajo men experience higher mortality rates than Navajo women throughout their lives (Howard 1993).

Significant Newsworthy Events

Among the newsworthy events that occurred during 1988 and 1989, several stand out because of their effects on the Navajo people and because they revealed values and attitudes held by Navajo women. National media focused on the plight of Alyssa Keetso, an eight-month-old Navajo baby girl, whose mother, Patricia Keetso, gave her up for adoption to a white couple, Rick and Cheryl Pitts, from San Jose, California. A California state court ruled that a decision must be made by a Navajo court under the provisions of the Indian Child Welfare Act. When Cheryl Pitts and Patricia Keetso arrived with Alyssa in the Phoenix airport to resolve the dispute, a Navajo tribal social worker grabbed Alyssa in the airport to take her to the Navajo Reservation, at the same time grabbing national media attention about the incident (Hardeen 1988). The settlement reached by the court allowed temporary custody of Alyssa to the California couple but required that they apply for permanent guardianship. Guardianship differs from adoption in that guardianship permits the natural family to maintain ties to the child. Rick and Cheryl Pitts willingly agreed to take Alyssa to the Navajo Reservation two or three times a year to visit the extended family (*Navajo Times* 1988).

In Crownpoint, the community buzzed with discussions about the Keetso baby, at times sparking widely disparate opinions about who was responsible for the baby and what the outcome of the custody battle should be. Opinions about the Keetso baby case often differed by generation, at the same time revealing fundamental attitudes toward family, parenthood, cultural identity, and individual well-being. Grandmothers often insisted that the baby belonged on the reservation, where she could be raised as a Navajo, whereas members of younger generations were divided in their opinions, some sympathizing with the Navajo mother, who had decided that her baby would be better off if she were raised by a white family, and some believing that the Navajo baby belonged with family members who lived on the Navajo Reservation. A question frequently asked was, "Why didn't the grandmother step in earlier?" suggesting that the grandmother had neglected her responsibility for her granddaughter.

A second newsworthy event involved the Navajo tribal chairman, Peter MacDonald, who early in 1989 presided over the opening of the first shopping center in Crownpoint, which offered a grocery store, laundromat, and video store. According to rumor, eight hundred people applied for approximately fifty available jobs. At the dedication of the shopping center on February 8, Peter MacDonald stated, "No longer do we have to travel many miles to Gallup, Grants, and Farmington just to obtain basic goods and services" (*Navajo Times* 1989). At the dedication, MacDonald disclosed that he had accepted contributions from contractors, initiating a chain of events that led to his removal from office. He protested, "So yes. I have accepted gifts. But that is not a crime," in response to allegations of wrongdoing by the Senate Select Committee on Indian Affairs (Donovan 1989). By the next week, 25 of 109 Navajo Nation chapters had passed resolutions calling for Chairman MacDonald to step down. According to the Shiprock Chapter's resolution, the chairman had received thousands of dollars in cash, vehicles, gifts, gratuities, and other favors from contractors while in office (*Gallup (N.M.) Independent* 1989).

The Navajo Tribal Council responded to the accusations that MacDonald had accepted kickbacks from contractors and profited from the sale of the Big Boquillas Ranch by voting to place him on administrative leave with pay. This action initiated turmoil until the Tribal Court prevailed and MacDonald was removed from office (Landon 1989).

A third event that hit close to home for Crownpoint residents in February 1989 was the March of Hope–Journey for Jovita, a grassroots effort initiated by Gallup, New Mexico, residents to bring attention to the issue of alcohol abuse and drunk driving. A white drunk driver in Gallup killed three Navajos, including a three-month-old infant named Jovita, in a tragic accident. All local ethnic groups participated in a walk from Gallup to Albuquerque on Interstate 40 and from Albuquerque to the state capital in Santa Fe on Interstate 25 to demonstrate for the need for legislative change. The groups supported alcohol-related legislation to close drive-up liquor sale windows, to increase the local share of the state liquor excise tax, and to fund an eight-million-dollar detoxification center (Locke 1989). New Mexico's high rate of alcohol-related traffic fatalities in the late 1980s, the highest in the nation (Davis 2001), was exceeded in Gallup, which had five times the national average (Locke 1989).

Rather than ignore the topic of Native American alcohol abuse to avoid promoting the demoralizing stereotype of the drunken Indian, I believe the issue must be confronted in order to bring about change. The drunk driving accident that motivated the march was caused by an Anglo driver who killed three Navajos, vividly underscoring the fact that alcohol problems involve all racial and ethnic groups. The March of Hope did more than focus attention on alcohol abuse, according to Herb Mosher, an alcohol program administrator, who emphasized the unity displayed among ethnic groups in Gallup, a border town where tensions among whites, Hispanics, Navajos, and Zunis have a long history. Mosher stated, "It was a coming together of cultures and a growth of understanding" (Locke 1989). The March of Hope transcended racial divisions and stereotypes to advocate for lasting change in reducing alcohol-related accidents.

The march began in Gallup on February 17, when tribal, city, and county politicians, health care personnel, pastors, priests, and nuns, and various other residents of Gallup and the adjacent Zuni and Navajo reservations joined together to draw attention to the problem of drunk driving. On February 27, when two thousand marchers completed the final stretch of the journey, I walked with Crownpoint senior citizens from Foster Grandparents in Santa Fe. The march ended on the capitol steps, where Governor Gary Carruthers addressed the marchers, and the Senate opened its chambers for an emotional session to hear the pleas for alcohol treatment and legislation.

The pervasive problem with alcohol abuse, often identified as the Navajo Nation's number one health problem (Kunitz and Levy 2000; May and Smith 1988), profoundly affects Navajo women and their families. I heard many painful stories about tragic incidents and of strained and broken relationships directly related to problem drinking. Women supported family members with alcohol problems in many ways: bringing intoxicated family members home, setting limits about drinking behaviors, and encouraging treatment. At the request of an anxious Crownpoint mother, I searched for an alcoholic son in Albuquerque who had been out of touch for weeks while he was drinking in town. A frequent reason given for divorce was a husband's excessive drinking.

The March of Hope brought results at the county level and ultimately contributed to legislation at the state level. McKinley County, with Gallup as the county seat, banned drive-up liquor windows, the first county in the state to do so, and passed a liquor excise tax. With the tax money, the county built Na'nizhoozi Center, a detoxification center that also conducts a treatment program tailored for Native American alcohol abusers (Ellis 2003). For March of Hope participants, the united effort offered the prospect of solutions to a seemingly intractable problem that devastates lives, creates family discord and dissolution, and can lead to disability and death. Those who participated in the march voiced the need to change a severe problem that needs long-term solutions.

After ranking first in the nation for alcohol-related fatalities from 1982 (when New Mexico began to compile statistics) until 1993, New Mexico's rates began decreasing (Davis 2001) to the rank of fourth in the nation in 2000 (Massey 2001). During the 1990s, McKinley County's rates also dropped, but deaths from substance abuse-related causes remained at a level 35 percent above the state's rate from 1995 to 1997 (Ellis 1999).

Conclusion

The transformation in Navajo women's lives during the twentieth century parallels Crownpoint's growth as an administrative center for the Eastern Navajo Agency. During the first half of the century, the major institutions from the outside world were the BIA boarding school and hospital and a few Christian churches, all utilized by only a fraction of the Navajo people. The grandmothers, who grew to adulthood during this period, represent this relatively unaltered lifestyle. Most grandmothers never attended school or attended for only a few years, gave birth to their children at home, practiced only the traditional religion, and lived in rural areas, where they cared for livestock and grew large gardens.

Corresponding to the acceleration of change that affected Navajo women's lives, dramatic growth in Crownpoint began at midcentury. In contrast to the grandmothers, midlife women who grew to adulthood in the 1950s, 1960s, and 1970s attended school throughout their childhood, gave birth to their children in the hospital, attended a Christian church as well as adhering to traditional religion, and lived in either Crownpoint or a rural area while depending on the cash economy for a livelihood.

In the latter decades of the twentieth century, the population of Crownpoint and surrounding chapters continued to grow, but the pace of growth in institutions and support services slowed. The established medical facility, agencies, offices, schools, and businesses offered only limited opportunities for employment to young people who reached maturity. The young mothers had more opportunities to pursue an education or training but suffered from lack of employment and housing opportunities, forcing many to rely on extended family members for support or to relocate to urban areas.

The incursions of Western society seen in Crownpoint tell only part of the story in regard to Navajo women. The other part lies within resourceful individual women who act from a position of strength as they develop cultural strategies to negotiate pathways in a bicultural world. The Navajo language, matrilineal family ties, and participation in and respect for traditional ceremonies remain intact as sources of strength and pride. Favored with cultural beliefs that value women's independence and decision-making abilities, Navajo women take into account the constraints on their lives while developing the skills and knowledge to take advantage of opportunities.

2

Three Generations of Navajo Women

Life history profiles of a grandmother, a midlife mother, and a young mother reveal the changes in the twentieth-century historical and cultural context that propelled the life course trajectories of Crownpoint area Navajo women. At the same time, various aspects of Navajo women's patterns of education, wage work, and family and childbearing patterns retain the unique characteristics of a Navajo worldview.

During the time span between the childhood years when Mary Cayaditto, the grandmother, grew up in the 1920s and 1930s, and the 1970s and 1980s, when the young mother, Diana Mitchell, grew up, dramatic changes greatly altered every aspect of Navajo lives, for both men and women. The life story of midlife mother Mary Joe personifies the transitional period, when young children began going to school and entered the labor force as young adults.

Mary Cayaditto, Grandmother

When looking for someone else who lived on the road to Mount Powell in the Smith Lake Chapter, we first met Mary Cayaditto. As we drove up, Bonnie Yazzie and I saw Mary and her sister sitting outside, surrounded by the two hogans where the sisters live and houses where Mary's children and grandchildren live. Freshly dyed gold-colored wool dried on a pole rack in the summer sun. Looking north across the valley from their vantage point on the mountain, they had a view of Hosta Butte and the Lobo Mountains. After that initial visit, I knew that I wanted to visit Mary again to learn about her life and traditional knowledge she had accrued over a lifetime.

Seventy-six-year-old Mary speaks Navajo, herds sheep, and weaves rugs from wool that she has carded and spun. A small woman, Mary gestures with her expressive, strong hands when she speaks. She is raising a three-year-old granddaughter, who sits with her at the loom and wants to learn to weave. Her handspun wools are left in their natural colors or dyed with mineral or vegetal dyes and woven in traditional designs. Mary showed us a rug she was weaving in a twill design with a natural cream-colored wool, gold wool dyed with lichen, and black wool darkened with mica and tree gum.

Mary recalled growing up in the Smith Lake area.

> My father told me to go to school. I went to a school run by the Catholics. My parents had land by the Continental Divide. There were no buses back then, and we would walk from that ridge of mountains. When I walked to school, it was with my siblings and my cousins. I don't know how long the school was operating. My father said he would not be around forever. We needed to learn how to make a living.
>
> Even when it snowed we went to school. We wrapped burlap around our feet and tied it.
>
> I went up to third grade. I wish I had gone to school more. I learned how to write my name, and I understand some English.
>
> At that time I grew up with most of my relatives. Mostly my maternal grandmother raised me. I took care of her in her golden years. When she died, she gave the allotment to me. That's why I live here. All of my children live around here and my sister. My grandmother died when she was 106.
>
> The first I learned was weaving from my mother and maternal grandmother. They knew a lot of designs. My grandmother knew how to make a design that came out like a diamond.
>
> I herded sheep ever since I can remember. I had as many as four hundred sheep. Now I have fifty sheep. I want to keep herd-

> ing; I want to keep busy. It makes me feel good. My kids told me to sell it. "You're tired," they told me. But the doctor told me to keep walking so I do.
>
> I had my own horse at one time that I used to herd sheep. My children thought it might spook, and I might fall off. My kids gave me a dune buggy, and I ride that sometimes to herd sheep. (11/22/96)

Mary had a Kinaaldá as a girl. She met her husband on her own, noting that "They didn't pay," meaning that her husband's parents did not pay the customary bridewealth to her parents. Following her younger sister's death, Mary raised her three young children. In matrilineal Navajo society, a mother's sister is also *shimá*, mother, to the children. Thus, although Mary and her husband had no children, she has thirteen grandchildren and recently became a great-grandmother. Like other grandmothers, Mary teaches her grandchildren by talking to them.

> I always remember my grandmother's words and talk to my grandchildren that way. "Get up early. Pray with some cornmeal. Chop some wood. Walk to the bus." My kids and grandkids walk quite a ways. I told them about the importance of education. I tell them not to lay around, not to watch too much TV, the importance of an education. When they see me coming, they turn off the TV.
>
> My grandchildren really love me, the paternal grandchildren. I wonder why the oldest two can speak Navajo and the youngest cannot. (11/22/96 and 12/11/96)

Mary adheres to traditional Navajo religion, preferring familiar prayers and ceremonies to those of one of the many Christian denominations that compete for Navajo members. She stated: "I have a strong belief in Navajo traditional religion. A lot of times people tell me to join a Christian church. My sister and I don't want to. We want to stick with our corn pollen. That's what we grew up with" (11/22/96).

One December morning, Mary had seen rainbows, an unusual occurrence for this time of year.

> This morning I saw a rainbow with seven colors. I am wondering about it. Usually rainbows move, but this one stayed in one place for a long time. I went outside and prayed with my cornmeal.
>
> The Holy Spirit will probably be with you, too. Yes, it is out of season for a rainbow. (12/11/96)

In her daily activities, values, and beliefs, Mary exemplifies the lifestyle referred to as "traditional" by younger Navajos who commute or move to town to take advantage of wage work and urban amenities such as education and health care.

Mary Cayaditto's life story is representative of those among grandmothers who did not go to school or attended only a few years because they were needed at home to help care for the large sheep herds. Some of these grandmothers remembered hiding when officials came around looking for children to send to boarding schools. As they reached adulthood, the grandmothers followed in the footsteps of their parents by depending on the land-based economy (Kelley and Whiteley 1989), which revolved around caring for livestock, raising crops, and gathering edible plants. Because they are fluent only in Navajo, they may be unable to communicate with grandchildren who speak only English. In contrast to those grandmothers who did not go to school, a few grandmothers in the Crownpoint sample were among the first generation of Navajo children to attend school throughout their childhood years. After graduating from high school, these bilingual Navajo grandmothers' lives took a different direction as their skills prepared them to enter the labor force, often in the growing agency towns on the reservation and border towns off the reservation.

Mary Joe, Midlife Mother

Born in 1942 and the oldest of seven children, Mary grew up north of Crownpoint, where she helped with the sheep until she started school at age nine. She vividly remembers the trauma and loneliness of adjusting to a strange and sometimes hostile environment.

And I guess my mother and my father didn't really think about putting me in school because I was the oldest, and they were depending on my help, and they had some sheep. They had a herd of sheep. And they wanted me to take care of the sheep. And my mother always tells me that she put me on the horse when I was five years old. Tied me to the horse, and she would pull the horse with me, and I was getting trained to be a sheep herder and a squaw!

But then my uncle, I guess he felt bad for me staying home. He thought that I should go to school. So he's the one that put me in school, my uncle. Yes, so he put me in school.

I remember I had the hardest time getting adjusted to being in school. I was always lonely; I was always homesick. I didn't want to go to school. Every time they would take me back to school, I would cry and try to run out after my mother. Out of the dorm. [Mary laughs.]

But I'm glad I was put in school. Otherwise, I don't know what I would be doing or how I was going to be. But the only thing I miss is my culture, the Navajo culture. I really don't know much. 'Cause I always think maybe the reason why is because I was always in school, being away from home nine months out of the year.

I know when I went to school in September I didn't get back until Christmas time. And then I would go back to school, and I wouldn't get back until school's out. We didn't make all these visits home for the school year. It was just once or twice out of the school year that we got a chance to go home. So it seems like I was away from home all the time. The only time I spent home was during the summer.

But when I got home for the summer, I had to herd sheep. I went after the horses, something like five o'clock in the morning, and then I brought the horses in. And then I would take the sheep out after I had my breakfast. I'd stay out there with the sheep all day, up 'til almost sundown. (10/5/88)

After attending Crownpoint Boarding School from kindergarten to third grade, Mary transferred to Central Elementary School in Gallup, New Mexico. From the fourth through the seventh grades, Mary lived in border town dormitories for Navajo students, first in Wingate and then in what was known as Gallup Dorm. Mary did not have a Kinaaldá as a girl "because I was in school when I had my first period" (10/10/88).

During her eighth- and ninth-grade years, Mary returned home and attended public schools in Crownpoint. Because the ninth grade was the highest grade in existence there at the time, she then transferred to Valley High School, in Albuquerque, for three years. Again, Mary lived in a border town dorm adjacent to the Albuquerque Indian School. After graduating, Mary attended Highlands University in Las Vegas, New Mexico, for one semester. "And I went to school there for first semester. The second semester I just came back. I came back, and I didn't go back because I went and got myself in trouble over the summer after I graduated. And I went to school carrying my oldest son. And during Christmas I just decided not to go back. I could have gone back, but I didn't. But I was carrying my son, and I had him in March. That's my older son" (10/5/88).

After her son was born, Mary went to work at the Crownpoint Boarding School as a dormitory aide.

> So I applied for a job there, and they hired me a month later! I was still breastfeeding my little baby, my little son, when I went to work. And right off hand they gave me a one bedroom quarter, too, a bedroom apartment. So I was really lucky. I was happy that I had a place to stay, and I had a job. But I had no vehicle though. But the place was near the school so I just walked back and forth.
>
> My mother and my father came out to visit me, and I had a little help from my sisters. They stayed with me off and on and babysat for me. (10/5/88)

Mary married a policeman who had checked on noises she heard outside the dormitory while working the night shift. She continued working after having three more children. "So we lived our years bringing up the kids, and he worked as an officer, and he tried real hard to help me. Sometimes there were times with my shift, he stayed home with the kids during the day, and I worked during the day. And it seemed like we were taking turns taking care of the kids" (10/5/88).

When Mary's husband got involved with a policewoman, Mary and her husband divorced, and she finished raising her children on her own. Reflecting on her situation, Mary stated, "I feel good about working and having a job. And raising my kids and having a home. I rented for about seventeen and one-half years. And I finally got this mutual help housing. It's rent to own" (10/5/88).

When asked if she would describe herself as modern, traditional, or somewhere in-between, Mary responded, "but just like I said, I'm kind of in-between because there's times, well, most of the time, I like to see the doctor if I'm having some problem, and if I don't feel any better, I feel like I should see a medicine man." When her daughter got sick, they sought help from a medicine man. "And then there's the time, in August, I told you my daughter got real sick on me. We had to turn to tradition, to hire a medicine woman. We had to say a prayer and use the corn pollen and all that. I try to tell my children that they should bring some of those things into their life which will help them" (10/10/88).

Mary has attended Christian churches at different points in her life. With her husband, she attended the Pentecostal Church, and as a student she attended the Christian Reformed Church. She stated, "I'm traditional yes, but I have my Bible from Christian Reformed" (2/20/96).

During her working years, Mary returned to school to earn an associate of arts degree in recreation at the Gallup branch campus of the University of New Mexico.

Mary's life course trajectory captures the midcentury transition in Navajo lifestyles, when school and jobs in the labor force began to eclipse the land-based economy. Her late start in school and her summers spent herding sheep indicate the conflicting expectations Navajo parents had for their children. Mary attended school during the midcentury expansion of schools aimed at making education available to all Navajo children. In fact, the Gallup Dormitory, where she lived during her later elementary school years while attending the Gallup public schools, was part of the Navajo Emergency Education Program implemented during the 1950s (Robert Roessel 1979). Mary's high school diploma, earned in 1963, qualified her for work in Crownpoint's BIA school. After working there for twenty-six years, Mary was laid off her job because decreasing numbers of students lived in the school dormitory.

Diana Mitchell, Young Mother

Before attending Crownpoint High School, Diana attended Christian boarding schools at Rehoboth and Saint Michaels, and one year at Fort Wingate, a BIA boarding school. During the summer, Diana stayed with her maternal grandmother in Crystal, New Mexico, where she helped with the sheep.

> In the summers, my mom used to have me go out to my grandmother's. And that's out at Crystal. I used to stay with my grandmother. I think it's like every summer because I wasn't with my mom. She was too much into her work. And I stayed up there, and it was fun. You had all this place to just do anything you wanted. And my grandmother told me a lot of things. The only thing is, I don't know how to speak Navajo. But I can understand it. And that's really hard for me. I don't know why I didn't learn because I was out there almost every summer.
>
> And it was nice. I herded the sheep. I don't know, it was just the same old summer like. It was good, too, because that's the only time I saw my cousins, I mean really got to know my cousins.

Upon reaching menarche, Diana had a Kinaaldá even though her mother had not had one. She recalls, "We had it at my grandmother's. That was hard work for me. I mean, my mom and my grandmother are real traditional! And you have your hair in front of your face, and you're not supposed to move it. And they say not to cut your hair before then, too. I don't know what that has to do with it, but I remember, I used to always tell my mom I wanted my bangs cut, and she said not until after you have your Kinaaldá" (7/1/88).

As a teenager, Diana and her friends drank and stayed out all night.

She and her friend reminisced: "We'd get like two dollars and say we're going down to the store. And end up drunk that night. And stuff like that. We'd laugh about it, but it's not funny because there's a lot of teenagers doing that now" (7/1/88).

Reflecting on her high school years, Diana marveled at the different direction her life had taken.

> When I was in high school, you know how teenagers party and everything, well, that's what I did. I hung out with the wrong crowd. My mom's really surprised at how I've changed. And I am, too.
>
> It's real funny. And now I see the friends that I used to party with. They have two kids, three. They're not working; they're not with their boyfriend or whoever. It's sad. And you wonder. That would have been me if someone didn't talk to me. And my mom's been a real big influence on me. I mean she talked to me and talked to me and told me, "There's a lot of people out there who don't make it in life. And they're the ones who take it out on people who make it in life." And I finally saw it for myself. (7/1/88)

Diana also attributed the change in her behavior to her daughter, who "just changed everything because you have a responsibility now" (7/1/88).

After graduation from high school, Diana completed a six-month veterinary assistant course in Phoenix, Arizona. When she returned to Crownpoint, the only job she could find was at an animal feed and supply store just north of Gallup, more than fifty miles away. When I first interviewed twenty-year-old Diana, she, her boyfriend, and her two-year-old daughter lived with her mother while she commuted daily to work. Diana's boyfriend also commuted to his work, more than forty miles away. When his schedule prevented him from taking care of their daughter, a friend across the street babysat. Diana's mother relieved the babysitter when she came home from her eight-to-five job in Crownpoint. Despite her long hours, Diana preferred working to staying home.

> Like that isn't for me. I can keep house real good. It's just that I can't stay home. I don't know how some ladies do it, staying home

and taking care of the kids, and you're into a routine. That's the way I am on Wednesdays. I clean and do laundry. Do everything. But I don't think I could do that every day.

And also it's better—I don't know, I see it that way—that both parents work. Because if the wife stays home, and the husband does everything, that's where all those arguments and everything come about. 'Cause when I stayed home, and I saw Nick every day we'd start arguing over every little thing. And now that we barely see each other we get along a lot better. But that's the way I see it; through my experience that's how it is. (7/1/88)

Diana Mitchell represents the majority of young mothers in this sample who had their first child during their teens and had a committed, long-standing relationship with the father of her child. Diana was in no hurry to get married. She reflected on the influence of her own mother: "I've been going with Nick for six years. We're still not married. . . . I think, I don't know, if you can make it I think it's real neat. I mean, my mom—I'm twenty years old, and she hasn't remarried. I think that's neat, just for her to do that." Diana continued: "But we will probably eventually get married. But it's still there that my mom made it, so could I. Sometimes we say things like we're not going to get married" (7/1/88).

For Diana and Nick, marriage was a process that accompanied their transition to adulthood. Parenthood became the first step that occurred when Diana gave birth to their first child at seventeen. Their relationship endured as they became parents, located housing, and gained financial independence. Diana and her husband later completed their family when they had two more children. Also, as the mother of three children she returned to school at Diné College in Crownpoint.

Like her own mother, Diana strongly opposed abortion. For her, an unplanned pregnancy was not reason to terminate a pregnancy. "If there's a medical reason why they have to have abortions, I don't have anything against it. Yeh, I think if I got pregnant again, I wouldn't go for an abortion because it would stay with you for the rest of your life," she explained. "And then sometime, the way I see it, God would probably punish you later on. Like if you wanted kids, you probably wouldn't be able to have them," Diana continued. "Or something will go wrong. Because he's the one that conceived the egg and the sperm to meet and all that" (3/22/89).

Diana Mitchell attended a Christian church and participated in Navajo ceremonies, considering them too different to be competing with each other or exclusive; both were worthy of her involvement. She explained that her orientation toward traditional ceremonies came from her mother and grandmother, whereas attending the Catholic Church was important to her and her husband. "I mean my mom and my grandmother are into, like I said, real traditional stuff, and that's what I'm more into, too. It's just learning from experience through them. But we used to go to church—I should say [my husband] and I and [my daughter]. We had her baptized. It's two totally different things" (7/1/88).

A Comparison of the Three Generations

The life histories of each of these three women on the whole represent major patterns that distinguish each of the three generations in the Crownpoint area sample. At the same time, in some respects they differ from others in their generation.

Like the majority of the grandmothers, Mary Cayaditto had too little education to enable her to speak, read, or write English fluently. She is comfortable speaking in Navajo and needed an interpreter for her interview. Mary Joe, the oldest child in her family, went to school during the transitional period, when the federal government first made universal education for Navajo children a reality through rapid expansion of federal and public school programs. Although Diana attended school in the 1970s and 1980s, when local public and BIA schools existed throughout the reservation, she attended public schools for only one semester in junior high and for three years during high school. Both Mary Joe and Diana continued their educations while raising their children, a common pattern for Navajo women.

As with other grandmothers who had little or no education, Mary Cayaditto worked in the land-based economy and wove rugs throughout her adult years. Meanwhile, Mary Joe herded sheep only during the summers after she started school. Mary Joe's graduation from high school coincided with the recent growth in Crownpoint as site of an administrative agency, enabling her to find work readily at the Crownpoint Boarding School. After finding work, Mary Joe worked throughout the years she raised children, leaving her job only when she was laid off. In contrast, both Diana and her husband entered the labor force in a period of high unemployment and had to commute long distances to work.

These representatives of three generations of Navajo women reflect the overall pattern found in the Crownpoint area for having a Kinaaldá. Although most grandmothers had a Kinaaldá, fewer midlife mothers did, either because they attended boarding school at the time they reached menarche, or because they were involved in Christian churches that frowned on Navajo traditional practices. Diana, whose mother did not have a Kinaaldá, had one when she began menstruating, after her family had returned to traditional ceremonial practices.

Many grandmothers adhere to traditional Navajo religion, although some have become Christians and participate in the Native American Church. Mary Cayaditto, meanwhile, prefers to practice only the Navajo religion. Among midlife and young mothers, a proliferation of patterns exists as women combine Navajo traditional ceremonies with a variety of Christian churches, as well as the Native American Church. Mary Joe and Diana both chose to participate in traditional ceremonies and Christian churches.

Like the majority of the grandmothers in the Crownpoint area sample, Mary Cayaditto remained married to the same man throughout her life. In the younger generations, divorce and single motherhood became more common. Among the young mothers, marriage became a process as young couples often became parents and lived together before getting married.

Unlike the majority of the grandmothers, who had large families, Mary Cayaditto had no children. However, after her sister's death, she raised her three children, and is now a grandmother to thirteen grandchildren. Among the younger generations, parents limited the size of their families as considerations of expense and time investment in children replaced concepts of children as workers essential to the land-based economy. The young mothers often gave birth to their first child during their teen years.

Among the three generations, motherhood and women's roles demonstrate persistent Navajo core values. The revered deity, Changing Woman, who raised her sons, the Warrior Twins, serves as a model for motherhood. Her high status parallels the high status of women in a matrilineal society. Respect for mothers as nurturers and childbearers combines with the high value placed on children in a pronatal society. Consequently, children are welcomed into the extended family and abortion is rejected as an option.

3

Navajo Women's Lives in Historical and Cultural Context

In the following chapters, two overarching themes connect the lives of three generations of women. The first is the impact of history on Navajo women's lives. Despite the pervasive onslaught of historical events, Navajo women have not been passive recipients; rather, women display agency in their responses to outside change (McCloskey 1998). Peter Iverson's history of the Diné "portrays Navajos as agents of their own destiny, rather than as victims" (2002, 2).

The second theme is the persistence of Navajo culture. Although publications on culture change among the Navajo (Bahr 1994) overwhelmingly outnumber those that consider Navajo cultural persistence, Navajo cultural practices, beliefs, attitudes, and values endure, as demonstrated in eastern area Navajo women's lives. The interaction between historical change and cultural persistence leads to both creativity and resistance. As Navajo women embrace education, wage work, and Western medicine, they adhere to principles that highly value reproduction, motherhood, and women as esteemed members of Navajo society.

Within this historical and cultural framework, related themes stand out as important in Navajo women's responses to all-encompassing historical change and to their adherence to their culture. First, complementary gender roles, which elicited comment from the time of first contact with the Spanish (Brugge 1980), continue in Navajo society today. Second, although Navajo culture may be contested, changing, and fragmented (Dirks, Eley, and Ortner 1994), a primary concern of Navajo women and men is the maintenance of their cultural identity. Third, Navajo women play a major role in cultural transmission, passing on threatened but valued customs, beliefs, and values to younger generations. A fourth theme is the creation of cultural strategies, patterns of behavior that combine Western and Navajo elements in new ways.

The Impact of History on Navajo Women's Lives

History sets the stage on which events take place, a performance site that does not write the script but prompts the cast of characters. The recent move to interpret social and cultural change in an historical framework, "the historic turn in the human sciences" (McDonald 1996), guides this study of three generations of Navajo women. For twentieth-century Navajo women, the historical context is crucial in defining the parameters of childhood, adulthood, and old age. As Tamara Hareven points out, historical circumstances affect the life course of individuals in each generation. "Each generation encounters a set of historical circumstances that shape its subsequent life history and that generation transmits to the next one both the impact that historical events had on its life course and the resultant patterns of timing" (Hareven 2000, 155). Changes in the life course of the grandmothers, midlife mothers, and young mothers attest to the impact of historical change on timing of transitions, particularly the transition to adulthood.

Navajo women's patterns of work, education, marriage, and childbearing, and of organizing and participating in ceremonies, demonstrate the impact of historical forces. The grandmothers, who were born between 1895 and the 1930s, grew up in a period influenced by railroads, trading posts, and stock reduction. During these years, the land-based economy shifted from subsistence-oriented herding to market-oriented herding (Bailey and Bailey 1986). The midlife mothers, born in the 1930s, 1940s, and 1950s, grew up in a period of rapid development of on-reservation infrastructure and expansion of educational and employment opportunities following the demise of the land-based economy, a period characterized as the end of independence (Bailey and Bailey 1986). Young mothers, born in the 1960s and 1970s, grew up in a period of growth of urban centers and schools, but of stagnation in a job market that has not kept pace with population growth.

Peter Iverson (2002) identifies four major themes in the history of the Diné. The first theme is defense and survival. From the time of contact with the Spanish to the present, Navajos have defended their land, their animals, and themselves as a people. Navajo women's determined search for ways to support their families exemplifies this theme.

The second historical theme is adaptation and incorporation. Throughout their history, Navajos have integrated new ideas, peoples, and patterns of behavior into the Navajo way. For Navajo women, the replacement of a Blessing Way Ceremony and traditional birth at home with prenatal health care and hospital births illustrates one of many ways in which women have incorporated new practices in their lives.

A third historical theme is expansion and prosperity. Not only to survive but also to prosper, Navajos have believed in the need to expand, which in the past meant expanding the land base. Today, Navajo women's pursuit of education and, if necessary, work off the reservation demonstrates this theme.

A fourth theme is identity and continuation. Tradition and the legacy of the past have sustained the Navajo people. As a current example, Navajo women plan and arrange for their daughters' Kinaaldá ceremony when they reach menarche, a powerful cornerstone for a girl's identity as a Navajo woman.

Reflecting on his childhood years on the Navajo Reservation between 1936 and 1940, William Adams (1993) realized that his family became part of the colonial enterprise when his mother became director of the Navajo, Hopi, and Southern Ute school systems. The Navajo lived as colonial subjects in the early days of tribal government, when "stock reduction and the resistance to it were at their height" (1993, 305). From the perspective of the federal range management and soil conservation people who enforced the policy, as soon as the land regained its productivity, Navajos would see that stock reduction was in their best interests. To the contrary, however, stock reduction dealt a devastating blow to the land-based economy and marked the beginning of the end of the Navajo pastoral lifestyle. Almost forty years later, the Navajo live in a postcolonial world, "in which the

Navajos really have assumed a large share of control over their own destiny, and when the relationship with the Bilagáana [white man] has moved from one of patronage to one of partnership" (Adams 1993, 310).

Twentieth-century federal programs that privileged men over women affected Navajo women. David Aberle's examination of 1937 and 1939 livestock counts found that "the final records were often inaccurate as to ownership, and those which I have seen are particularly surprising in listing almost no women as owners, although it is well-known that Navaho women owned livestock in their own right" (1982, 66).

In addition to its failure to recognize women's ownership of livestock, the federal government failed to develop wage labor opportunities for Navajo women. Mary Shepardson observed this pattern after stock reduction. "The federal work program offered in compensation for the enforced stock reduction involved jobs mostly for men. Those jobs that were available for women were fewer and less highly paid" (Shepardson 1995, 174).

Consistent with assimilation policies, Navajo men were targeted as wage earners and heads of household. Navajo women, meanwhile, secure in their position in Navajo society, pursued family strategies available to them. When men left for off-reservation jobs, women stayed at home to care for the reduced herds of sheep, crops, and their families. More recent studies (Klein and Ackerman 1995) point to diverse ways in which Native American women have retained or regained power in their societies regardless of federal policies and legislation that privileged men over women. As a case in point, Navajo women have resisted the onslaught of Western formulations of women's roles in the family by contributing economically and maintaining their egalitarian position in a "partnership" society (Shepardson 1995).

Cultural Persistance versus Culture Change

Overshadowing cultural persistence, culture change has been the primary focus of many studies of the Navajo. In a review article, Bahr (1994) categorizes dozens of articles in twenty-one genres that consider Navajo culture change. In contrast, studies of cultural persistence are rare. However, the tenacity of cultural values, beliefs, and behaviors attests to the need for a reoriented perspective that highlights cultural persistence (Inglehart and Baker 2000; Spicer 1980). Navajo women's lives document the continuity of culture amidst a multitude of twentieth-century changes, as the following chapters demonstrate.

In "Change and Persistence in an Isolated Navajo Community," Shepardson and Hammond (1964) consider the impact of change on the Rainbow Plateau community on the northwestern border of the Navajo Reservation. At midcentury, Navajo social organization, the land-based economy, and ceremonial practices remained intact after the introduction of a primary school, local chapter government, Navajo tribal regulations, and increasing sources of cash income. The Indian Bureau and the Navajo tribal government "support, rather than replace, the traditional structure" (Shepardson and Hammond 1964, 1049).

By sidestepping threats to the traditional lifestyle, the Navajos preserve old ways. Thus, "the area is seriously overgrazed; compulsory education is a dead letter; resolutions against polygyny are conveniently ignored; eligibility requirements for tribal work are not strictly applied" (Shepardson and Hammond 1964, 1048). Almost four decades ago, selective and nominal adoption of Western as well as tribal innovations protected against the destruction of Navajo traditional ways.

According to Ruth Roessel, Navajo cultural persistence depends on two key elements. "The Navajos have always said that, as long as they have cornfields and Kinaaldá they have nothing to worry about. These two elements of Navajo life remain of vital importance, and in both elements the women play the vital role." She continues: "The cornfield, with its fertility and growth, and the Kinaaldá ceremony, with its recognition of the coming of age of the Navajo girl to womanhood, combine to focus on the cycle of reproduction, without which there can be no food and no people" (Ruth Roessel 1981, 105).

Of Roessel's two quintessential elements of Navajo life, the Kinaaldá ceremony endures as the most viable. As the cash economy replaced the land-based economy and many Navajos moved to urban centers, most Navajos stopped growing corn. Midlife mothers who did not have a Kinaaldá ceremony because they were away at boarding school when they started menstruating now arrange the ceremony for their daughters. The Kinaaldá ceremony continues to be vital and important to the Navajo people, an affirmation of the primacy of reproduction, of the fertility of women, and of Changing Woman's example (Frisbie 1993). Cultural persistence among Native Americans often resides in frameworks of meaning typified by shared values (O'Nell 1996; Rushforth and Chisholm 1991). Rushforth and Chisholm, in their analysis of cultural persistence among the Bearlake Athapaskans of Canada, identify a "distinctive cultural framework of meaning and moral responsibility" (1991, 36). Guiding Bearlakers' behavior are the basic values of industriousness, generosity, restraint, autonomy, and control. When expressed in behavior patterns, cultural values lead Bearlakers to hesitate to impose themselves on others, but otherwise they act generously to help and cooperate with others when the need arises.

Rushforth and Chisholm's survey of the literature of other Athapaskan peoples suggests that a common heritage, both genetic and historical, is manifest in shared beliefs, values, and norms. For the Navajo, a southern Athapaskan people, generosity, cooperation, and helpfulness appear repeatedly as paramount values. Also, Rushforth and Chisholm cite Kluckhohn and Leighton's Navajo guide to behavior: "Act to everybody as if they were your own relatives" (Kluckhohn and Leighton 1974, 299).

The relative scarcity of studies of Navajo cultural persistence may reflect the difficulty of assessing aspects of continuity in contrast to the ease of assessing change. Visibly apparent changes in Navajo life are abundant. They include the growth of reservation towns and dressing in Western clothing, living in houses, and driving cars and trucks. Meanwhile, as indicated by Rushforth and Chisholm, cultural persistence is less obvious, implicit in enduring values, attitudes, and belief systems that guide behavior.

Arising from shared beliefs and values are persistent cultural practices. In Maureen Schwarz's study of Navajo views of the human and personhood (1997a), baskets, cradleboards, looms, and hogans incorporate symbols of the Navajo worldview. The endurance of traditional practices also demonstrates the continuity of deeply held beliefs and values. During pregnancy, both the mother and father of the baby avoid witnessing any traumatic event, such as an automobile accident, or watching an eclipse because the baby can be adversely affected. After birth, parents influence the direction that a child's life will take by burying his or her umbilical cord under a corral or loom, objects that suggest a future occupation. A baby's First Laugh ceremony heralds the ability to express emotion. The Kinaaldá ceremony conducted for girls and a variant performed for boys at puberty honors the transition to adulthood.

Emphasis on persistent traditional customs and beliefs associated with reproductive events—pregnancy, childbirth, infancy, and puberty—indicates the deep significance of birth and renewal to the Navajo. The Navajo women's value system in regard to motherhood, children, and family is a cornerstone of Navajo cultural persistence.

Complementary Gender Roles

Navajo women writers such as Jennifer Denetdale (2001) portray Navajo women as powerful and autonomous, respected in their families, clans, and tribe. Navajo women, like other Native American women, establish complementary relationships with men (Ackerman 2003; Albers 1989; Caffrey 2000; Frisbie 1982; Schwarz 1997a, 2003; Tsosie 1988).

The cultural construction of gender in Navajo society derives from the beliefs, practices, and values embedded in Navajo traditional religion, matrilineal social organization, and the pastoral economy. Changing Woman, the Navajo deity and beloved cultural heroine, acts as a role model for all Navajo women. At the time of their first menstrual period, girls reenact the first Kinaaldá, instituted by the Holy People to celebrate Changing Woman's new capacity to bear children. Young women's ability to bear children is noted and honored when relatives and friends attend the four-day ceremony. Later, when nurturing their own children, mothers mirror Changing Woman's devotion to her twin sons.

Besides being the source of matrilineal clan membership, the females in a family—grandmother, mother, and daughter—embody clan continuity through the generations. Parents welcome the birth of a baby daughter as an assurance of the perpetuation of the clan. Although the cash economy and wage labor have replaced the pastoral economy, the essential contribution of women's work to the family economy remains. A willingness among extended family members to share responsibilities for children enables Navajo women to work while raising their children.

Changing Woman is associated with the earth, the seasonal cycle of life, and the power of the earth to provide food for her children. She sustains vegetation with female rain, the gentle steady rain that nourishes crops. As an encompassing symbol of motherhood, Changing Woman is identified with reproduction, sustenance, and nurturance. Witherspoon states, "Changing woman or Earth woman is called mother. Agricultural fields are called mother. Livestock are called mother. Changing Woman is in charge of female rain and all vegetation" (1975, 60).

Ruth Roessel identified principles from stories and ceremonies about Changing Woman that apply to motherhood and mothering. Changing Woman counseled her sons, Monster Slayer and Born-for-Water. She taught them many skills and provided protection and security for them while they were growing up. Her sons, in turn, learned to take responsibility, maintained a strong sense of identity, and grew up to be independent, resourceful adults (Roessel 1981).

Emmi Whitehorse, an artist who grew up east of Crownpoint in Whitehorse Lake, expresses the agency of Navajo women in her paintings. "In my family, the female owned everything, the women ran everything. They owned the land and the sheep. They nurtured and carried the family. The woman was responsible for the survival of the people. So in my work, the female is always very big, she is imposing, she is like this big Goliath in the work. The male image is tiny" (Whitehorse 1995, 56). In Emmi Whitehorse's family, female agency is integral to all family activities.

Motherhood is intrinsic to Navajo women's conceptions of being female. As mothers, women are sources of nurturance, strength, and life itself. The associations, in turn, extend to the earth, crops, and livestock, which sustain humans. The cultural, social, and economic context of Navajo motherhood reveals an ideology that continues to elevate and empower Navajo women.

Cultural Identity

Deborah House outlines the challenge to Navajo cultural identity. "The supreme challenge was and continues to be the maintenance of an identity that feels satisfyingly authentic and secures for Navajo people an adequate degree of economic and political autonomy in the face of pervasive American domination" (2002, 12). An authentic Navajo identity recognizes the lack of a homogeneous or static Navajo culture on which to base this identity. Similar to other cultures, Navajo culture is always changing as a result of interactions in a dynamic world. The core values that shape Navajo identity may themselves undergo alterations even while maintaining their uniqueness.

Replacing the former concern with acculturation and assimilation, cultural identity more accurately reflects Navajos' attempts to reconcile what it means to be Navajo in a society dominated by whites. Although Navajo women work in schools, stores, offices, and hospitals and dress in contemporary Western styles, they nevertheless consider themselves Navajo and value various aspects of "the Navajo way." Their sense of place, rooted in parents' or grandparents' rural homes, their vision of family that includes extended family and matrilineal clan members, and their worldview, anchored in specific Navajo stories and ceremonies, all contribute to a distinct worldview.

Navajo cultural identity is not either-or, either dependent on adherence to Navajo traditions or Bilagáana (white man) ways, or consisting of varying proportions of Navajoness or whiteness. In her reflections on indigenous identity, Hilary Weaver, a Lakota woman, states, "Rather than determining where someone fits on a continuum between two cultural identities or worlds, it may be more accurate to say that indigenous people live in one complex, conflictual world" (2001, 249). She notes multiple levels of identity: self-identification based on individual perception, community identification maintained relative to other communities, and external identification formed by nonnatives. Besides a lack of consensus on what indigenous culture identity is, there are no adequate measures of identity such as appearance and blood quantum.

Three recent articles address the issue of Navajo cultural identity. Thomas Csordas (1999) proposes two identities: the first a collective identity rooted in a Navajo worldview in opposition to Euro-American society, and a second, individual Navajo identity expressed as allegiance to three healing traditions: traditional ceremonies, the Native American Church, and faith healing in fundamentalist Christian churches. Navajos frequently combine allegiances to these spiritual traditions, even participating in all three.

Navajo women in the Eastern Navajo Agency likewise vary in their choice of multiple spiritual traditions. Some Navajo grandmothers who exclusively participate in local ceremonies were never baptized in a Christian church. At the other extreme, some Navajo women belong to Christian churches and oppose any participation in traditional ceremonies. The majority of all three generations of Crownpoint area Navajo women at various times became involved in more than one of the religious traditions.

In a second article on cultural identity, Amy Schultz (1998) emphasized the role of different historical contexts in shaping Navajo women's cultural identity. Women born before 1960 were more likely to identify solely as Navajos, whereas younger Navajo women born after 1960 were more likely to incorporate their tribal identity into a broader American Indian one. The younger Navajo women responded to the social movements of the 1960s that fostered a pan-Indian identity.

Regardless of whether or not Navajo women identified with other American Indians, they stressed the pride they felt in being Navajo, a unique people who felt strong ties to the land, their own language, a network of kinship and clan relationships, and a complex ceremonial system. Furthermore, "Respondents repeatedly linked Navajo identity with the ability to survive and endure in the face of adversity" (Schulz 1998, 347).

Two major challenges faced by younger and older Navajo women were a lack of knowledge of the Navajo language and culture and racist views that judged Navajos and other Indians to be inferior or less worthy. Women who lived a good part of their youth away from their families while attending boarding school or who grew up in cities during the mid-century relocation program lacked a speaking knowledge of the Navajo language. The time spent away from the reservation and their inability to speak Navajo contributed to their feelings of being outsiders when they returned to the reservation. Navajo women resisted and distanced themselves from negative identities related to major social problems such as lack of education, unemployment, poverty, and alcohol abuse. Even when overcoming limited familiarity with Navajo culture and harmful stereotypes, Navajo women created identities that preserved core values, beliefs, and practices.

In the third article that analyzes the sources of Navajo identity, Donna Deyhle (1998) argues that the notion of a bicultural identity fails to consider the realities that Navajo youth face in a racist environment. A more accurate portrayal of the world in which Navajo youth grow up and attend school is a "complex, messy, conflictual, contemporary world" where youth enact "performances of resistance" (1998, 6).

On the basis of Deyhle's interactions with Navajo youth at a border town school, in social settings outside of school, and in their homes in a southeastern Utah community, she interpreted music preferences as metaphors for Navajo cultural identity. During the mid- to late 1980s, the Navajo youth who had better scholastic records preferred soft rock, whereas those whose performance ranged from average to poor favored break dance music. In the 1990s, the less motivated students preferred heavy metal music.

In the border town where Deyhle worked, 48 percent of the students were Navajo. Almost 80 percent of the district's dropouts were Navajo, with one out of three Navajos leaving school before graduation. Many of the marginalized Navajo youth who preferred break dance or heavy metal music were the same ones who eventually dropped out of school. Their music of choice became a form of resistance, an oppositional identity compared to that of the whites, who had advantages in the economic and political structure of the community.

The current focus on cultural identity investigates the multiple options and facets of an identity. Navajos construct an identity based on personal and family histories, activities, and abilities as well as feelings of pride in being Navajo. A Navajo cultural identity becomes more important to women as they mature and learn more about family and tribal history, beliefs, and traditions.

Cultural Transmission

The writings of Beatrice Medicine, anthropologist and respected elder of the Standing Rock Sioux Tribe, address the concern about preserving Native American culture. Medicine asserts that "Repression of Native belief systems and Native languages has been countered by concerted efforts of many women to preserve cultural ways, languages, and a worldview that reflects unique tribal life. The adage 'women are the carriers of Indian culture' sums up this important fact of Indian life" (2001, 163).

In a study by Weiss (2000), concern about cultural loss and transmission united the lives of three generations of indigenous women from Canada and Australia. One common theme expressed by these women is their desire to reclaim their culture while negotiating a life largely shaped by the political and historical events that originate in the Western world. At the same time, these women expressed their concern for their children and grandchildren as they endeavored to transmit their culture as well as prepare them to survive in the Western world.

As with women in other cultures, Navajo women work to ensure the transmission of culture from one generation to the next. As carriers or keepers of the culture (Berman 2003; Billson 1995; Medicine 2001), women are concerned about the preservation of the language, ceremonial knowledge, social organization, weaving, and former subsistence patterns. Navajo grandmothers often prioritize their role as bearers of tradition and guardians of Navajo culture.

The desire to transmit Navajo culture is, of course, not limited to Navajo women but is shared by men and women of all ages. Elders often use stories from the oral tradition as the preferred method of passing on core tenets of Navajo beliefs and values (Schwarz 1997a, 2001). "Contemporary Navajo turn to the stories making up Navajo oral histories as the most important sources of information about their world, for these stories contain the ancestral knowledge that is the charter for life" (Schwarz 1997a, 16).

In a collection of essays, *American Indian Grandmothers: Traditions and Transitions* (Schweitzer 1999), Karen Benally and Ann Hedlund emphasize the role of Navajo grandmothers as transmitters of the culture. With excerpts from life history narratives, Benally illustrates the multiple roles of Navajo grandmothers from a single kin group. They acted "as substitute parents, kin keepers, teachers, role models, storytellers, and transmitters of tradition" (1999, 50). Grandmothers emphasized "good thinking" and "forward thinking" as important principles for adhering to Navajo values. As one grandmother stated, "Good thinking means teaching our children that we must know one another in the family. We must maintain harmonious relations. We must share with one another. We must be able to depend on one another" (1999, 49). This grandmother's statement espouses cultural values associated with the enduring principle of *k'é*, in which family and kin group cooperation and interdependence stem from feelings of love and loyalty.

Anne Hedlund, in her discussion of Navajo grandmothers who weave, recognizes that weaving contributes to a "positive status for older women and helps provide a pathway to successful aging" (1999, 54). It is often grandmothers who pass on the skill of weaving to their granddaughters, who learn by watching, not by any formal instruction or teaching. At the same time, through their weaving, grandmothers model and impart traditional values such as hard work, patience, humility, and moderation.

Grandmothers may be thwarted in their attempts to pass on traditional knowledge and customs to the younger generations for multiple reasons. Navajo-speaking grandmothers often cannot communicate with younger generations who speak limited or very little Navajo. Some Christian churches denounce Navajo traditions and ceremonies, which leads younger generations to avoid learning about them. Younger generations now see only remnants of the former land-based economy among their elders, who may have small herds of sheep and goats.

Cultural Strategies

The concept of cultural strategy, introduced by Mary Grantham-Campbell (1998) to analyze Alaska Native students' ways of dealing with their educational experiences, may be applied more comprehensively to a wide range of plans, intentions, and behaviors employed in multicultural environments. Grantham defines cultural strategies as "attitudes, behaviors, and activities that enable individuals and communities to participate in their own culture(s), as well as in other cultures with minimized risk of cultural conflict" (1998, 386). Adapting this concept to eastern area Navajo women, I will define cultural strategies as attitudes, behaviors, and activities that enable individuals and communities to preserve their own culture while participating in other cultures.

Implicit in this definition of cultural strategies is the notion that they are culturally constructed by individuals who revise and tailor strategies to fit situations, demands, and contingencies of the moment. Cultural strategies assume that culture is dynamic, that both cultural persistence and cultural change are involved as individuals meet both possibilities and constraints in their actions. At the same time, cultural strategies are distinct from adaptive strategies in that rather than adapting to another culture, cultural strategies select cultural principles and practices to incorporate into new strategies. Thus, rather than leading to the loss of one culture that is absorbed by another, cultural strategies allow individuals to adjust yet preserve their own cultural identity.

The concept of cultural strategy represents eastern area Navajo women's behavior and lifestyles better than the labels *traditional* or *modern*. Although women refer to themselves and others as traditional, modern, or somewhere in-between, women vary in their adherence to Navajo or Western culture in different aspects of their lives. The concept of cultural strategy implies that an individual will develop numerous flexible strategies and that the process is dynamic as needs and conditions change.

Cultural strategies are likely to be anchored in family strategies, which Hareven describes as "a set of interrelated family decisions and plans governing the family or household membership, migration, demographic behavior, labor-force participation, and consumption patterns" (2000, 78). A family must look forward as well as backward, acting as "both a custodian of tradition and an agent of change" (2000, 23). To adapt effectively to contemporary circumstances, families operated with a principle of selectivity when faced with changing socioeconomic conditions. "The family selected those aspects of traditional culture that were most useful in coping with new conditions and adapted them to new needs" (2000, 22).

In this selective process, Navajo women make decisions that weigh the advantages and disadvantages of a course of action for themselves and their children. Fortified with the model of independent female family members who are decision makers, Navajo women devise and negotiate cultural strategies designed to benefit themselves and their families.

Conclusion

In accounts of their life experiences, Navajo mothers and grandmothers acknowledge the competing influences that inform their plans, decisions, and courses of action. An array of federal programs, Christian missionaries, Western medicine and education, and technology and material goods, all exert powerful influences on Navajos. In response, Navajo women actively select and create strategies in light of constraints and possibilities.

Historical forces in the form of modernization, colonialism, and capitalism form an inescapable power differential between the Navajo people and Western people to produce inequities in lifestyles. The desire for modern amenities exists side by side with the reality of scarce resources that result from only partial control of the Navajo economy. Navajo culture remains the foundation of identity, the template for interactions with non-Navajos, the guide for plans and decisions, and the core of values and belief systems. Although culture change is readily apparent in many aspects of Navajo life, cultural persistence is a steady, underlying presence. Long sustained by Navajo elders and more recently promoted by Navajo government and educational programs, Navajo women adhere to "the Navajo way" while negotiating a path in a complex, contested world. In the following chapters on education, work, family life, and children, Crownpoint area women will be seen to forge a lifestyle that builds upon a cultural and historical legacy of multiple influences yet manages to sustain a Navajo identity.

4

Navajo Women and Education

At the Crownpoint High School gymnasium, we decided to forego Roxanne's graduation ceremony when we found we could barely squeeze in behind the standing crowds that arrived too late to find seats. Instead, we opted to go directly to her graduation party at her maternal grandmother's home nearby and deliver our gift and contribution of watermelon for the upcoming dinner. Extended family members and friends were already gathering while her grandmother and aunts prepared the food for the dinner. On outdoor grills, steaks cooked while mutton stew simmered on the stove inside. Women skillfully shaped thin Frisbees of flour dough to cook fry bread in skillets filled with hot melted lard.

I recognized many local relatives and family friends and met others from Lukachukai, in the Arizona portion of the reservation. Also, Roxanne's paternal grandmother, a monolingual Navajo speaker, was pointed out to me. After we ate under a blue plastic awning in back of her grandmother's house, relatives and friends stood up to give speeches, in both Navajo and English, congratulating Roxanne and encouraging her to continue her education. Her mother advised against marriage until she had completed a college education. One uncle discussed the values promoted in the school program, Character Counts. Roxanne, in turn, opened the gifts displayed on one of the tables and acknowledged the givers of each.

The most recent of many graduation parties that I have attended, these events signify an important life course event for Navajo youth. High school graduation announces a major milestone, the conclusion of the years of school that equip Navajo youth with English literacy skills and fundamental knowledge for a move into the Bilagáana world, a move impossible for those Navajo elders who never attended school. Younger generations recognize the necessity of further training and education to compete in the labor force, and high school graduation remains symbolic of the vast gulf between the elders who never attended school or attended for only a few years and those who attend longer.

Navajo Grandmothers' Two Distinct Lifestyles

In the early decades of the twentieth century, many parents and grandparents concentrated on outwitting officials who came to take children away to boarding schools. Nellie Becenti, a woman in her eighties from Dzil Abee', Milk Hill, was one of the grandmothers who never attended school. Her first memories extend back to the time when she was about seven years old. Through an interpreter, she stated:

> At seven years, I remember cleaning the house, sweeping, grinding corn, preparing food. I helped my mother work with the wool and prepare the wool. I didn't start weaving until later.
>
> I remember a time when I was almost put in school. But my maternal grandmother prevented it. I was in the hospital with throat trouble. I was being bathed when my grandmother showed up and yanked me out of the water. I remember her praying, "Please let the policeman leave my granddaughter alone." She took me home and hid me. It wasn't long before the policeman came. She locked the hogan. My grandmother was a really strong talker. (3/20/97)

Sarah McCray, who was born in 1934, also remembered how her mother kept her out of school. "I didn't attend school. My mother hid me in a sweat lodge. John Perry [the policeman] was the one who was going around collecting young Navajo Reservation boys and girls to take off the reservation to go to school. I wished I went to school, but I didn't. I have five brothers who went to school for a short time, but they came back after a few years" (7/16/97).

On her living room wall in Crownpoint, Sarah proudly displays the mortar boards that her eleven children received when they graduated from high school. She also encourages her twenty-six grandchildren to finish high school in preparation for finding a job or pursuing higher education.

Loretta Benally, who was born in 1919, represents the grandmothers who never attended school. She recalled her childhood years working at home.

> I did a lot of sheepherding and gathering of horses because I was the oldest. I didn't get an education. I didn't have shoes, just animal skin leggings. I suffered a lot. I used to eat roots when herding and went hungry. I drank water from ponds.
>
> We had a big garden. It was hard in the winter. We used to gather a lot of seeds from vegetables. We used to dry watermelon in the fall. We used to dry wild spinach, corn, and berries. We went on a wagon to gather wild foods in certain places where they grew. We gathered crow's onions, which were called that because crows loved them.
>
> We used to weave a lot and took the weaving to a trading post here or in Dalton Pass. We didn't get money for the weavings, but we traded them for food. We didn't have candy then. We used to buy coffee beans and flour. We went to a pueblo for bread. We had speckled plates and ate out of one big bowl. We made fry bread in mutton fat. We used a lot of corn meal.
>
> My brother and I used to go out and catch skunks and badgers. My brother would make me butcher them, and then we took the skins to the trading post. We would eat jackrabbits and prairie dogs. We would put water in prairie dog holes and flush them out and get several at a time.
>
> My brother and I were the only ones in my family who didn't go to school. My father told us to carry on the Navajo way. Now I feel I have nothing. (9/19/88)

Those grandmothers who did attend school frequently left after a few years because they were needed at home. Seventy-three-year-old Nellie Chavez went to school at her grandmother's insistence. "I started school in kindergarten when I was ten. My grandma brought me in on horseback."

Her grandmother said to her, "You need to talk English." Her school days ended when she was needed at home. "I had six years of school all together. My mom brought me home from school. I came home and herded sheep. I would herd sheep with my grandma and my sister" (5/22/97).

June Kalleco, a woman from Standing Rock born in 1932, completed second grade at Crownpoint Boarding School before she went home to help care for her sick grandmother. She never returned to school. The first time I met June, she was herding a small number of sheep on her land in Standing Rock, west of Crownpoint. She cards the wool, dyes it, and continues to weave traditional rugs today.

Seated in a chair in her rural home, June's dignity, self-confidence, and composure gave her the appearance of a queen seated on her throne. She dresses traditionally, in full skirts and blouses and wears her hair pulled back in a bun. She instigates and participates actively in ceremonies by planning, cooking, and singing with the medicine man. Despite her orientation to Navajo culture, she nevertheless stresses the importance of education to her grandchildren. "I talk to my grandkids and tell them that education is very important. I tell them to keep up with school and graduate and go back to school for further training. All of my kids graduated and have further education" (9/27/88). Her own immersion in Navajo culture and her desire to pass it on to her children and grandchildren does not preclude encouraging her children to pursue an education to prepare them for the labor force.

Navajo-speaking grandmothers who never attended school or attended only a few years currently regret not having an education. Their inability to speak, read, and write English handicaps them in the contemporary bicultural world. Monolingual grandmothers' inability to communicate with grandchildren who speak only English is a constant reminder of their lack of education.

The few women born in the early decades of the twentieth century who attended school throughout their childhood years and graduated from high school differ from their contemporaries in their appearance, their fluency in English, and events they have experienced throughout life. Loretta Benally's younger sister, Nuse Capitan, who was born in 1923, is one of the few grandmothers who graduated from high school. She attended Crownpoint Boarding School and then went to high school at Fort Wingate Boarding School, near Gallup, New Mexico.

> I don't remember how old I was when I went to school. Then I guess they forced us to go to school; there were a lot of us who went to school. I don't know how many of us went to school. I went up to eighth grade at Crownpoint.
>
> They used to wash for us at the school, all our clothing. I lived in the dorm. We had a nice place to sleep, clean bedding and all that.
>
> Sometimes we got lonely. One time, we were planning to run off. We got a little ways behind a hill. We heard a cow. We thought it might be a bull. We ran back. My parents used to come visit us, and they used to bring mutton and fry bread and candy. Candy cost five or ten cents then. They wanted to make us feel good at school.
>
> Then I went on to Fort Wingate High School. I finished twelfth grade over there. My boys didn't believe me. They wanted to know where my diploma was, and I told them I didn't know. "Oh, Mom, you didn't graduate," that's what they tell me.
>
> It was in 1944. The boys were going off to war. We had farewell dances every week. It was sad. It was really sad for us.
>
> I almost didn't go back to school in the twelfth grade. My mother was sick at that time. My dad said, "Go back to school."
>
> And my mother said, "Go back to school."
>
> So I went back to school. (9/20/88)

After graduation, Nuse worked at the Crownpoint Hospital as a ward aide for two years before her parents and the groom's parents arranged her marriage. Later, her education enabled her to return to work. "My husband came home [one day] . . . and said, 'I'm laid off. I'm not going back,' " she later recalled.

"I said, 'Good. I'm going to work, and you can babysit!' So I got a job at Standing Rock [Boarding School] as an education aide. I worked there for thirty-three years. I retired in '85" (9/20/88).

Since retirement, Nuse has babysat for her grandchildren and, with one of her six sons, cares for their sheep and goats. She also participates in traditional ceremonies. Whereas Nuse dresses in slacks, her sister wears traditional long three-tiered skirts.

Exceptional for her high level of education, Gladys Wilson stands out among the grandmothers as well as the entire sample of women in the Eastern Navajo Agency. The youngest of the grandmothers, Gladys was born in 1937, and was almost fifty-one at the time I interviewed her. She had a master's degree in education and was working on a second master's degree in administration. When she graduated from high school in the late 1950s, few Navajos were earning secondary diplomas. The estimated number of Navajos graduating from high school in 1956–1957 was 185 students, a number that would be multiplied by ten in the mid-1960s (Young 1961, 64). She was a pioneer in her pursuit of higher education, and at the same time she typified the future pattern of Navajo women who often return to school after they have had children and worked in the labor force. Also, Gladys exemplified the Navajo women who took advantage of the Navajo Teacher Education Development Program, the jointly sponsored project of the Navajo Department of Education and the University of New Mexico that began training Navajos to be teachers in the early 1970s. The majority of those enrolled in the program were Navajo speakers with experience as teacher aides (Emerson 1983).

After graduation from high school, Gladys married and had five children. When her youngest child was old enough to be left with a babysitter, she began to work as a dormitory aide at the Crownpoint Boarding School. Gladys's mother, who also worked at the dormitory, often babysat when their shifts at the school came at different times. During the summer, Gladys attended school at Fort Lewis College, in Durango, Colorado. She stated:

> When I was working, that's when I started taking classes. I went to summer school at Fort Lewis every summer. And then I transferred all my credits to UNM [the University of New Mexico]. Then I finished there. And then I decided to get my master's. I went back to UNM while I was still working. I'm still taking classes, this time from Western [New Mexico Western Univer-

> sity] in Silver City. And I take classes from them when they come up to Gallup. They have a branch with administrative courses.
>
> My mom was very supportive. She was always telling me there's nothing here, just like I'm telling [a local youth], "There's nothing here for you." "You don't want to end up like me, just working in dormitories. Go ahead and be a teacher." (6/21/88)

After completing her bachelor's degree in 1975, Gladys taught fifth grade at Crownpoint Boarding School for seven years and then became a school principal at an elementary school. She has since completed her second master's degree from Western New Mexico University.

Steps toward Universal Education for Navajo Children

The Treaty of 1868, signed at the release of the Navajos from their four-year imprisonment at Bosque Redondo, New Mexico, mandated education for Navajo children. This provision failed to materialize until almost one hundred years later, when universal education became a reality. The faltering beginnings of Navajo education changed little until 1928, when the Meriam Report described the harsh, militaristic character of conditions in Indian boarding schools. School days were divided between a half-day of academic instruction and another half-day of vocational instruction that entailed student labor with livestock and in gardens and kitchens to make the schools self-sufficient. Describing the eight Navajo boarding schools and nine day schools in operation in 1928 as decrepit, the Meriam Report (Meriam 1928) advocated replacing the boarding schools with day schools.

In response to these recommendations, fifty new day schools were built for Navajo children, which added thirty-five hundred new spaces for students who could reside at home and ride buses to and from school (Young 1961). Despite efforts to provide local schools for Navajo children, the day schools achieved only moderate success. "The attendance in day schools was sporadic, children were older than six when they started, and the total school capacity of 3,500 seats was never more than half filled" (Thompson 1975, 64).

A revealing indication of the early meaning of education for Navajos, the literal translation of the Navajo word for teacher, *bá'ólta'í*, is "the one for whom reading takes place" (Bowman 2002). Students learned to read for the teacher rather than for themselves. Continued reluctance of Navajo parents to send their children to school arose from family priorities that realistically assessed children's labor in the land-based economy as more vital to family well-being than the pursuit of an education. The forced stock reduction of the 1930s, which resulted in the traumatic slaughter of families' sheep, goats, and horses, exacerbated Navajo avoidance of white men's ways.

Navajo parents objected to the undesirable conditions in schools and the treatment of their children. Children might not be allowed to return home for months at a time and often received strict and harsh treatment from boarding school personnel. The alarming frequency of illness and death at school made parents "fear the institutions as a kind of death trap from which their children would not return" (Iverson 2002, 86).

Exposure to the outside world during World War II convinced Navajo parents that their children needed to be educated. After Navajo enlisted men returned from the war and men and women returned from wartime jobs, Navajos recognized that even if their children had to attend boarding schools, education was essential for living in a rapidly changing world (Adair 1947). The Navajo Tribal Council, outlining the major problems that faced the people in 1946, prioritized education as the greatest need (Iverson 2002). Navajo parents reversed their position on sending their children to school; as the need for an education became apparent, they demanded more and better schools for their children (Robert Roessel 1979; Szasz 1999; Thompson 1975). Robert Young noted that "the interest in education increased greatly during the war; Navajo servicemen and former war workers alike returned to the Reservation with a new understanding of the role of education in the life training of their children" (1961, 13).

Key legislation passed in 1950 laid the groundwork for universal education of Navajo school-aged children. The Navajo-Hopi Long-Range Rehabilitation Act funded twenty-five million dollars in numerous projects on the Navajo and Hopi Reservations, including the renovation and building of schools (Bailey and Bailey 1986; Young 1961). Enrollment of Navajo students in public schools was made possible by legislation also passed in 1950: Public Law 874, which compensated local school districts for educating children of military personnel and Indian children, and Public Law 815, which authorized money to build schools in districts where these children lived (Thompson 1975). Two major programs after World War II—the Navajo Special Education Program, commonly known as the Five-Year Program, and the Navajo Emergency Education Program—expanded the enrollment of Navajo students in schools. Navajo children's enrollment expanded from one-third of the school-age population in the 1930s and 1940s to 90 percent of the Navajo school-age population by the 1960s (Robert Roessel 1979).

The Five-Year Program

Immediately after World War II, in 1946, the BIA instituted the Five-Year Program for twelve- to eighteen-year-olds who had little or no schooling. The program's objectives were to teach adolescents the English language and basic literacy skills during the first three years and to devote the last two years to equipping the students with job skills (Robert Roessel 1979). By 1950, the Five-Year Program had brought Navajo student enrollment up to more than 50 percent of school-age Navajos for the first time (Johnston 1966).

Crownpoint women who attended the Five-Year Program made modest progress in their ability to speak, read, and write English. For example, Rita Chee, who began herding sheep with her mother as a young child, started a Five-Year Program at the Phoenix Indian School when she was twenty-two. Through an interpreter she stated:

> I went for three years to the Phoenix Indian School. I was supposed to go for five years, but I came home because of an illness. I went to school when I was twenty-two. I didn't go when I was younger; I stayed home with my mom.
>
> I learned how to spell my name, a few simple spellings and writings. I can do only simple writings today. I learned to sew,

> make dresses, make buttonholes by hand. I attended home ec classes and learned how to cook. (10/14/88)

Limited by her lack of education, Rita has had few opportunities for employment, and she and her husband raise livestock.

Midlife Mothers and the Transformation of Navajo Childhood

The impact of Navajo education irreversibly changed Navajo life. Bailey and Bailey in *A History of the Navajos: The Reservation Years* assert that "The universal education of children had a more profound influence on Navajo life and attitudes than did economic change. This was particularly true during the 1950s and even into the early 1960s. Indian schools trained students in skills they needed to survive in the Anglo-American world, but also indoctrinated them with Anglo-American cultural values" (1986, 277).

Midlife mothers from the Eastern Navajo area reached school age during the 1950s and 1960s, decades during which schools available to Navajo children multiplied both on and off the reservation. The older midlife mothers, those who reached school age in the 1950s, went to boarding schools, at least for their secondary education. The younger midlife mothers, those who reached school age in the 1960s, had the opportunity to attend local Crownpoint public schools from kindergarten through twelfth grade because the Gallup–McKinley County public junior high and high school had opened by the time they reached their adolescent years.

The nature of Navajo children's experience in boarding school sometimes depended on how often they got to see their families and visit home. As a young child, Angie Bahe, born in 1941, attended elementary school at Crownpoint Boarding School, which was located about two miles north of her home. She reminisced:

> I remember that my mom, my dad used to take us to Crownpoint where we used to go to school, and we used to be in boarding school. And they just left us there on Sunday afternoon, I think, and then we come home every other weekend, I think.

> But I know sometimes my mom and dad would come see us, just to visit. They used to give us fifty cents. And they used to make a lunch, fry bread and meat. I don't know how long that lasted, but anyway we used to share it with the girls in the dormitory.
>
> And then my mom and dad, they sent me off to Brigham City, Utah [Intermountain Indian School]. And then I would come home in the summers, just to help out with herding the sheep. Water the horses, just everyday things. Stay home and help with this and that with my sisters and brothers.
>
> So my dad used to depend on me because I was the oldest one, sort of, in the girls that is. And my brothers, I don't know where my brothers were. I guess they were out working somewhere. So it was like they sort of depended on me, just everything. Herding the sheep and being there when they need me. In the fall I go back to school. (12/15/88)

Representative of the younger midlife mothers who attended Crownpoint public schools through all or most of their school years, Bonnie Yazzie, Mary Joe's younger sister, was born in 1956. In contrast to Mary, who went to boarding school for most of her school years, by the time Bonnie reached school age, a preschool had opened at the Becenti chapter house and public schools had opened in Crownpoint. She remembered:

> I remember walking about three miles to the chapter house to attend the preschool with [my sisters]. And I remember walking back afterwards, and those two girls had longer legs than I did. I had to . . . I don't know, I didn't like it then, walking back. Especially in the hot summer, it's really dry.
>
> That I remember, and after that my father was a bus driver. That was easier for me. Kindergarten we'd get on the bus steps from my door, and I went through all, kindergarten to high school here in Crownpoint. And from kindergarten to fifth grade I rode the bus. Then we moved here to Crownpoint around when I was in sixth grade. (5/17/88)

From the sixth grade on, Bonnie attended the Gallup–McKinley County Public Schools in Crownpoint, graduating from Crownpoint High School when she was almost eighteen.

The Mormon Placement Program

Beginning in 1954, the Indian Student Placement Services Program, also known as the Mormon Placement Program, grew rapidly in the 1960s and 1970s and then declined in the 1980s and 1990s when local Navajo schools increased in number and improved in quality. Indian students, mainly from southwestern tribes, traveled from their reservation homes each school year to live with Mormon families while attending local schools. Children who were at least eight years old and baptized members of the Mormon Church lived with families close to their own age and received free clothing and room and board. At its height in 1972, the program placed 4,997 students, then gradually declined before ending in the 1990s (Dehoyos 1992).

Opposing views of the Mormon Placement Program either praise the educational and social opportunities offered or criticize the program as a traumatic psychological experience that demanded a painful adjustment to life in a social and cultural environment vastly different from the one from which the students had come. In a study funded by the Church of Jesus Christ of Latter-Day Saints, Chadwick, Albrecht, and Bahr (1986) concluded that participating students had a higher educational attainment than nonparticipants and that the placement program "fostered assimilation of the Indian students into white society" (1986, 524).

In contrast, Martin Topper (1979) analyzed the reactions of twenty-five Navajo students at home during summer vacation from the Mormon Placement Program. He divided students' behavioral responses into three groups: (1) two students who continued to identify with their Mormon families and religion, (2) twenty-one students who acted out their Navajo identity in a gender appropriate pattern, and (3) two students who refused to go back at the end of the summer. Eventually, all twenty-one students in the largest group also dropped out of the program, leaving only two students among the group of twenty-five who remained in the program, graduated from high school, and became adherents of the Mormon religion.

Similar to the pattern found in Topper's study, only one of the seven Eastern Navajo area women in the sample who left home as children to live with a Mormon foster family and attend school stayed and graduated from high school. Most returned home after one, two, or three years. The one placement student among the Crownpoint women who graduated from high school while living with a Mormon family, Rachel Morgan, maintains strong ties with her foster family in Utah, celebrating birthdays, graduations, weddings, and anniversaries. Rachel considers the Mormon Placement Program a positive formative experience in her life. As a young child, she started school in California, where her family lived during the Relocation Program. After her family moved back to Crownpoint, she attended the Crownpoint Elementary School for two years before her parents decided that the placement program promised a better education.

> We all moved back here and went to this school. My parents put us at the elementary school here. It just didn't seem right with them for some reason. Because I think the school systems here are so much different than in the cities. And maybe it has a lot to do with being in a remote area. I don't know. Being reservation, they felt like the quality of the schools wasn't up to par, and we had the best schools and were educated in really good schools [in California]. And so, I think we spent two years here.
>
> At that time, well, my family was always religious. We have a very firm religious upbringing, not traditional, but you know. And so at that time, there were some Mormon missionaries here, and they introduced the placement program to my parents. Living in a white foster home and getting basically a good education like we were getting and teaching us spiritual aspects of life.
>
> So they sent us up there [Utah] when I was in seventh grade. So from seventh to my senior year, that's where I was. I was raised with a white family that I chose to call my folks. They're the same as my parents here. They're parents to me. (9/14/88)

Rachel's Navajo parents chose the Mormon placement program as a way to provide a good education for her and her siblings. "But my parents knew what they were getting into. And my mom says now it was really hard for her. 'But I did it because I loved all of you, and I knew that you would thank me years later.' And we have. And I know she did it because she loved us" (3/10/89). Although Rachel's mother never attended school, she recognized that her children needed an education in a world vastly changed since her own childhood, when Navajos depended on their crops and livestock for survival.

The Crownpoint women who participated in the placement program gave favorable reports of their placement experiences, no matter how brief they were. For example, Geraldine, who moved to Idaho after the first semester of the ninth grade in Crownpoint, lived with a Mormon foster family for an entire year without visiting her natal family. She stated, "I really liked it. My foster parents were real nice to me. They told me to come home for Christmas. I did, and never went back" (5/2/89). The competing pull of home led her to stay there for good after the first semester of her tenth-grade year in Idaho. Once at home, she did not return to high school. Married and the mother of two children at the time I interviewed her, Geraldine was taking classes at the Crownpoint Institute of Technology to prepare for the General Equivalency Degree (GED), an alternative to a high school diploma.

Although Crownpoint area women spoke positively of their placement program experiences, other reports reveal a darker side. For example, one Navajo school principal told me about a student who had been kicked out of his host family's home and was sleeping in the park. He had to borrow money to make a phone call to ask his family for money to buy a bus ticket to get home.

Midlife Mothers and Higher Education

Unlike the grandmothers, midlife women had all attended school long enough to learn to speak, read, and write English. The major factor that distinguished midlife women's lives became graduation from high school, the stepping stone to further training and education. Within the group, older and younger midlife mothers differed in the type of higher education they pursued. The older midlife mothers were most often advised to get some vocational training, whereas the choices for the younger midlife mothers expanded to include college. Vocational training for the older midlife mothers met the need for employees in the newly created on-reservation jobs in schools, agencies, and hospitals for teacher aides, nurse aides, secretaries, and technicians.

One Crownpoint community professional, Marilyn Gilmore, who was born in 1937, attended Saint Michael's High School, a Catholic school, where the sisters decided on careers for the students. "The sisters chose our careers for us," recalled Marilyn. "The sisters characterized students. The smartest girls they encouraged to be nurses, the smartest boys, engineers. The next group of girls they encouraged to go to secretarial school. I think that's how they manipulated us." Marilyn continued: "I wanted to be a teacher, but the sisters suggested I go to business school. I never realized until I worked here that I could have gone ahead. They made us think we should be happy with that little bit of training" (5/24/88).

After high school, Marilyn attended Draughon's Business College, in Albuquerque, for one year. Later, she earned an associate's degree in sociology from the UNM, Gallup Branch. She hopes to complete a bachelor's degree in the future. She reflected:

> Sometimes I think about my life and the way my career was chosen. I didn't see that I could have gone on. Now I'm waiting for UNM to have a four-year program at the Gallup campus.
>
> I tell my son, when he gets out of high school, not to waste his time working. He has this dream, and they say that's how to reach a goal.
>
> My parents weren't educated. They told us to get up and go. "Get up early, go on. We won't be here forever for you." No one ever explained that there was something big ahead of us. Well, my sisters tried, but they gave up. They went to school for a while and just got married. My parents never told us. (5/14/88)

More Navajo high school graduates are pursuing higher education. The Navajo tribal community college, Diné College, prepares students for jobs and acts as a bridge to four-year institutions. According to Margaret Szasz, "Tribal colleges have become the institutional cultural intermediary for Native college students, reaffirming Native identity and training for survival in the contemporary world" (1999, 235).

Many Navajo women defer their education until they have had children and have had some experience in the labor force. According to the 2000 Census, more than twice as many Navajo women as men are enrolled in undergraduate and graduate programs in colleges and universities (Choudhary 2003). The mature Navajo woman student is motivated and dedicated, seeking a means to provide support and a better life for her children (McCloskey 1993; McReynolds 1997). Instead of being guided by a vague, less-relevant notion of education as preparation for a career, women further their education in order to find a job and achieve financial stability for their families.

Typical of Navajo women who become "nontraditional students," Sadie Goodluck made a decision to return to school after she was divorced.

> I went about my work, and I continued working, and when I was going through a divorce, I really told myself that I wasn't gonna, . . . you know, life can't be reversed. I can't just go back, and, you know, feeling sorry for myself. I've got to do something. I've got to do something better than what I'm doing here. There's got to be something out there that I could do.
>
> So right away, that's when I enrolled back in school. I started taking classes at UNM, and then I started taking classes through NCC, Navajo Community College, NCC [now Diné College]. Okay. I went to NCC for two years. I got all my basics out of the way and everything, and then I went to Highlands, and I got my bachelor's. And that's when I, that's where I got stuck! I haven't gotten any further than that. I want my master's so bad. But it seems like money's always the problem.
>
> But anyway, that's what I did. I advanced myself, and that's what I wanted to do was right there. I wanted to be a social worker. I wanted to get out there and help my people. Because when I was going through this crisis situation, I studied a lot

> about it. Physical abuse and the neglect. Learned about it myself. I learned, and I went through the experiences that I felt. It really encouraged me. It really motivated me to go on if this is what you want to do.
>
> And when I started my schooling, that's when I told myself, I want to help. I want to help my people. I want to help the children that are suffering out there. I made up my mind that was what I was going to do. And that's what I'm doing now. (7/19/89)

As Sadie awaits the right time to return to school to earn a master's degree, she is fulfilling her dream of helping the Navajo people.

Young Mothers and Contemporary Patterns of Education

The legacy of American Indian education has created an enduring adversarial relationship between the needs of Indian students and educational policies. The 1969 Kennedy Report characterizes schools attended by Indian children as battlegrounds in which children attempt to protect their integrity and identity, a strategy that often results in poor academic performance and a high dropout rate. In a step taken to begin to alleviate these conditions, the 1998 Executive Order on American Indian and Alaska Native Education recognizes tribal sovereignty and self-determination and calls for consultation with tribal governments about their "education-related needs and priorities" (Szasz 1999, 232).

The same educational challenges affect Navajo youth. One study of Navajo reservation high schools found that 31 percent of students dropped out before graduating (Platero et al. 1986). Young Crownpoint women's reasons for dropping out of school included pregnancy, "not caring," falling behind because a disrupted home life contributed to frequent absences, disliking school, and wanting to be independent.

Deyhle and Margonis (1995) argue that a clash of values stemming from the unfamiliar expectations and objectives of Western education contributes to Navajo female students' poor academic performance, high dropout rates, and high rates of teen pregnancy. The individualism promoted in Western nuclear families and duplicated in the classroom contradicts Navajo families' patterns of cooperation within matrilineal, extended family networks.

Although I do agree with Deyhle and Margonis's thesis that some fundamental values and attitudes encountered in Western education create a dilemma by focusing on the individual rather than the family and the community, I disagree that the reliance on the family eliminates women's desire to achieve. Rather, young women rely on extended family networks, but as they mature they develop goals and strategies that will enable them to contribute to the family economy, just as their mothers and grandmothers had done. In the past, Navajo women worked in the pastoral economy by caring for livestock, crops, and weaving, but contemporary Navajo women pursue training or higher education in order to qualify for jobs. Children act as a source of motivation to pursue higher education because mothers seek a dependable source of support for their children (McCloskey 1993; McReynolds 1997). Education qualifies mothers for dependable jobs in the labor force and assures them that they can provide for their families.

In contrast to Deyhle and Margonis's study, a recent study of Navajo high school students by a Navajo sociologist, Angela Willeto (1999), reports that Navajo girls had a higher level of academic achievement in high school than did Navajo boys. Among 541 Navajo high school students in 11 Navajo Nation high schools, girls were found to be more committed to school, had higher grade point averages, and had higher college aspirations.

In the 1960s and 1970s, when the young mothers were students, Crownpoint families confronted a multitude of options among schools. Besides the local Gallup–McKinley County Elementary School and the Christian Reformed Church elementary school, students at the BIA school, now called Crownpoint Community School, can attend as either day school or boarding school students. Also, a daily bus takes Crownpoint children twenty-six miles south to and from the Saint Bonaventure Catholic School in Thoreau, New Mexico. Middle school students can attend sixth to eighth grade at the public Crownpoint Mid School or at Crownpoint Community School. Locally, the only option for secondary students is

Crownpoint High School, a Gallup–McKinley County public school. In addition, a few parents sent their children to the Navajo Academy, now Navajo Preparatory School, a boarding school that provides bus transportation Monday and Friday to and from Farmington, eighty-seven miles north of Crownpoint.

Education and Teen Pregnancy

Representing a selective bias of the research design, the Crownpoint sample includes only young women who have started their families. Accordingly, the sample does not include young Navajo women who are not yet mothers or those who have left Crownpoint to further their education or training. The majority of the young mothers in the Eastern Navajo area sample did not graduate from high school, which may or may not be related to adolescent pregnancy.

Findings from a study by Upchurch and McCarthy (1990) contradict the popular belief that adolescent pregnancy causes students to drop out of high school. Using National Longitudinal Survey of Youth data on 5,347 young women between the ages of 14 and 21 who have complete schooling and fertility histories, they found that having a baby does not predict dropping out of high school. Adolescent pregnancies more often occurred among girls who had already dropped out of school more than nine months previously, "suggesting they did not drop out because of an impending birth" (1990, 230).

Jennie Thompson is a young mother who dropped out of school long before she became pregnant. Twenty-seven years old when I interviewed her, Jennie had dropped out of school after completing the seventh grade. Although she wanted to join the Mormon Placement Program to continue her education, her mother never completed the application. Jennie recalled: "I slowly drifted away from school. All I know [was that] I was having school problems. It was bad. Some of the kids were mean. I guess they were advanced, and I was having problems. I guess that was what was bugging me" (12/9/88). Jennie later married and gave birth to her son when she was twenty-four years old.

Some young women finished high school despite adolescent pregnancies. For example, although Clarissa Mason and her husband began having children when she was in her junior year, they both finished high school. Clarissa lived with her husband's family, and both her sister and her mother-in-law helped with child care.

> Well, when I was in school, I had Raymond.
>
> So we were to ask for a babysitter. We could take him back down to my mom's house, but it was too far away, and I was going to nurse him, but I was in school so I just put him on bottle.
>
> Well, my sister took care of him from February up to July. That's when she took care of him, and then that was kind of a little bit easier because she was there. And then when we used to come home, she would always have supper ready or something like that. She used to take care of my little boy for us. And then my mom and dad came by and picked her up, and she went home. And it was my turn to take care of him.
>
> Before that, we used to have a full day of school. And then that's when I started talking to my counselor. And I talked to him about the problem I have at home. I have a little kid, and I have to do this and that. And so he just arranged some classes for me so I could go to school for half a day and then go home and stay with my little boy.
>
> So he was on bottle, but his [her husband's] mom used to take care of him for us when we were in school. So we'd just go to school up to noon time, and the rest of the day, I used to take care of him myself. So that's how we worked it out, and then when I was having Valerie, I did the same thing, too. I just went up to school in the afternoon. (2/24/89)

Clarissa graduated from high school and encouraged her husband to attend summer school in order to catch up so that he, too, could graduate.

Earning a GED

Among the sample of young mothers I interviewed were five taking classes at the Crownpoint Institute of Technology (CIT) to prepare for GED tests. A day care center and buses that ran to outlying rural communities made it possible for these women to attend school. All of the young mothers and their children lived in extended family households. They viewed a GED as the essential first step toward being able to make a financial contribution to their extended family household and to establish an independent nuclear family unit. Sandy Etcitty and her sister, who was also working on her GED, want to be able to contribute to their mother's household, where other siblings and their children live. "We have a hard time helping my mom so we decided to go back to school and try to help out" (5/3/89). When asked what goals she had for herself, Sandy replied, "Well, I'm going to try to get a job for my family and move away from Crownpoint. It's hard" (5/3/89).

Conclusion

Different levels of education among the three generations of Navajo women reflect historically contingent views toward education and opportunities for going to school. The majority of grandmothers, who did not go to school or went for only a few years, now express regret that they did not receive an education. When young, they were needed at home to help with sheepherding and chores, when the land-based economy provided subsistence for most Navajo families. Even under the best circumstances, the prospect of leaving home for long periods to attend a distant boarding school had no apparent benefits.

Parents and grandparents sometimes hid children when officials came to their houses to take them to school. Those few grandmothers who spent their childhood years in school and subsequently graduated from high school lived markedly different lives than those who did not. These grandmothers worked in the labor force throughout their adult lives in contrast to those with little or no schooling who worked in the land-based economy.

By the time midlife mothers reached school age, parents recognized the value of an education due to the decline of the land-based economy and their increasing exposure to the Bilagáana world. Even if parents had to send their children to boarding school, they wanted them to have the advantage of learning to speak, read, and write English, and to learn math skills. The widespread growth of on-reservation schools occurred during the years the midlife mothers were growing up. As a result, older midlife mothers attended boarding schools, whereas the younger midlife mothers were more likely to attend public schools and ride buses daily to and from school. No longer did they need to endure the loneliness of the boarding school experience. Those who graduated from high school often had opportunities for further training or education, often pursuing higher education after they married and had children.

Although the young mothers routinely attended school throughout their childhood years, most often in public schools, various factors interfered with completing a high school education. Some lost interest in school; some who grew up in socially disrupted families fell behind in school; and some became pregnant and dropped out. Whether at the high school or college level, young mothers wish to further their education in order to qualify for jobs and contribute to the support of their families.

5

Navajo Women's Transition to the Labor Force

The work lives of a grandmother and her granddaughter depict the twentieth-century transition from dependence on the land-based economy to reliance on the cash economy. The oldest grandmother that I interviewed, Marie Tsosie, did not know her date of birth but estimated that she was about ninety-three years old. An alert, small woman, she gestured energetically as she talked in Navajo while her granddaughter interpreted. During her childhood, she lived west of Gallup and worked with livestock while her mother wove and her father did silversmithing.

> I remember at age ten where we lived, which was close to that trading post, and the transportation was mainly horseback, and getting places by foot. The only thing that was in existence at the time as far as strangers coming into the area was concerned was at Fort Wingate. They had the cavalry there, and a whole platoon of soldiers. I remember they were moving into there and establishing that fort and spending several years there.
>
> My activities at that time were mostly taking care of livestock. I had to go out and find our horses and bring them back and feed them so they can be used for whatever daily needs we needed to use the horses for. The sheep was our main concern. My folks let me take care of the sheep a lot. So that was my main duty, was to take care of the sheep. At the time, I was the only child with my mother and father. It wasn't until much later that another baby came along. (6/10/88)

After her marriage, which was arranged, Marie at first lived in the Dalton Pass area, west of Crownpoint, where her husband was from. Here she gave birth to eleven children, eight of whom survived to adulthood.

After her husband left her, she returned to her parents' home. Throughout these years, she raised sheep, harvested crops, and wove rugs.

> Most of the activities with the kids were to take care of the sheep. Just like I grew up, I brought them up in the same manner, taking care of stock, mainly horses and sheep. And a lot of times they helped me around the home area, too. I brought most of the kids up by myself because my husband began to leave me at that time, going off.
>
> Milan, they had big farms out there where they grew different kinds of vegetables—carrots, potatoes. And I worked there a lot. With the money I earned I bought clothes and shoes for my kids. And then I put them in school.
>
> I made money whatever way I could, mostly by weaving rugs to keep them clothed, and to give them shoes. So they would have something at school. (6/10/88)

Because education for her eight children was a priority, Marie sought multiple sources of income to prepare her children for school. Her work enabled them to finish high school and complete at least one or two years of higher education.

Marie's granddaughter, Renee Chavez, a forty-two-year-old midlife mother, exemplifies women's work in the labor force. When Renee gave birth to a son the year after she graduated from high school, her mother immediately took over the care of the infant, insisting that her daughter go to work. Renee's politically active mother stressed education and assimilation to the dominant lifestyle. Renee recalled:

> She [my mother] volunteered to take care of the baby and took him over the day after we came home from the hospital. She was concerned about her reputation, the family reputation. More or less people looked up to her in the community, being the politi-

> cian that she was. So literally she pushed me out of the reservation. As much as I hated to, I left.
>
> I worked in Washington, D.C. When I first went, I looked for a job for a while. I worked for the Department of Interior for one year. I was transferred to IHS [Indian Health Service] in Rockville, Maryland. I worked there for fifteen years. Most of my jobs were secretarial jobs, as administrative assistant, and then Grants Administration. That's where I was at when I left.
>
> I went to Federal City College for two or three years. I was always turned down for scholarships. I had to support my son and pay for my parents' taking care of him. I helped out my brothers, too. For a while, it seemed like I was sending money to all of them when my brothers were in school.
>
> I moved back [to New Mexico] in 1985. My husband got a job here. So we all followed him back. He works in Gallup for the government. (3/25/88)

Since moving to Gallup, Renee has found a job that requires her to commute three days a week to Fort Wingate and two days a week to Crownpoint. Although Renee and her husband had a son, her second, she now regrets that she didn't have more children, but as she stated, "I was busy with school, my career, and now I'm sorry" (3/25/88). In her case, "We were being pushed and pressured to do good, get an education, and assimilate, and live as well as anybody else" (4/19/88). At the same time, she is proud of her successful assimilation. She regards her small family the result of a trade-off that allows them to be successful. "I feel in my family we've advanced out of the Navajo traditional beliefs and practices. We're so much a part of American society, and I think it is concerned with family planning." Marie continues: "We know now, to have a big family, you don't get to acquire much in life. You don't get a new home, a new car every few years, you don't get to go on vacation. We've become too assimilated into that culture" (4/29/88).

As documented by Marie and Renee's work histories, during the twentieth century, wage work replaced dependence on herds of sheep. The move away from a subsistence economy had already begun during Marie's childhood in the early twentieth century, when her mother and father earned cash income by weaving and silversmithing. For Renee, this lifestyle no longer existed as an option.

Other American Indian women have also experienced the transition to wage labor. "Over the century dependence shifted from rural primary-sector employment characteristic of the nineteenth century to the urban industrial and service sectors, and Indian women participated more than ever in the formally recognized labor force" (Knack and Littlefield 1996, 15).

During World War II and, later, during the BIA-sponsored relocation program, many American Indian women and their families, some of whom never returned, worked in urban areas. Major changes occurred in American Indian women's participation in the labor force between 1960 and 1980, when employment opportunities expanded from unskilled jobs to positions in skilled, professional, and technical occupations. However, income-earning strategies within extended family groups remained diverse, with some family members continuing to maintain older subsistence patterns, to market crafts, or to provide child care for extended family members (Knack and Littlefield 1996). Likewise, Navajo extended families exhibit a variety of income-earning strategies, with some herding, weaving, silversmithing, and caring for children or older family members, whereas others find jobs in the labor force.

Twentieth-Century Changes in Navajo Women's Work Strategies

The cultural strategies that support Navajo women's work patterns highlight the importance of contributions by all members of the extended family. Although Navajo women, like many other American Indian women, grew up in a society that stressed cooperation and egalitarian relations between men and women (Amott and Mathaei 1996; Berman 2003; Fast 2002; Lamphere 1989; Powers 1986), their work strategies developed in light of the options available to them and their husbands. The transformation of Navajo women's work patterns coincides with the profound changes that affected the overall Navajo historical and cultural context during the twentieth century. Navajo men preceded Navajo women into the labor force when federal work programs and other off-reservation jobs offered employment for men to replace dependence on sheep and goats after stock reduction. Off-reservation jobs available in ranching, mining, and construction, and on the railroad were designated as men's jobs, according to Western categories (Knack and Littlefield 1996; Maltz and Archambault 1995; O'Neill 1999).

Federal programs, World War II enlistment, and war-related job opportunities softened the blow of stock reduction. However, Navajo men most often found employment elsewhere; Navajo women stayed at home to maintain the depleted herds. "The blow fell heaviest on Navajo women who were offered few alternatives—federal jobs were in forestry, irrigation, road building and the construction of schools—man's work" (Shepardson 1982, 151). As a result, during the years they were raising their children, the strategies of the majority of the grandmothers I interviewed focused on the remnants of the land-based economy, still the primary option open to them. Married before midcentury, Navajo grandmothers came to marriage as livestock owners who participated in caring for and managing the extended family's herd, raising crops, preparing wool, and weaving. Wage work opportunities were limited to seasonal farm labor, domestic work, and cooking at schools. For the few grandmothers with several years of education, opportunities included work as nurse or dormitory aides.

The midlife mothers' work lives contrast sharply with those of their own mothers in the aftermath of stock reduction and the implementation of universal education for Navajo children. As the midlife mothers reached young adulthood, they entered the labor force in school, hospital, clerical, and sales positions or sought ways to earn money in the informal economy, where they made crafts, cooked and sold food, cleaned houses, and babysat.

Young mothers found that they needed to continue their education beyond high school and confronted the specter of unemployment, a problem for young men as well. Limited employment opportunities at home and the availability of higher education and training elsewhere often led them to move to nearby cities.

Navajo midlife women in Crownpoint actively pursue some form of income-producing activity regardless of their marital status or the age of their children. In 1990, the U.S. Census reported that 56 percent of Navajos fell below the poverty level (Etsitty 1994), and in 2000, 43 percent lived in poverty (Choudhary 2003). Unemployment in the Eastern Navajo Agency consistently ranks highest among the five Navajo agencies, with rates ranging from 67.93 percent to 70.44 percent between 1996 and 1999. The overall unemployment rates for the Navajo Nation during the same years ranged from 43.65 percent to 45.81 percent (Choudhary 1997, 1998, 2001). Employment in such an environment is a privilege; for many, work in the informal economy is necessary for survival.

Grandmothers' Work Patterns

Without thinking about my choice of words, I asked the grandmother, June Kalleco, "What were your jobs as a child?"

She responded, "There were no jobs back then. I was raised herding sheep. When I came back from herding sheep, I was told to prepare the wool for weaving. That was the main thing that I did. When they sold the rug, they bought their supplies" (9/27/88).

June still maintains a small herd of sheep. She cards, spins, and dyes wool, and weaves rugs to sell. Like June, the majority of the grandmothers worked in the land-based economy throughout their adult lives, continuing the work they began as children. Foreshadowing the changes to come, the few grandmothers who attended school and spoke English diverged from this pattern when they found jobs in the labor force. Those grandmothers who graduated from high school readily found jobs in BIA schools and the local Crownpoint hospital. A few other grandmothers with little or no education worked as cooks in the local schools. While the majority of grandmothers maintained herds of sheep, Navajo men earned wages in various off-reservation jobs, often seasonal and temporary.

Work in the Land-Based Economy

Annie Burnside, fifty-seven years old when I first met her, never attended school but spent her childhood caring for livestock, tending crops, preparing wool, weaving, and grinding corn. She recalled her childhood:

> I remember when I was seven or eight I lived east of Little Water. I remember herding sheep. I remember hoeing. My parents had a large garden. I remember crying after my older sister who was in school. I myself didn't have any school. They told me to milk the goats, to tie the horses so they wouldn't wander off, and to herd sheep.
>
> I used to clean wool and card wool a lot when I was younger. I started weaving when I was a little bit older. The main thing was grinding corn on the metate.
>
> We didn't have very much when we were growing up. We didn't have as much as other Navajos. We didn't have a big flock. My mother used to weave a lot. My father tended the garden a lot and hauled wood.
>
> I think the reason that we didn't have very much was that my mother and father were married before. My two older sisters had a different father. They [my parents] didn't get back on their feet.
>
> My father was the one that told me to stay home and keep the Navajo culture alive and keep my traditions. My older sister and younger brothers went to school. I kind of regret that now. It's hard for me to get money. (10/28/88)

Annie married her husband when she was twenty and he was twenty-seven. Following the prevailing matrilocal residence pattern, he came to live with his new wife and her family.

> I had no Navajo wedding because Harry was shy. I was introduced to him by my sister. My sister was going around with one of Harry's relatives. My mother wanted to have a Navajo wedding, but he was shy.
>
> He came to live with me in Little Water. I brought him home,

> and thankfully he hasn't left. When he first came to live with me, he herded sheep. I did a lot of weaving. I stayed home a lot to take care of the children while my mother was herding sheep, taking care of the livestock. My husband used to work with the railroad a lot. (11/10/88)

A skilled artisan, Annie taught arts and crafts in the VISTA program when it was active on the reservation during the 1960s and 1970s. "My father was a silversmith. I was taught silversmithing. I learned by watching. I started doing silversmithing in my marriage," she recalled. "I also make baskets, weave rugs, and do hide tanning. I can do a lot of things on my own without people telling me what to do. Back then, I had to do what people wanted me to do. Now I make my own arts and crafts and get the income from them without other people keeping it" (11/10/88). Although Annie and her husband now live in Crownpoint, they still have their land and home east of Crownpoint, in Little Water. Since she finished raising her children, Annie began herding sheep and raising some cattle in Little Water again. She now participates in the informal economy, as well, selling Navajo tacos and mutton stew at the busy four-way intersection in Crownpoint.

This industrious woman is active in traditional ceremonies and is respected in the community for her knowledge and wisdom. At a Kinaaldá for Bonnie's older daughter, Annie acted as her sponsor, exemplifying the high ideals of Navajo womanhood.

Seasonal Farm Labor

One of the few alternatives to the land-based economy available to the grandmothers while they raised their children was seasonal farm labor and harvesting of crops. A study by Victor Uchendu (1976) carried out in 1964 and 1965 demonstrates the singular importance of seasonal farm labor as a means of earning a cash income for Navajos in the Crownpoint area. Out of 518 households in the Eastern Navajo area—which includes Standing Rock, Borrego Pass, Smith Lake, and Pinedale—263 (51 percent) engaged in seasonal farm labor. Based on estimates current in 1964 and

1965, Uchendu found that seasonal farm labor was the second most important source of wage labor after employment in full-time jobs. Women and children often accompanied their husbands to the fields, and some single women with children worked in the fields.

Because grandmothers did not have the education to qualify for newly created jobs, seasonal farm labor became an important source of a cash income in midcentury. During the years they were raising their children, they traveled with their husbands or on their own to work in the fields. Navajo women actively participated in the transition to wage work in agricultural labor, just as they had fully participated in the agrarian economy.

Theresa Bia, her children, and husband worked together on New Mexico farms throughout the agricultural season.

> During May we would work in the fields wherever there was work available. Until November. My husband worked on a tractor when we used to work in the fields. He worked mostly on machinery and watering. I used to thin out plants and weed.
>
> At noon, I would build a fire and cook lunch under the trees. Then I would bathe the children and put them to sleep in the back of the truck and then go back to work in the fields.
>
> I feel that I was a very strong, hardworking woman compared to my daughters now. And I would put the children in the back of the truck, and they would wait for me. My grandchildren get restless. (6/8/90)

Now a medicine woman, Theresa conducts Yeibichai and Enemy Way ceremonies. Also, she is knowledgeable about healing herbs that she uses to treat her grandchildren when they get sick.

Foster Grandparents

One current source of employment for Navajo-speaking grandmothers is Foster Grandparents, a tribal program that employs elders on a part-time basis in local schools and agencies to pass on traditional knowledge. Mary Ann Tso worked as a Foster Grandparent in the preschool for four years before transferring to the girls' home in Crownpoint. Coming from all over the Navajo Reservation, the girls have been sent to the home because they ran away from home or got into trouble with the law. The girls' home presented a big challenge. In her attempt to counsel the girls, Mary Ann found it "very hard to work over there. They are very rebellious and don't want to listen to advice" (10/11/88).

Foster Grandparents attend workshops that emphasize Navajo traditions, arts, and crafts, as well as ones that provide information about issues that affect children. At one workshop, Thelma Curtis played the shoe game, a winter game in which two teams, representing daytime and nocturnal animals, compete in their ability to select a ball hidden in one of four shoes. While one team chooses the shoe, the other sings traditional songs about the animals. The winning team indicates whether night or day will prevail. Thelma also attended a workshop that demonstrated how to butcher a sheep and prepare dishes made from all parts of the animal. She observed demonstrations on making blood sausage and cooking a sheep or goat intestine. I attended a Foster Grandparents talk presented by an IHS dentist, who explained that putting a baby to sleep with a bottle could cause dental caries.

Wage Labor

In sharp contrast to the grandmothers who worked in the land-based economy, sometimes supplemented by laboring in fields or making crafts, the few educated grandmothers worked in the labor force throughout their adult lives.

Gladys Wilson, a grandmother with two master's degrees, began working in Crownpoint at the BIA school. "And I worked as an education aide for about five years, maybe more," she recalled. "Then I went to Standing Rock Boarding School as dormitory supervisor and worked there for three years, still going to school nights and during the summer. And then I transferred back to Crownpoint in '75." Gladys continued: "That's when I got my bachelor's from UNM. Then I got a job as a teacher at the boarding school, and I taught fifth grade. I taught there until 1982. I got this job as a principal, and I've been here ever since" (6/21/88). When I asked Gladys what her most difficult decision had been as a woman, wife, or mother, she replied that it was "Becoming an administrator. It's a twenty-four-hour job. You never really leave it. That was a hard decision because it took me away. I do a lot of traveling, too. When I got married," she continued, "my husband and I had to sit down and talk about it. I tried it, and I like what I'm doing. There's always something new. It's never the same. I guess that's what I like" (7/1/88).

Gladys received many forms of support as she worked toward her goals. Initially, jobs in the dormitory and classroom were open to her because they were designated for women. Once she held these positions, her pursuit of higher education was supported by family, local schools, and the program designed to train Navajo teachers, the Navajo Teacher Education Development Program, which recruited teacher aides who had classroom experience (Emerson 1983). Of great importance, Gladys had the support of her husband, mother, and aunt, who cared for her children while she took classes at night and during the summer.

Chapter Projects

Chapter work projects provide short-term employment to chapter members. Offered by all Navajo chapters, the projects are funded by the Federal Revenue Sharing Program, with amounts based on the number of registered voters in each chapter. Ten- and twenty-day projects give large numbers of persons opportunities to earn some of the available money. Work projects for men include home and fence building, cutting and hauling wood, and fixing irrigation dams and ditches. Women are paid to weave rugs, make quilts, and sew items such as hot pads, which are later sold by the chapter (Bingham and Bingham 1987). At the Becenti chapter work project, I observed women making quilts and sewing. I knew two of the women, one grandmother, Loretta Benally, and one midlife mother, Margie Yellowhair. Following a typical work schedule, the workers took a coffee break at ten o'clock in the morning. Besides being paid while working at the chapter, women offer their crafts for sale at the chapter house.

Midlife Mothers' Work Patterns

Among the grandmothers, work patterns dramatically diverged between the larger group, which remained tied to the land-based economy, and a smaller, educated group that worked in the labor force. Midlife mothers, in contrast, all of whom attended school at some point in their adolescent years, looked to the cash economy as their source of support at the end of their school years. The proliferation of federal and tribal schools, hospitals, and agencies on the reservation provided job opportunities for Navajo women whose number eventually surpassed those for Navajo men (Etsitty 1994).

During the middle decades of the twentieth century, Mary Shepardson (1982) witnessed the growth of Navajo women's participation in the labor force. Earlier, the few Navajo women who worked did so as waitresses, cooks, or house cleaners, but rarely did they work in governmental offices. By 1975, Shepardson was "surprised to see so many Navajo women working in important professional positions." By then, Navajo women worked as "teachers, professors, school principals, administrators in education, public health, nurses, social workers." (1982, 158). In addition, Claudeen Bates Arthur worked as the first Navajo attorney general (Iverson 2002).

In the western rural reservation community of Shonto, Arizona, Scott Russell and Mark McDonald (1982) documented the transformation in Navajo women's work patterns. With the opening of the Shonto Boarding School in the 1960s, women's local employment began to increase. In 1974, a higher percentage of men were employed in either community or off-reservation jobs, but in the school equal numbers of men and women worked. However, the majority of women's income came from three sources of unearned income: Social Security, Bureau of Indian Affairs General Assistance, or state welfare, which was used for food, clothing, monthly payments on vehicles, and gasoline.

Among the Crownpoint midlife women in the labor force, the older women in the group, those in their forties, fared better than those born a decade later. These women finished school in the early 1960s, when the first wave of women who graduated from high school and received additional training went to work in the schools, the hospital, and the growing number of agencies in the headquarters for the Eastern Navajo Agency.

Ellen Mitchell, a forty-four-year-old single mother, worked throughout her child-rearing years. After attending Parks Business College in Denver, she stayed in the city for two years to work for an insurance company. Back home on the Navajo Reservation, she at first worked in Arizona for the BIA and the tribal government. During this time, she married and gave birth to her daughter but separated from her husband after two years because he drank and physically abused her. Since her divorce and relocation to Crownpoint, she has preferred not to remarry. As she explained to her current boyfriend, "I told him from the beginning that marriage is out of the picture" (3/21/88).

An independent career woman, Ellen described how she feels about marriage. "Me, as an Indian woman, I don't like the man to cater to me. I would rather work out what's best for my family. I'm just completely on my own, and I do what I want all the time, and I don't think about anyone else" (3/21/88).

Ellen's mother serves as a role model for Ellen's own sense of purpose and resourcefulness in caring for her family. Although her father worked, he spent his earnings on himself or his truck. "It was all my mother. She worked late into the night, weaving." Ellen avowed, "My children come first. I have to think of the betterment of my children" (4/18/88). Like her own mother, Ellen relies on her own earnings to support herself and her children.

Because of the nature of jobs available on American Indian reservations, as well as women's higher levels of education, women may hold more stable professional jobs than do their husbands. Among the Oglala Sioux, for example, women are employed in the reservation workforce in responsible positions such as educators, judges, and community leaders (Powers 1986). In general, reservation jobs favor women over men. "The distribution of labor opportunities was based on location, education in skills relevant to the larger society, and white-defined gender roles. As groups were absorbed into the national economy, employment opportunities were often more available for women than for men" (Maltz and Archambault 1995).

Mary Jo Morgan and her husband personify reservation employment patterns that force men to seek jobs away from the reservation. When I interviewed Mary Jo, she had worked for the BIA for seventeen years after completing business school in Albuquerque. Her husband belongs to the boilermakers' union, which sends workers to sites throughout the country on jobs that vary in length. "He works at the union, out of the local area. So when there's a job, they call him, and then he goes. And then he's laid off." His intermittent work makes it difficult to budget. "I have to really budget. If my husband could get a permanent job, that would really help" (3/2/88).

While he is not working, Mary Jo's husband helps care for their four children, but when he is working she takes the entire responsibility because he is away from home. Anticipating that her husband would be leaving soon on a job, she said, "And then I'll be here by myself with the kids. It's kind of hard" (3/2/88). In his absence, she must make other arrangements for child care during her work day.

Representing women who are currently the sole source of support for their families, Karen Dennison worked as a substitute teacher before she finally found a job as a child development specialist after the family moved from Phoenix to Crownpoint. Meanwhile, her husband was unable to find a job even though he has had training in three different fields.

> We moved back because I needed a change of jobs. He was going to be getting laid off soon. And I just wanted something else, too, and we were looking at Albuquerque. We were going to be moving to Albuquerque. In Albuquerque when we came back I tried putting in applications. I ran into. . . . I filed a suit against employment for discrimination. I ran into that.
>
> I had applications all over Farmington, Gallup, and as far down to Silver City, and Las Cruces. All over. And then the McKinley County Schools came through for me. And I started substituting there.

> My husband got his certificate as administrative assistant, and he went into carpentry, and he went into electrician. So he's got three trades now, but no job. Around here, there's no job. He's got applications all over, but it's still pending, still pending. Check, come in and check. So we're going through this now. (4/26/89)

While waiting to locate a job, Karen's husband is taking care of their younger child at home.

Child Care Arrangements

Child care arrangements varied widely for working mothers, but they often depended on family members and in-laws who were willing to babysit. High unemployment rates in the Crownpoint area contributed to the availability of sitters. When Evelyn Yazzie's oldest son was a few months old, she started working and continued throughout the years when she had two more sons. Evelyn's mother, who cared for Evelyn's three children when they were young, welcomed the opportunity to help raise them. Evelyn stated: "At the same time, she's a mother who was like, I don't know, she didn't feel good if other people were taking care of my kids. She feels that she should take of the kids. If someone else took care of them, that would be something that's not right. So she did it." Evelyn continued: "Now that they've grown up, they feel they owe her. They do things for her and chop wood and bring water in and stuff like that for her. It kind of just makes a cycle" (3/2/88). The employed midlife mothers in the Crownpoint area sample held on to their jobs through their childbearing and child-rearing years, recognizing that they were privileged to work in a community plagued by high unemployment rates.

The Informal Economy

The midlife mothers who were not employed, regardless of marital status, all sought ways to earn money. Only three women herded sheep, either daily or occasionally. Two of these women also wove rugs. The large herds that the grandmothers had cared for had disappeared, and the smaller

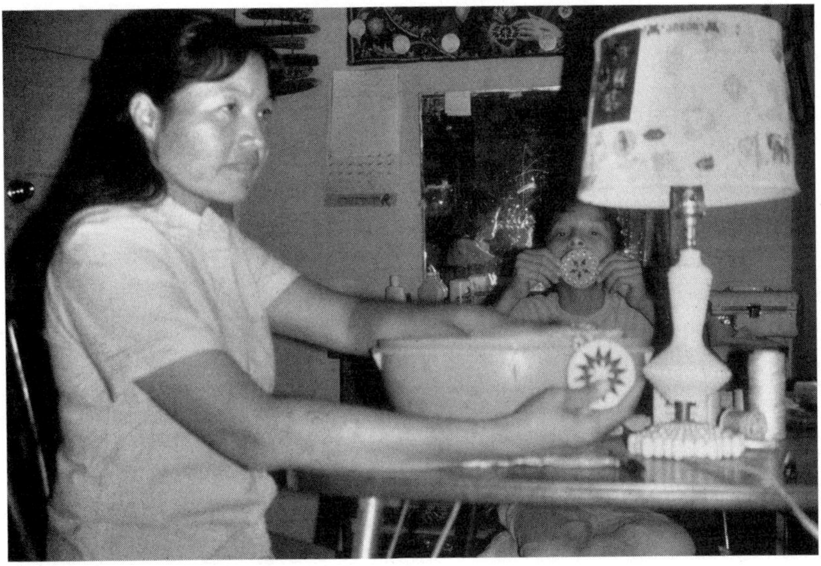

Cindy Negale displaying her beadwork.

existing herds failed to support the herders' families. The Navajo women in the informal economy earned money selling food, making crafts such as beadwork and silver jewelry, weaving rugs, babysitting, and cleaning houses. Besides their entrepreneurial activities, women depended on various other sources, most often a form of welfare, either the New Mexico's Aid to Families with Dependent Children or the Navajo Tribe's general assistance.

Angie Bahe earns a steady income from her sale of burritos, which she cooks and sells daily during the workweek to supplement her husband's earnings.

> It's hard when you're out here by yourself. Just on weekends my husband's home, but he comes home and he's tired. He can hardly do anything because he's up there.
>
> He's in Albuquerque working, and he only comes home on weekends, Friday. Then he goes back, sometimes Sunday night or early in the morning, about four o'clock in the morning.

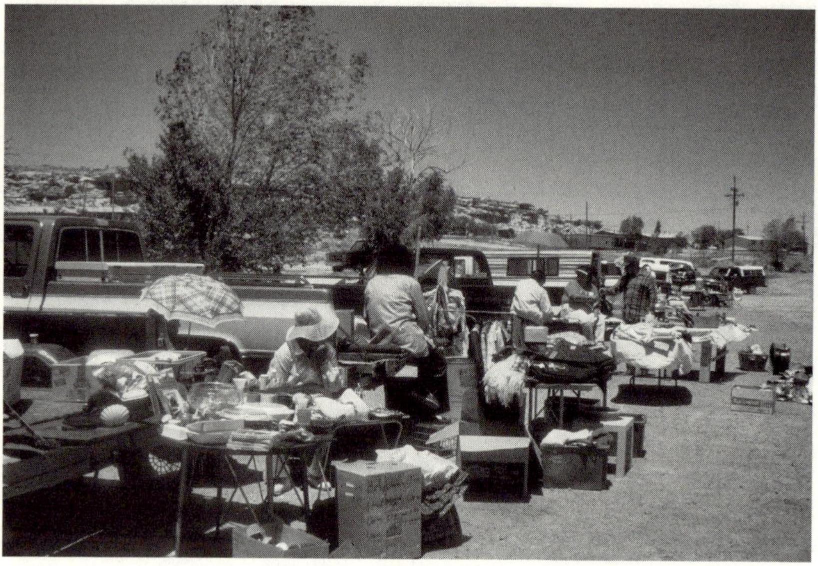

Noon at the Crownpoint four-way stop, where food, clothing, and miscellaneous items are sold.

> That's why I make my burritos every morning to sell and try and help with the bills. He makes the house payment every month, and sometimes there's not enough to go around. So I pay the water and electricity and sometimes butane. (12/15/88)

Angie sells her burritos in Crownpoint at agencies such as the police department, the BIA and welfare offices, public schools, and the Crownpoint Community School.

Nevertheless, Angie tries to find employment. Other than a ten-day job at the Crownpoint Chapter in January, when she prepared meals for senior citizens, she has not been able to find work. Since Angie did not graduate from high school, she qualifies for few jobs.

> So I went to see this lady at DOL [Department of Labor], and she said for me to go back to school. I don't know. I like cooking, I like being in the kitchen. So she told me to go back to school

about that in the fall. It's only going to take six months, and then she said she'll place me somewhere at work in the kitchen. That way I don't have to depend on my husband.

There's another job that's open over there at the high school as janitor, and my son told me not to work there. I said, "Why?"

"I don't want you over there, Mom," he told me. "Look for a job elsewhere."

I said, "Where am I supposed to get money when you need it?" And he didn't say anything.

He says, "I don't care. Don't work there." He was telling me that. Oh, shucks.

I guess he doesn't want the kids to see me as a janitor. So that's out of the question. (1/19/89)

In the meantime, Angie was attending classes at the Crownpoint Institute of Technology in order to earn her GED.

Often, midlife mothers who depend on welfare supplement their income by making crafts. Cindy Negale, a single mother who took nurse's training at Intermountain Boarding School in Brigham City, Utah, worked at the Crownpoint Hospital before she married. She did not complete her education and feels more comfortable speaking Navajo than English. She divorced her husband when his behavior became a threat to her and the children. To supplement her limited income, Cindy does beadwork, which her brother sells for her because she has no transportation.

From 1976, I started having problems with my husband, and he left in 1980. He was an abusive husband, and I made a choice to be alone with my kids. I have been on welfare since 1976 because I don't have enough education.

My kids' father doesn't support them so the welfare people said to give up on him, and they would be the ones to try to contact him.

I'm trying to make two hundred of the [beaded] headband belts. My brother in Farmington is trying to help me get a used vehicle so I can get around and take my kids to activities. (4/11/89)

With her earnings, Cindy later purchased a vehicle so that she had her own transportation.

Weaving, although the most common supplemental source of income for midlife mothers in the informal economy, did not provide enough income to replace either tribal or state assistance. Bonnie Yazzie learned to weave from her former mother-in-law when she and her ex-husband lived with his parents in Arizona. She does creative pictorial weavings, which she finds more challenging than other designs. "I like to do pictorials," said Bonnie. "I don't like to do Two Grey Hills. It's just too repetitious. I put in everything, like an appaloosa horse and a horse trailer, skunks, rabbits, rabbit brush, hogan, corrals, birds. And I put them in, and he [the trader] just grabbed it." Bonnie continued: "That was the most expensive rug I wove; after that I didn't weave. For that reason, 'cause the wool's expensive. I don't have any livestock of my own so I have to buy from other people" (5/17/88). Women in the informal economy, whether married to a wage earner or dependent on a form of assistance, found diverse ways to supplement their income.

Young Mothers

As young Navajos reached adulthood on the reservation, their prospects for finding employment were more bleak than those of their mothers' generation. Because the Navajo Nation's rich energy resources have failed to build a viable economy for the Navajo people, David Aberle's portrayal of it as an internal colony of the U.S. government still applies.

> The traditional sector provides the people with insufficient support, while the industrial sector provides almost no employment; the major employer is government. Direct welfare and public works are required to support many people. Conditions would be worse if Navajos did not share income in cash and kind so widely. The major modern technological developments are capital-intensive and use Navajo energy resources for the benefit of large corporations and their customers far from Navajoland.

> Navajo resources have been developed; a rounded economy for the benefit of the Navajo people has not. (1983, 655–56)

Many Navajo young people leave the reservation to find employment because insufficient opportunities exist in the traditional and industrial sectors of the economy.

In the Crownpoint area, the young Navajo mothers in their teens and twenties have yet to fully assume the roles and responsibilities of mature Navajo women. Whereas all grandmothers and midlife mothers engaged in productive activities either in the land-based economy, the labor force, or informal economy, fewer of the young mothers contributed to the income of their nuclear or extended families. The majority of the young mothers did not work in the labor force and depended on extended families, boyfriends or husbands, or a form of welfare for support. The lack of employment opportunities combined with the young mothers' lower education levels preclude the possibility of obtaining work. Of the three young mothers who were employed at the time that I interviewed them, two commuted to jobs some distance from Crownpoint, one in Thoreau, approximately thirty minutes' driving time, and one in Gallup, approximately one hour away.

Jennie Thompson, whose disrupted family life during childhood interfered with her school attendance, worked part-time while going to boarding school before she dropped out during her eighth-grade year. Later, while living with an aunt and helping her with child care, Jennie worked for a year as a teacher's aide in a special education class. She also worked for a short period in a retail store in Crownpoint.

At the time I interviewed her, both Jennie and her husband were unemployed and unable to get any form of assistance from the tribe. "They give you hell just to get a few groceries," Jennie remembered. "I tried to get food stamps, but they turned us down. We are living with Travis's parents. We don't have any income. My mother-in-law helps us, and Travis's dad. General assistance is unreliable," Jennie continued. "When you apply, they give you a long list of job search. If you don't have that filled out after four months, they cut you off. That's what they did with us. We got tired of it" (12/9/88). Jennie's frustration emerged when she considered Navajo women's sometimes limited opportunities. "I sometime wish I were a man. I could work construction. A lot of people don't hire women. They get pregnant" (12/9/88).

Jennie found work at a retail store in Crownpoint, where she proudly reintroduced me to her son, a tall adolescent. She appeared self-confident and energetic since she was working and independent. As a mature Navajo woman, her positive attitude has replaced discouragement from her days as a dependent young mother with no job prospects in sight.

Michelle Jimmie's skill as a weaver provided a major source of support for her family. Living with her mother, her unemployed husband, and four children, twenty-five-year-old Michelle filled orders for Navajo rugs. I first met Michelle at a youth leadership conference, where she was giving a weaving demonstration on a loom she had set up in a classroom. Seeing that I was left-handed, she explained how I needed to use the shuttle differently, inserting it to the left of the warp.

Michelle often wove late into the night to meet deadlines on her rugs. "I worked all week on that rug," she stated. "I stayed up until like three o'clock every night, and I went to bed, and I had to get up at five o'clock. Oooooh! I went bananas, but I got it done! 'Cause I had a deadline on it. I had to get it done so I got it done" (2/19/89). Michelle used both commercial yarn and hand-spun wool, which her mother spun for her. She experimented with dyes for the yarn, such as coffee grounds used to color the wool.

Besides weaving, Michelle babysat. "I've done a lot of babysitting 'cause I love kids. I had six kids last summer." The ongoing need for child care in Crownpoint has prompted the suggestion that she start a day care center. "And they wanted me to start my own day care center. I just don't have the money for it" (9/8/89).

The one young mother married to a white man, Cathy Howard, found that her husband objected to her intention to look for a job. His conception of his role as the male breadwinner conflicted with her desire to work. She recalled:

> Well, I used to work in the chapter house, and I told him that I was going to see if I could get a job at the chapter house. And

then right away he said, "What's wrong? I'm not making enough money for you?"

And I told him, I said, "That's not it," I said. "I just want to do something [other] than stay home."

And he says things like, "I make enough money. You don't need to go to work." That's what he said. And right there I just dropped the subject, and I never brought it up again. (3/22/89)

In this clash of cultural values, Cathy acted on the traditional expectation that Navajo women will contribute to the family economy, whereas her husband's Western value system led to his belief that she belonged at home while he worked.

Welfare

Income derived from general assistance from the Navajo Nation or Aid to Families with Dependent Children (AFDC) from the state of New Mexico constitute essential sources of livelihood for some Navajo women. Among the midlife women in the informal economy and the young mothers, approximately one-fourth (eight out of thirty) receive one of the two forms of assistance. Unstable relationships with men and the extremely high unemployment rates for all Navajos, which is even higher in the Eastern Navajo Agency, heighten the need for a form of welfare. Widespread shortages in human capital among Navajos (Rank 1994)—in education, training, experience, and skills—limit prospects for finding jobs elsewhere. The welfare reform legislation of 1996, which replaced AFDC with Temporary Assistance to Needy Families and slashed the number of recipients, has exacerbated the plight of struggling Navajo families.

The scarcity of jobs in the Eastern Navajo Agency does not alter Navajo women's eagerness to work, consistent with the attitudes of women on welfare throughout the United States (Edin and Lein 1997; Rank 1994; Seccombe, James, and Walters 1998). Navajo women want to work. Their lack of education and training, plus the acute shortage of employment opportunities, motivates them to seek income-earning activities in the informal economy. Navajo women who rely on a form of welfare are also active in the informal economy. Like women nationwide, they find it difficult to survive on limited income from welfare and do not have fertility rates higher than other women in order to increase their benefits (Rank 1994).

Of the three generations of Navajo women, the midlife mothers and young mothers were more likely to depend on welfare as their major source of income. Grandmothers, both widowed and married, had reached the age at which they received Social Security and veteran's benefits, most often through their husbands. Such benefits are small, but absolutely essential for survival. One grandmother in 1988 received $134 a month from the Veterans' Administration and $188 a month from Social Security.

Jennie Thompson found the application procedure for general assistance formidable. At the time I first spoke with her, the only benefit she received was Women, Infant, and Children (WIC) coupons for food supplements for their son. With the coupons, she purchased foods such as cereal, milk, juice, eggs, and cheese. Meanwhile, she and her husband lived with his parents.

Sharing resources within an extended family network ensures that all members of a family will be able to meet their basic needs. Because Evangeline Benally, who receives AFDC and food stamps, does not have a vehicle, she borrows her mother's to do grocery shopping. In return, she shares food and money for gas. Evangeline explained, "Well, I help my mom a lot with the money that we get from food stamps. I share some with her. Like for borrowing the truck from her, then I give her about twenty-five or thirty [dollars], something around there. I give her the food stamps so she can use it for herself to get something to eat. Then I give her twenty dollars on top for using the truck" (6/1/89).

In spite of patterns of reciprocity among extended family networks that stretch limited resources, unexpected expenses force women to pawn their possessions to obtain cash. Evangeline had to pawn her jewelry and shawls when her family ran out of propane. "I used to have a lot of 'jewelries' and some shawls. I pawned them for that. Like I would say, we ran out of propane 'round about the middle of the month, and we used it a lot first, and then we were running out, and it ran out in the middle of the month. So I had to go into these pawn stores and take my jewelry over there to pawn it" (6/1/89). Evangeline was not sure whether or not her jewelry was considered dead pawn because of the lengthy period it had been at the pawn store.

Evangeline enthusiastically expressed a desire to work so that she could buy things for her children. When asked how she would feel about working and being a mother, she replied, "I'll be really happy because if I'm working, I wouldn't be working for myself. I would have been working for my kids. I'll probably be still thinking about them and buying something for them while I'm working there, when they pay me, hey. So I'll be very happy to be working someplace" (6/1/89).

Gradually collecting building materials, Evangeline and her boyfriend were planning to build a house to replace the hogan in which they lived. Her fifteen-year-old daughter objected to the hogan, threatening that she would join the Mormon Placement Program and live with a foster family if they did not build a more modern house.

Regardless of their sources of financial support, midlife mothers shared resources within their kinship networks. In contrast to the coresidential kin groups that grandmothers relied on during their childhood and childbearing years, the midlife mothers in the Crownpoint area were far less likely to live with extended family members. Nevertheless, reciprocity among family members prevailed as a cultural survival strategy whenever pooling of scarce resources could make the difference between being able or not being able to buy groceries. One midlife mother whose husband had a steady job told how the couple had helped her parents, his parents, and a sister in Crownpoint. Another midlife mother on AFDC told how she periodically helped an aunt and uncle.

Unemployment affected whites as well as Navajos who lived in Crownpoint. Sarah Forrestal, a midlife mother, and her Anglo husband received general assistance. She described how she would feel if she were working. "Once in a while I go to work, but it makes me feel a lot better just working. I'm not saying that I'm not happy with only taking care of them right now. I think I'll be content with being both, just working and just being a mother. So I guess it's not hard for me" (5/2/89). Like other Navajo women, Sarah believes that providing economic support for her children is integral to her role as a mother.

Conclusion

Eastern Navajo area women's work histories exhibit both generational differences and similarities. Changes in work patterns of the grandmothers, midlife mothers, and young mothers reflect the unrelenting twentieth-century economic changes. However, Navajo women also preserved cultural values in regard to expectations that women work and contribute to the family economy. The shift from the land-based economy to the cash economy at first favored Navajo men, who had opportunities to work in construction, mining, and ranching, and on the railroad, while women maintained reduced herds of sheep and goats. Seasonal farm labor provided an important supplementary source of employment for both men and women. Meanwhile, Navajo women maintained their complementary gender roles with men and contributed to the family economy with their subsistence activities and weaving.

Grandmothers followed two main work trajectories, dependent on their levels of education. Those grandmothers who had little or no education continued the work begun during childhood by herding sheep and goats and weaving. For the able and healthy among them, there was no such thing as retirement, as they pursued their traditional economic activities. The grandmothers who had a high school education worked in the labor force, even as they raised their children.

Among the midlife mothers, education no longer always determined the type of work women did. Even with a high school education and additional training and higher education, women might not be able to find employment in Crownpoint and the Eastern Navajo Agency, which were afflicted by the highest unemployment rates on the reservation (Choudhary 2003). Although all midlife women worked, they worked in either the formal or informal economies. Those employed in the formal economy often had long work histories in their relatively scarce and prized positions. Those in the informal economy developed their weaving and craft-making skills or sought other opportunities in domestic work, babysitting, or food sales.

Rather than detracting from mothering their children, work fulfilled the expectations for Navajo women's productive role. In an environment of high unemployment, women held on to coveted jobs throughout their reproductive years. Navajo women's economic contribution to their families assumed even greater importance in the latter half of the twentieth century as more on-reservation employment opportunities became available to Navajo women than to Navajo men.

Young mothers face even more limited employment opportunities than did midlife mothers because the expansion of employment opportunities has not kept pace with the growing population. Most young Navajos must commute to jobs or relocate to urban areas to find employment. Since few young mothers in the Crownpoint sample were prepared to contribute to their nuclear or extended families, they relied on extended family members, boyfriends or husbands, and state or tribal assistance for support.

6

The Family as Custodian of Tradition and Agent of Change

In the late 1920s, Loretta Benally moved with her family from Mariano Lake, New Mexico, where she had spent her early childhood with her mother's family, to her father's family home north of Crownpoint. Eight years old at the time, she helped herd more than nine hundred sheep and goats on the seventy-mile journey north, over Dalton Pass, to Whiterock. Prompting the move was Loretta's maternal grandparents' disapproval of her father's marriage to two sisters, her mother and her mother's older sister. In their new home, the family lived with her paternal grandmother for a year before they moved to some nearby land in Becenti given to her father by his older sister. Here they built their permanent home. Loretta's mother, Alice, had nine children and her aunt, Mary, had twelve. Loretta's mother was the youngest of the two sisters and her father's second wife.

> I often wonder how my father had enough guts to have that many children. We all stayed in one big hogan. My mother stayed on the north side. She was the cook for everyone. My aunt was on the south, and my father was on the west side.
>
> There was a sheep pelt for each child to sleep on. So we could identify each one, my mother attached a color of yarn or wool. We all laid down in the hogan like a can of sardines. . . .
>
> Mine was red. Sheep skins were used as blankets, and there were also army blankets. (5/24/96)

When she compared the personalities of her aunt and mother, Loretta remembered how different they were:

My mother was more calm and patient, and Mary was more dominant and barking orders. As a result of that, as we got older the children were different in the way they were treated. The dispute started from there. Mary's children started dominating us.

There was a lot of difference in personalities. Mary's children told me that to this day. Mary was louder.

We learned more from my mother about living life. My mother was the one who raised the children and all her sister's children, cooking for them and talking to them. My father and aunt would be gone for days, taking off in the wagon.

My mother was the cook of the house. I remember her making a stack of tortillas and a stack of corn bread that high [spreading her hands about eighteen inches apart]. My mother was the weaver of the house, too. She made the clothing, the blankets, if a child needed a coat. I think that's why my mother didn't live that long. She was a slave to her sister.

My mother hauled her own water. She would take her sister's kids in the wagon with her because she didn't want to leave them alone. (5/24/96)

Loretta was responsible for herding the sheep and gathering horses.

I did a lot of sheepherding and gathering of horses because I was the oldest. I didn't get an education. I didn't have shoes, just animal skin leggings. I suffered a lot. I used to eat roots when herding and went hungry. I drank water from ponds.

My brother, Ben Cowboy, and I were the only ones in my family who didn't go to school. My father told us to carry on the Navajo way. Now I feel I have nothing.

In the early years, we didn't have a hogan after the move. Logs were hard to get. At times, we had no water. We walked great distances for snowmelt. We used brush for firewood. We had no hay then. My father used a big knife to cut grass to get ready for winter.

I cried sometimes when herding sheep in the winters because it

> was so cold. At times I had frostbitten toes. We didn't have pants then, and the cold air would go up under my skirts. (9/19/88)

When Loretta grew to adulthood, her parents arranged her marriage with her husband's parents. She didn't see her husband until the day of her traditional wedding ceremony. The groom's parents paid seven horses as a bridewealth payment to Loretta's parents. During the early years of her marriage, the couple lived with her husband's parents until they moved about a mile away after her husband's father gave them one hundred sheep to start their own herd.

> A month after Mary [her oldest daughter] was born, my husband left for the war [World War II] and was gone two years. After the war, he worked for the railroad. It was hard when I was by myself and used to herd sheep with one of the kids. We had a clan relative help, a young girl, until Mary reached puberty and could help.
>
> I took my mother in when she had TB. They wanted her to go to Albuquerque, but she wouldn't do it. She wanted to go home and died at Mariano Lake. Then my father died about a month later.
>
> I raised my younger brothers and sisters after my mother died. I made sure they went to school. I sent my brothers and sisters to border town schools, and my kids got on the bus. After that, I didn't get along with my aunt. (9/19/88)

I met Loretta's aunt, Mary, on several occasions when she was visiting with family members. Frail in body but indomitable in spirit, she participated in family decisions and gave advice about ceremonies for family members until her death at approximately one hundred years of age.

In Loretta's childhood and adulthood, many aspects of traditional family life were present. Loretta's father's marriage to two sisters represented the most common type of polygyny among Navajos, sororal polygyny. As a child and a young married woman, Loretta's moves and residence patterns encompassed the options open to Navajo families. Relatively untouched by Western society during her childhood and early years of marriage, Loretta later witnessed the profound modernizing changes that Bilagáanas brought with them. After more than forty years of marriage,

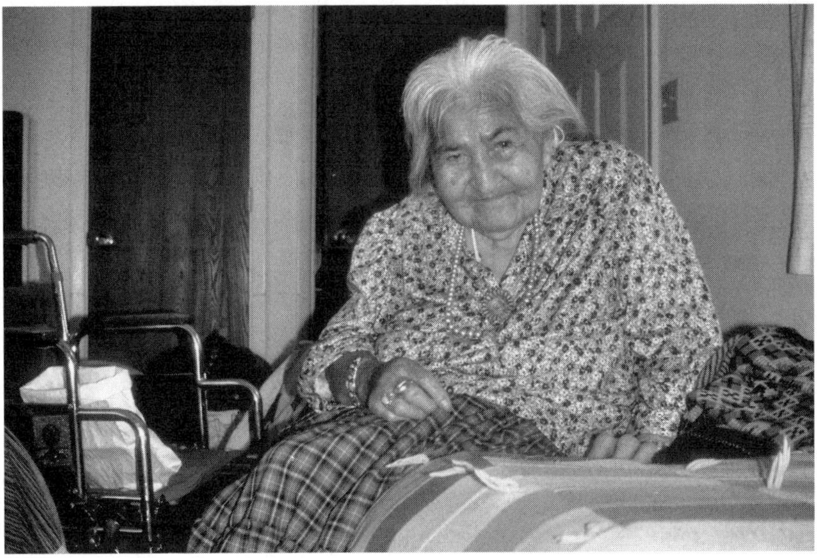

Mary Vicenti, Loretta Benally's aunt and Loretta's mother's sister and co-wife, when she was about a hundred years old.

Loretta was widowed in 1982. All of Loretta's seven children, as well as many of her numerous grandchildren and great-grandchildren, live in Crownpoint.

Navajo Women, Family, and History

"The family was both a custodian of tradition and an agent of change" (Hareven 2000, 23). This finding of Hareven applies to Navajo families as well as the New England families that she studied. "As people encountered new circumstances, they modified and reshaped their plans and strategies in the context of their own culture and traditions" (Hareven 2000, 23). Kinship networks and the extended family were important. "Members of the nuclear family were engaged in various forms of mutual assistance, collaboration, and rituals with extended kin" (Hareven 2000, 15).

In this chapter, I examine the changes and continuities in marriage and family formation among the three generations of Navajo women in the Crownpoint area. Traditional patterns of arranged marriage and establishment of a home in an extended family camp still prevailed when grandmothers like Loretta married. By the time the midlife mothers married, traditional patterns had given way to voluntary marriages, wedding licenses, and church weddings. Among young couples, unemployment and housing shortages act as barriers to marriage and promote reliance on extended family members for economic and social support.

Amidst a plethora of changes in patterns of family formation, family structure, and residence patterns during the twentieth century, Navajo women's preeminent role in the family, egalitarian relationships between men and women, and the importance of cooperation among kin groups have endured.

Tall Woman (Mitchell 2001) and her husband, the esteemed medicine man Frank Mitchell, agreed on her central role in the family. Her husband told their children that "the mother is the one who holds everything together in the hogan and because of that, they had to listen to what [she] said and do what [she] asked whenever they were [t]here" (Mitchell 2001, 237). The mother is the heart of the family, the one who plans the daily activities and gives assignments to the children.

The fundamental principle that guides the relationship between Navajo men and women is that of complementarity rather than the assumption of hierarchical relationships inherent in Western thought (Ackerman 2003; Caffrey 2000; Schwarz 1997a, 2003; Tsosie 1988). Egalitarian relationships in domestic groups (Lamphere 1974) translate into spheres of influence in different areas of life. In the land-based economy, men often assumed responsibility for farming and watching over horses and cattle, whereas women took responsibility for the hogan and the surrounding area (Leighton and Kluckhohn 1947). Because husband and wife each typically owned sheep and goats of their own, responsibility for the herd was shared.

Navajo women from the Crownpoint area almost invariably described Navajo women's roles in terms of their strong position in the family. Ellen Mitchell stated, "Women are the backbone of the family" (2/26/88). Loretta Benally said, "A lot of women believe in Changing Woman and are the head of a household" (9/19/88). Women are respected decision makers, planners, and nurturers.

One underlying value that guides relationships among family members is *k'é*, meaning kindness, love, cooperation, thoughtfulness, friendliness, and peacefulness (Witherspoon 1983, 524). K'é is the ideal for interactions with relatives, including family members, extended matrilineal kinship networks, and clan members. In daily life, k'é means helping others, a way of life important for a positive Diné identity. "To be Diné is to fulfill one's responsibilities to one's relations" (Waller and Patterson 2002, 73). For Crownpoint women, the principle of k'é is enacted in diverse ways, such as babysitting, helping prepare and carry out ceremonies, transporting people, and sharing housing, food, money, and other resources among family members.

Navajo Marriage in Sociocultural Context

The diversity in Navajo women's relationships with men in Crownpoint and the surrounding Eastern Navajo area raises the question, "What is marriage?" Numerous attempts by social scientists to define marriage (Bell 1997; Burton 1997; Gough 1959; Hua 2001) falter when applied to Navajo marriage, an institution characterized by its variability. In the past, as summed up by David Aberle, "Among the Navaho, marriages may occur with or without ceremony, with or without prior arrangement through the parents, and with or without bride price [bridewealth]" (1961, 124).

Since a Navajo child receives clan membership in the mother's clan at birth, the status of the parents' relationship becomes irrelevant to legitimacy. According to Navajo educator Ruth Roessel, "No such thing as a bastard or illegitimate child exists in traditional Navajo society. All children have a father and become part of a kinship network that supports them and provides them with parents and love" (1981, 38). Regardless of the marital status of the parents, maternal and paternal extended families rally to recognize and welcome an infant. The values and practices of a matrilineal, egalitarian society that cherishes children as sources of wealth and as evidence of the continuity of generations eliminate the need present in other societies for a defining role of marriage.

A legacy of variable ways to initiate marriage persists among young people today. A couple that begins to raise children without formalizing a marriage demonstrates its commitment over time. Marriage becomes a process, with the birth of children as the valid first step. In New Mexico between 1989 and 2000, 66.9 percent of Navajo births were to single mothers (New Mexico Vital Records and Health Statistics 1995, 1997, 2002). However, a sizable proportion of Navajo women who are labeled as single mothers have a committed relationship to the father of their child. A father's dependable financial contribution and his emotional support of mother and child validate the relationship. In the Navajo cultural context, such relationships are recognized as marriages, although they would not be in Western society.

Selecting a Marriage Partner

Over the course of the twentieth century, the responsibility for selecting a marriage partner shifted from the parents of the bride and groom to the young couple themselves. The former pattern of arranged marriage at first gave way to a transitional type, and then to voluntary marriages. For young people today, marriage becomes a process as they begin committed relationships but postpone marriage.

In an arranged marriage, the bride's parents negotiated with the parents of the groom to create a match that would benefit both families. The bridewealth given by the groom's family to the bride's family sealed the transaction between individuals who might not meet before the wedding day. Integral to the arrangements was the provision of livestock and land, most often located at the bride's family home, where the couple could build a dwelling of their own and establish a resource base within an extended family unit.

The federal stock reduction program, however, undermined arranged marriages by reducing the availability of livestock to give to children at marriage and by severely limiting the potential value of the animals to sustain young people as they embarked on a life together. Federal bureaucrats did not recognize a wedding ceremony performed by a medicine man as valid, and instead required a marriage license and an official marriage. Superintendents in the Indian Service put regulations into effect to eradicate the "vices" of polygyny and child marriage (Bailey and Bailey 1986), and later the Tribal Council outlawed polygyny (Young 1961). Although currently rare, these practices have continued covertly among the Navajo to the present. In the Crownpoint sample, one of the grandmothers had a sister who was also married to her husband, but she did not disclose that information. Missionaries sought adherents to Christian denominations, advocating church weddings and teaching that only monogamy was acceptable.

A transitional form of marriage surfaced when parents acknowledged a growing bond between a young man and woman and intervened to negotiate the bridewealth payment and plan a traditional wedding ceremony.

The transitional marriage soon gave way to the voluntary one, initiated and carried out according to the wishes of young couples. Today, young couples may obtain a marriage license, marry in a local church, engage a medicine man to conduct a traditional wedding ceremony, or combine any of the three forms. Most couples decide to marry after a period of living together. References to the obsolete arranged marriage sealed by a bridewealth payment surface when friends and relatives joke about "driving the horses over" to acknowledge a couple's wedding plans.

Although relationships ranged from casual and temporary to stable and caring, most of the mothers from Crownpoint and the Eastern Navajo area had long-term partners who fathered their children. The identity conferred by membership in their mother's clan at birth was supplemented by that of their father, whose clan they are "born for." Even in the case of a tenuous relationship between a mother and a father, a child receives recognition and acceptance by both the paternal and maternal grandparents, who demonstrate their feelings with gifts, financial support, and visits.

Marriage as a Process

From the Navajo perspective, stable, long-term relationships that begin when a couple simply decides to live together are marriages. Women in all three generations describe these relationships as marriages. For the young mothers, this pattern prevails when young couples delay marriage in the face of formidable obstacles, economic factors foremost among them (Seltzer 2000). Marriage becomes a process in which steps toward it take place over a period of years, as demonstrated in African societies (Bledsoe 1990; Comaroff 1980; Richards 1956). In the marriage process, the birth of a child to a couple is a major validating event that secures their relationship.

In a very real sense, young Navajo couples are stranded between the former arranged marriages and current patterns of dating before marrying and independently establishing homes and families. Whereas in the past younger generations depended on their parents to find marriage partners and provide sound economic bases for their future life together, contemporary young people form relationships on their own but lack the means to survive as independent married couples. Economic barriers exist for many Navajo couples, who often confront high unemployment rates (Choudhary 2001) and housing shortages. In the absence of economic independence, parenthood is an alternative route to adulthood that is valued culturally.

Residence Patterns

Contemporary residence patterns in the Crownpoint area are highly reminiscent of former extended family residence groupings even though the economic basis of the kinship group has changed. Three generations of family members may live together in housing developments in order to share scarce resources. As they enter adulthood, young people face socioeconomic uncertainty due to unemployment, incomplete educations, and housing shortages. Underlying the similarities in residence patterns among the three generations of Navajo women are core values that lead to strong ties to family, kin, and other clan members.

Most Crownpoint area grandmothers lived in rural, extended family residence groups at least some of the years after they married and were raising their children. Although Navajos express a preference for matrilocal residence after marriage, actual decisions allowed for flexibility to match individual family resources, needs, and preferences (Chisholm 1986; Kluckhohn and Leighton 1974; Lamphere 1977). In accordance with the preferred matrilocal residence pattern, Annie Burnside's husband went to live with her and her mother in Little Water after marriage. Nuse Capitan, in comparison, worked at the Standing Rock dormitory while living in a patrilocal residence group with her husband and his family. Currently, some grandmothers live in Navajo Housing Authority (NHA) housing in town or in chapter housing units, whereas others live in more rural extended family residence groups. For example, Elizabeth John lives west of town with her husband, and nearby live two adult sons, their wives, and children.

Among the women in the Eastern Navajo area, the midlife mothers in the labor force were the least likely to live in extended family residences. Many lived in nuclear family residences in NHA or BIA housing in Crownpoint. However, even those in town often lived with a relative, either occasionally or on a regular basis. Lillian Kaye, a single mother of three children, lived in Crownpoint with her sister and her son while sharing child care responsibilities. More often than women in the labor force, midlife women in the informal economy lived in extended family residence groups, either sharing homes or living in houses or hogans located near relatives' homes.

With few exceptions, young mothers lived with extended families, sharing homes with their own parents or those of their boyfriends. Although the family structure was similar in principle to the residence patterns of the grandmothers, their economic bases differed. No longer did extended family members live clustered together in order to cooperate in the land-based economy. Instead, young families depended on kinship networks to provide economic and social support as they took tentative steps toward independence.

Family Formation Patterns among Three Generations of Navajo Women

As grandmothers reached adulthood prior to midcentury, they followed diverse but largely traditional patterns of family formation (Kluckhohn and Leighton 1974; Leighton and Kluckhohn 1947; Reichard 1928). Changes in ways to select marriage partners, in residence patterns, and in additional areas became more pronounced in the younger generations. In contrast to the comparatively stable marriages among the Crownpoint grandmothers, separation and divorce became more frequent among midlife mothers. Among the young mothers, adolescent pregnancy and childbearing often guided young people's commitment to each other. Whereas the grandmothers and midlife mothers had given birth to their first child in their early twenties, more young mothers gave birth to their first child during their late teens. Early parenthood contributed to decisions to live with either the young mother's or father's parents.

Grandmothers

The oldest of the grandmothers, Marie Tsosie, had an arranged marriage, customary in the early twentieth century. Based on her estimate that she was born in 1895, she married in 1913 when she was eighteen years old. In contrast to other reports of marriages of young Navajo girls, her parents considered her too young to marry and at first objected to the marriage request from the parents of the groom. Through her interpreter, Marie stated:

> But at the time, the way that they conducted weddings was that the parents of the man had to request the parents of the girls to marry into that girl's family. To marry the girl, a formal request had to be made, which my husband's folks did. They came by one day and asked me, sat down with my father and mother and asked if they could marry their son into the family.
>
> But it took a long time for a decision to be made because my parents didn't like the idea of my getting married at age eighteen. They wanted me to wait until I became at least twenty years old. That was the proper way of doing it, I believe, that we had to be much older than eighteen before we got married. So there was a lot of negotiating that was done back and forth before they finally agreed that I could go ahead and marry my husband. And after I got married, it was another year before I had my first baby. And now he's getting as old as I am! (6/10/88)

Marie and her husband were married by missionaries and got a marriage license, practices essentially unknown at that time.

> The missionaries from Rehoboth were there at the time, and we got a license, a marriage license filled out by them. We were taught by the missionaries that once that marriage license was made and we were married by the missionaries that meant that we had to stay together for life and that we couldn't deviate from each other anymore. That there was only one path we could follow. We couldn't switch to any other path. As long as we were married, we had to follow that one path together and not deviate from each other. And that's what was explained to us at the time, but I remembered it so I led a good life and never deviated, but after a time, my husband left me. (6/10/88)

After her husband left, Marie moved from her husband's family's home to live near her parents while she finished raising her children. "My main concern was my kids all the time, struggling to keep them fed and clothed and active, doing their chores and things. My main concern also was keeping them in school. During their very young childhood days, they took them to Oklahoma, that was where they went to school. They began their lives from there" (6/10/88).

Marie's agency, strength, and determination guided her as she wove rugs, herded sheep, and worked as a seasonal laborer harvesting crops in order to support her children and send them to school.

Conflicting reports on the frequency of divorce in traditional marriages make it difficult to assess the stability of Navajo marriages. "In spite of the ease with which such divorces took place," contends Ruth Roessel, "Navajo marriages generally were stable" (1981, 62). However, anthropologists have observed that divorce occurred frequently (Aberle 1961; Kluckhohn 1966), particularly in the early years of marriage (Lamphere 1974). The majority of the grandmothers in the Crownpoint sample maintained long-term marriages to one husband, and these ended only at death. As in the case of Marie, if divorce did occur, the extended family cushioned the impact, with other male family members stepping in to interact with and guide the children (Ruth Roessel 1981).

Although the most common age for marriage in the Crownpoint sample of grandmothers was in the early twenties, marriage often did occur shortly after puberty. Theresa Bia was fifteen years old when she married. Through her interpreter, Theresa recalled the events that led to her marriage:

> My mother was still alive. How they got to know who I was—my husband's father was at my puberty ceremony and observed me. I ran the distance, and I did things really well, and that's what he admired about me. He noticed how I helped around, how I cooked. I was a good girl, a good lady.
>
> My husband's parents went to visit my family. My father was gone by then. They needed a man's help with the work at home. They made plans.
>
> I had no say-so. It was between my mother and his parents. I had to go along with what was planned. I was asked if I was afraid of men. But I had a cousin sister who was already married, and she was doing real well.
>
> When I got married, I had corn meal and a Navajo basket. And I was told by my mother that at the dawn of the day I was to make suds of the yucca and grind corn.
>
> I was told that my husband's father told that I made the Navajo cake real well, and I ran the distance real well, and that's what he wanted to see.
>
> And I said, "What does he care? I won't be running for him." But in those days they said that you shouldn't be saying that. But nowadays it's different. (5/18/90)

Married forty years when I interviewed her, Theresa had ten children, most of whom were married and had children of their own. The absence of a wedding license, an imposed formality, is irrelevant to extended family and clan members, since her marriage was sanctioned by her traditional wedding ceremony.

Sarah McCray's marriage represents the transitional marriage because her father stepped in to arrange the bridewealth after she met her husband.

> I met him when I was seventeen, and he was twenty-one. My brother took me to go to the movies in Grants to meet young

> people. One offered to pay for me; I didn't know that was the one who was going to be my husband.
>
> We continued meeting, and we brought him home, and my father found out. I don't know how much my husband's family paid for me. We didn't have a ceremony. My father said that once you meet a man he is your husband.
>
> We left for Idaho. We worked as migrant workers in the fields there. I was with him for two months straight, and I used to cry because I missed my family.
>
> My husband was a very gentle man. It took me a long time to get over my grief when he died. He never raised a fist towards me. He never drank. He talked to his kids, "I never drank. I don't want you to drink. I don't want you to fight. Do you see your mother and I fighting?" (8/7/97)

One of the few grandmothers who graduated from high school, Stella Larson, got to know her future husband at school. Her marriage represents the transitional marriage type because her husband's mother intervened to arrange a traditional wedding for the young couple.

Explaining how she met her husband, Stella stated, "He was my friend at school. And so I guess his mother saw us together and said, 'Well, are you going to go after that girl?' He was just going to go into the army. So I had a big Navajo wedding. He brought a cow and a calf. And my relatives butchered that the next morning. They all took a piece. We didn't get any" (9/26/88).

Stella accompanied her husband when he was stationed at bases around the country. After three years in the service, they returned to the Navajo Reservation, first to Window Rock and later to Crownpoint.

Among the grandmothers, the voluntary type of marriage appeared in which couples met on their own and agreed to live as man and wife. Dorothy Reed is typical of such grandmothers who voluntarily began living with their husbands without a wedding ceremony. Similar to other grandmothers who met and married on their own, she stated simply, "I never had a Navajo wedding. We just met on our own and made a good life" (4/11/89). Dorothy and her husband were married for twenty-seven years until his death in 1970.

Midlife Mothers

Among the sample of midlife mothers, voluntary marriages became the most common type, and divorce occurred more often. Arranged and transitional marriages became the exception rather than the rule. Women became acquainted with their future husbands, often in high school or in vocational school, before deciding to marry. Women who had an arranged marriage were likely to have had less education.

Rita Chee, a monolingual Navajo speaker from a remote rural area north of Crownpoint, attended three years of a five-year educational program, and later married when she was thirty-one. Through her interpreter, Rita described her wedding. "I didn't know the groom. They asked for my hand in marriage. The groom came with his family, and the ceremony was held. I remember eating corn meal mush in a basket with him. We were married in 1967. The groom's family paid fifty dollars for me" (10/14/88). At the time I interviewed Rita, she and her husband lived in the same area where she had grown up, caring for their livestock with the help of their two sons.

Another woman who had an arranged marriage, Sadie Goodluck, was a high school graduate whose arranged marriage took her by surprise. She still resents the role that her brother and parents played in planning the marriage. As a teenager, Sadie babysat for her older brother and his wife, whose brother later became her husband. Sadie recalled:

> It's like I said, my older brother is married to his sister, right. Okay. During the summer I used to be used as a babysitter in that home there. So oftentimes this man would come by. And one year, one summer, I was babysitting again, and this talk came around, something about arrangement for marriage. But it never really dawned on me that it was about me and him. . . .
>
> My sisters used to tell me that your brother was the one, our brother was the one, that came to force mother to say yes, that I could marry that guy. So I guess all this time the talk and arranging was made behind my back. He started asking me out to go to the movies and stuff like that.
>
> And it was kind of like arrangement type, I would say, because

> I've never gotten used to him. I really didn't know him when I got together with him. (7/19/89)

The marriage ended in divorce because of her husband's drinking, abuse, and jealousy. After her painful divorce, Sadie returned to school and earned her bachelor's degree and remarried "a wonderful person. He's got a lot of things going for him" (7/18/89).

As arranged marriages disappeared, transitional marriages became less common among the midlife mothers. Cindy Negale recalled that her mother and her boyfriend's mother took matters into to their own hands to arrange a wedding. "When I was a nurse's aide at Crownpoint Hospital, he was a patient. He was discharged, but he kept coming to see me. I didn't know that his mother and my mother knew each other, and they got us together. They paid for me" (4/11/89).

Cindy and her boyfriend were married at her parents' home, near the location of her present home. "I was living with him. A day before the wedding, I was brought back over here. I had a green velveteen outfit. I had jewelry, concho belt, necklace" (4/11/89).

Parents' intervention in planning marriages between young people declined as more young couples decided to marry before their parents consulted each other. Young Navajos, who then had many opportunities to become acquainted with each other, initiated relationships on their own. If a couple had a traditional Navajo wedding, it was likely to be their own idea or a mutual decision made by the couple and their parents.

Carla Harwood's marriages typify the most common pattern of voluntary marriages among the midlife mothers. She has had two marriages, both of which were voluntary. Carla met her first husband in school when she was in the seventh grade but didn't marry him until she was twenty-one. After they divorced, she met the man who became her second husband at work. They decided to marry, and together they planned a traditional Navajo wedding as well as a Las Vegas wedding. Her husband's grandmother, a medicine woman, conducted their traditional Navajo wedding.

> You have to have a basket, wedding vase, and a gourd water scoop. So I got those things. Sometimes the man's parents would ask for buckskins.

We had a traditional wedding at my older sister's house. We cooked up a storm. The women's side cooked lunch for the men's relatives. So we gave it to them, and they went home. That's how we had our wedding. . . .

In white society, they both eat the wedding cake. In a Navajo wedding, it is corn mush. We both fed it to each other. Then later we got married in Las Vegas. We thought it would be fun. (3/14/88)

My husband helps me. We're equal partners. When I go to school, my husband is there for the kids. He cooks for them. I know it's not like that for all families. My husband supports me completely in my desire to go to school. (5/26/88)

Carla compared her second husband to her first husband.

My husband is a lot different from my first husband. He is a very responsible man. I think family comes first to him. I think his brothers and sisters look up to him.

I am going to school at the Gallup Branch of UNM at night and on Saturday. The first time I decided to go to school, he's behind me all the way. He got his bachelor's from UNM in 1973. Education is really a goal for his family. His mother has a degree, and he has a sister working on her doctorate. So I've been going to school in the evenings. I'm going for an associate in computer science. He says, "When you get it, go ahead and go full time to get your bachelor's." It's the traveling, it's a lot of traveling. I go Monday through Thursday, and Saturdays all day. (3/14/88)

As with the grandmothers, an egalitarian relationship between husband and wife remains the ideal in a marriage. Among the midlife mothers, equal contributions involve both work and education.

In contrast to Carla Harwood's husband, who encouraged her pursuit of higher education, some women's husbands object to their efforts to go to school. For instance, Christine Tsinnijinnie's second husband left when she decided to go to the Crownpoint Institute of Technology.

> I had a choice to forget it or go back to school. My husband told me that if I went then he would go, so I had to really think about that. I didn't think that he meant it, but I just took that chance.
>
> But it sort of made me wake up to a lot of things. I can do a lot of things myself, too. I don't really have to depend on somebody to help me. But I think that the kids are the ones that really kind of suffered then, too. Even though it was their stepdad, they really cared for him, and they thought of him as their real dad. They didn't think of the other one. They didn't think of their real dad as their real dad. They thought of him as their real dad, and they suffered a lot. (11/22/88)

Christine's husband's reaction to her going to school was not an isolated example. Some returning women students in my classes at Diné College also had to struggle with the resentment and jealousy of husbands who opposed their decisions to further their education.

Divorce, Single Mothers, and Female-Headed Households

Marriages that ended in divorce increased among the midlife mothers, as did households headed by females. Midlife mothers acknowledged the unsettling trauma involved in going through a divorce.

In Sadie Goodluck's family, her parents and seven siblings all had stable marriages, making it far more difficult for Sadie to divorce her husband. Her sisters' marriages had lasted as long as twenty-five years, and her parents' marriage endured more than fifty years before they passed away.

With her oldest daughter's encouragement to end the abusive cycle in her marriage, Sadie overcame her hesitation.

> But it got to where my husband started drinking heavy, abusing me. Even sometimes when he doesn't drink, he still abused me because he was so jealous. I was working. And I just didn't know how to cope with it, and I didn't know how to live with it. So the best thing, I got advice from my family, my immediate family,

> 'cause I didn't want to. . . . I didn't want no divorce, or anything. I tried to hang on to it for as long as I could because of my children, because of my daughters.
>
> I tried so hard. One day, my daughter—I think that she was the most supportive, and she was the most encouraging person in my life. She came up to me one day. She was not maybe more than thirteen years old, twelve years old.
>
> Anyway, she came up to me, and she says, "Momma, we can't carry on this far, we can't carry on like this no more." Because a lot of times I would, when I get abused, I would like to leave. When I leave, when I leave the house, I don't know where to go. And my kids would be with me. And we end up going back to the same place. And I guess they just couldn't put up with it any more.
>
> So finally she's the one that really supported me. She told me, "We can't go on like this anymore. There's got to be some way that we can move away or move out of that place." And I finally decided, and I talked to my family members, my mother and my father, and my sisters, my brothers. 'Cause nobody has ever experienced anything like that in the family. Mom and Dad, I had Mom and Dad all the time, nobody else, and it seemed so different when you have to go through something like this. It was very, very stressful for me. (7/19/89)

Sadie's divorce motivated her to return to school and earn a bachelor's degree.

In the context of Navajo culture, the label *female-headed household* bears reexamining. Single and divorced mothers who either live with their extended families or visit them often do not assume sole responsibility for their children, as do women isolated in nuclear family residences. Instead, male and female relatives nurture and support mothers and children, providing a cushion that absorbs changes in family structure. Ruth Roessel states:

> Further, living in the general area of the wives' parents provided a group of relatives around the children that kept divorce from

> being devastating. Men were always in and around the camp, regardless of whether the father himself were present. Those individuals would react with the children in ways which were not different from the interaction of the father with his own children. Further, the various aunts and other relatives surrounded the children with the cushion of love and attention which provided a degree of security for the divorced family that rarely is seen in other societies. Thus, the very nature of Navajo culture made divorce far less destructive and traumatic than it often is in a nuclear family culture such as we find in the dominant American society today. (1981, 62)

Thus, the extended family compensated for a father's absence and rendered the concept of the female-headed household insignificant when a single mother was supported by caring family members.

Whether mothers are married or single, persistent Navajo values accord them high status. Also, because single mothers who hold stable jobs in the labor force have adequate resources to support themselves and their children, the complications of poverty that hamper many single mothers may not apply to these women. In general, employed single mothers expressed pride in what they had accomplished on their own, and sometimes they preferred to remain single or not to remarry. "My present friend, I have been going with him for six years," explained Ellen Mitchell. "I don't want no problems. So I'd rather stay single. He treats me really good. He's always there with his helping hand" (3/21/88).

Another midlife mother, Lillian Kaye, lives with her three children and her sister and her children. Lillian stated, "I sometimes regret that I went with all these Navajo guys. I tell my sister that there's no Navajo man that's going to make a difference" (5/3/89). When the father of her two younger children visits, her children are reluctant to spend time with him. "He wants to know if we need anything for the kids. Sometimes he wants to take them out. They don't want to go to his mom's house [with him]." Lillian went on: "When I take them over, they fit in the family. They give their [paternal] grandma and grandpa a big hug. They don't want to go with their dad. I guess maybe he thinks he asked at the wrong time. They'll go there for the day," said Lillian, "but in the evenings they always want to come home" (5/3/89). Regardless of the nature of the relationship with the father, ties with his parents typically remain strong.

Some midlife mothers never married, a pattern not represented among the grandmothers. In this category, I include temporary relationships and occasional visiting relationships, but not long-term common law relationships.

For example, Charlene Gray met her daughter's father when she was attending the Southwest Indian Polytechnic Institute in Albuquerque, New Mexico. Charlene recalled, "In September, we played a lot of basketball, volleyball. It was in October I started going with him. In February I found out I was pregnant. He was drinking a lot. I told him I was leaving," said Charlene, "and I did. I thought he would come after me, but he never did. I stayed home and made rugs. I kind of forgot about him. My mother was the one that helped me" (5/31/89).

Charlene's former boyfriend's sisters initiated contact when her daughter was one year old, and she invited them to visit. Later, when her daughter reached grade school age, the father began to visit her on a regular basis and arranged visits at his home even though he had a family by then. "He started coming to see her [my daughter] regularly. She got used to him," recalled Charlene. "Now it's to the point that she looks forward to seeing him. Like she wants to go to the reception tomorrow. My sisters really encourage her. 'You have a father that loves you' " (5/31/89). While growing up, Charlene's daughter built a relationship with her father, despite the short-lived relationship between her parents.

Priscilla Curly does not consider her former relationship with the father of her children to have been a marriage. During their intermittent relationship, Priscilla gave birth to three children over an eight-year period. Priscilla recalled:

> I met him in Roswell when I was going to school there. He is from Arizona. We didn't really live together. The only time, in '80 and '81 was when my baby was young. He used to help us out a lot. He was working.
>
> My older ones knew him. One time, I was talking to him in

> town. I saw him in Gallup. Later, my younger girl asked why I was talking to a strange man. I told her, "That's your father." Now she talks about him sometimes. Kids like to talk about their daddy, and she does.
>
> His family came out when I had that ceremony for my daughter. One of the in-laws was the medicine man for the Kinaaldá. He [the father] didn't come. I found out later that he was afraid to. I think that he had another woman, and I think his family knew that. Maybe he was even married.
>
> We don't keep in touch. He helped us out a lot. We asked him before he left because my daughters needed some braces and glasses. But he didn't [provide any financial help] so we don't bother him anymore. (3/25/88)

Priscilla's steady job and close ties to her own extended family enable her to raise her children within a supportive kinship network. Because Priscilla lives with her mother and three uncles, her children are growing up surrounded with caring relatives.

Mothers who were divorced or never married may be categorized as female heads of household, a family type that became more frequent among the midlife mothers than among the grandmothers. The 1980 census reported that 24.3 percent of Navajo families had female heads, with no husband present (Technical Support Department, Navajo Nation 1988).

Young Mothers

Young mothers formed relationships with boyfriends and gave birth to their first child at younger ages than did mothers and grandmothers. One major trend among young mothers was a delay in marriage until after the birth of one or more children. In the Crownpoint sample of young mothers, the formally married mothers tended to be in their twenties, whereas those in their teens were in the process of marriage. Unmarried couples often had stable, committed relationships despite early parenthood and dim prospects for employment and housing.

Twenty-two-year-old Rosie Slim had chosen not to marry the father of her child, Amanda, and no longer had a relationship with him. Rosie declared:

> He wanted to get married, but I told him, "You aren't ready for it." At that time he was twenty-three. I was nineteen. I told him, "You're not ready, and I know I'm not ready."
>
> "I started going with you, and you're the only guy I've been out with. I started going with you and getting married right after just because I got pregnant, I don't think that's right." And I told him, "I don't think you're ready to settle down either. So it's best we just see what happens." I said, "If you care enough for both of us, then you'll come back. Then if you don't, you won't. So I can live with or without you. It won't bother me." [She laughs.]
>
> So that's what, I just let him do what he wants now. And I do what I want so I still got some of the freedom that I never had to do what I wanted to do without someone telling me you can't do that or something like that. So I enjoy it. I'm glad I made that decision not to get married.
>
> His family and my family, they were like having it to where we were. . . . They were already planning for us to get married and all that. And I'm like, . . . I mean, I was crying, begging my dad, "I don't want to," and all that.
>
> Yeh, I see the family and all that. I used to talk to him a lot more and stuff like that. We still saw each other, but then after he started seeing this other girl, he didn't . . . she wasn't fond of the idea of my being around, or Amanda being around. So I just left it like that. I just told him, "You picked her, so it's up to you who you're going to pick, Amanda or her." (11/2/88)

Amanda's father occasionally contributes financially, but Rosie and her parents avoid pressing him to support his daughter. Rosie explained: "People tell me to take it to court and get child support and all that. My dad said, 'We don't need to do that. We have enough money. We don't want, like his family saying this and that about how he had to help us. If he wants to help, he can do it on his own,' her dad continued, 'but we're not going to force him.' So I said, 'That's fine with me.' So he'll give her money every once in a while, but we don't go to him asking for money" (11/2/88). Judging that a future relationship with Amanda's father would be rocky, Rosie chose to remain single and raise her daughter with her parents' help. Like other young Navajo mothers, Rosie turned to reliable kinship networks for emotional, financial, and social support (Dalla and Gamble 1998).

After living together and having children, young couples often marry to solidify a promising and committed relationship. Victoria John, for example, married her husband when she was seventeen years old and her oldest child was two. Victoria started going with her future husband when her older sister was going with his brother. She recalled, "My sisters used to tell me about him. I guess they didn't like me going with him. He's really changed. He was a big flirt. My mom didn't like me going with him," said Victoria. "She didn't approve of it. We had a hard time seeing each other. Also, we went to the same church. I guess that's how we knew each other" (2/24/89).

I asked Victoria to tell me about when she and her husband got married. "I remember that day he went to ask my mother. He barely made it up the steps. He was so scared," Victoria recalled. "They talked. My mother was crying. He could barely understand what my mother was saying. My oldest daughter was only two years old then" (2/24/89). When I last talked with Victoria, she and her husband had just had their fourth child after ten years of marriage.

Conclusion

The customs that guide selection of a marriage partner, postmarital residence patterns, and family formation and dissolution demonstrate both change and continuity among the grandmothers, midlife mothers, and young mothers. When the grandmothers married, before or around midcentury, arranged marriages and sororal polygyny, although decreasing, were still practiced. Rural residence in large extended family camps predominated at a time when families still partially relied on herding and farming. Some couples began their married lives with a wedding ceremony, often a traditional one conducted by a medicine man. Meanwhile, civil weddings or church weddings were becoming more common. Other couples simply started living together. Among the grandmothers in the Crownpoint sample, marriages were relatively stable, irrespective of whether the marriage was initiated by living together or formalized by a traditional, church, or civil ceremony, but divorce and separation did occur.

Sororal polygyny disappeared, and arranged marriages became rare among the midlife mothers, whereas voluntary marriages became the norm. Couples who initiated a marriage with a ceremony may have had a Navajo traditional ceremony, a civil ceremony, or a church wedding, either with or without obtaining a marriage license. Separation and divorce became more common among midlife mothers than among the grandmothers, and some mothers never married. Midlife mothers were far more likely to live in nuclear family residences and in town than were grandmothers.

Many of the young mothers formed relationships and gave birth to children at younger ages than did their mothers and grandmothers. The young mothers who married tended to wait until after the birth of a child, and, like the midlife mothers, initiated marriage in a variety of ways. Adolescent marriage and parenthood, high rates of unemployment, and housing shortages dictated the need to live with extended family members. Residence patterns resembled those of the grandmothers in that young couples lived with extended family members, either the parents of the mother or the father, but differed in that homes were often located in Crownpoint or in Navajo Housing Authority housing developments in surrounding chapters, or in rural areas.

Although arranged marriages, the bridewealth, and sororal polygyny gave way to voluntary, monogamous marriages, other customs remain. The strong ties among extended family members and the central position of women in the family persist in spite of more fragile marriages, proliferation of nuclear family residences, and the dispersion of family members to find work or pursue educations.

7

Wealth in Children

Cindy Negale cherishes memories of a childhood she spent with her maternal grandparents, who gave her special attention and made her feel loved and wanted. When she herded sheep with her grandfather in the winter, he would tell winter stories. Because her grandfather was a medicine man and often away from home conducting ceremonies, she and her grandmother spent a lot of time together.

> I was very close to my grandmother. When my grandfather went to a sing, my grandmother used to tell about her childhood years. I used to sleep on a sheepskin with my grandmother. I think children now would be afraid to sleep on a sheepskin. Some are afraid of sheep.
>
> I remember herding sheep with my grandmother. We had dried meat for lunch. My grandmother would chop it up and cook it, and I was satisfied with it. That's all we ate. Now we eat food the Bilagáana gave us, and then they say we're diabetic.
>
> After I quit school here at Crownpoint, my parents took me away from my grandmother and put me in Intermountain School in Brigham City, Utah. I was there a couple of years and came home because I heard my grandmother died. I came home and had nowhere to go and went to my mother's. I had nurse's aide training at Intermountain. I came back and got a job at Crownpoint Hospital. (4/11/89)

When I first became acquainted with Cindy, she was a divorced thirty-six-year-old mother of three children whose focus centered on her children. When I asked her how her life changed after she started to have children, she replied:

> To this day, I'm still enjoying it. Some say they don't like to have kids. But I like to have kids.
>
> I prefer the traditional life because I was brought up very traditional by my grandparents. My children are leaning towards English, but I am telling them that Navajo is important. I talk to them in Navajo. My daughter is learning how to cook, to peel potatoes, make dough. I tell her she needs to learn how to cook. I'm teaching my boys how to cook, too. I tell my daughter and sons, "If your husband or wife leaves you, you'll know what to do."
>
> I'm teaching them how to build a fire. They bring in firewood. I leave them a simple message and food on the table if I'm not home. (4/11/89)

Although she is one of nine children, Cindy used family planning methods advocated by IHS and tribal staff members to limit the size of her family to three children. The tribal family planning staff pointed out the negative economic consequences of having large families.

> The hospital warns us not to have too many children because there's poverty, no place to go when they grow up, unemployment. But then the children keep the earth moving!
>
> I prefer to have children because the children give me the strength in life to go on. My children teach me a lot, and life teaches me a lot when I have children. When they grow up, they'll help me back financially. Some people who don't have children tell me that I am lucky to have children. (4/11/89)

When asked her opinion about the Keetso baby, whose Navajo mother gave her to the Pitts family in California, Cindy expressed her disapproval. "I don't think that's right. If somebody raped me, I wouldn't give it away. I would keep it. I don't approve because the baby is her flesh. The Holy People gave it to her. Even though a man and a woman make the baby, the Holy People have a lot to do with giving her the baby." Cindy continued: "I heard about it, but other people saw it in the newspaper. We were saying only a dog would do that. Something must be wrong with her reproductive organs" (4/11/89).

In her experiences and attitudes toward pregnancy, childbirth, and child rearing, Cindy illustrates the dual influences of Navajo traditional practices and more recent Western teachings and innovations. Strongly rooted in Navajo tradition, she observed the taboo against contact with the dead when she didn't attend her grandfather's funeral because she was pregnant with her first child. Yet her children were born in the hospital and bottle-fed. Her belief that children are central to life was compatible with use of family planning methods to limit family size. As a way to avoid behavior problems in her children, she welcomed Christian teachings, but also encouraged them to speak Navajo and to prepare traditional foods.

Navajo Women's Reproductive Patterns

Navajo women's reproductive patterns, like marriage and family formation patterns, incorporate cultural values that prioritize childbearing and raising children. Navajo women from the Crownpoint area prize children as one of life's greatest gifts. Children represent the blessings of life, renewal, and growth, and they affirm the continuity of generations by extending the matrilineal descent group, *da'ahołchihigii*, "those who are linked together by a chain of births" (Witherspoon 1975, 41).

According to Leighton and Kluckhohn, "Children are highly valued by The People and are almost invariably wanted" (1947, 13). This statement, written at the time the grandmothers were having their children, still holds true. Pronatal values, integral to matrilineal clan membership, were expressed in pride in children, grandchildren, and even great grandchildren. The birth of a baby is a time of joy and goodwill for extended family members, who provide support to the parents and new baby. Reflecting the paramount value placed on children, Navajo women reject abortion as an option. In addition, Navajo women and their husbands follow pregnancy taboos to ensure an easy childbirth and a healthy baby.

In family life, Navajo women, like other American Indian women, rely on a wide circle of kin during the years that they are raising their families. Medicine (2001) refers to the concentric nature of Indian families, with the family of procreation at the center, radiating outward to extended family and clan members. Family structure, including male-female relationships, tends to be flexible, due in part to the effort to maintain economic viability. Pivotal members of the kinship network are the grandparents, who act as primary socializers of children for short or extended periods. Most often, grandmothers relish the opportunity to develop close relationships with their grandchildren. Medicine found that the most devastating thing Dakota grandparents could say about their children was, "They are stingy. They deprive us of our grandchildren" (2001, 245).

The twentieth-century whirlwind of change has altered many aspects of Navajo pregnancy, childbirth, family size, and child rearing. Programs of prenatal care and hospital births have largely replaced Blessing Way Ceremonies during late pregnancy and home births attended by midwives, family, and friends. Unlike the grandmothers, who bore children throughout their reproductive years, mothers and fathers choose to limit the size of their families. The three generations of women also differed in their opinions about birth control and optimal family size. Without exception, the grandmothers opposed the use of birth control and desired large families, a reality for most grandmothers. The midlife and young mothers favored smaller families, but varied in their opinions of birth control, some endorsing it for themselves or others and some opposing it for Navajos. As illustrated by the three generations' reactions to the Keetso baby case, the grandmothers' opposition to having a white family raise a Navajo child has given way to mixed opinions among the midlife and young mothers.

In her influential study of Navajo women and the reproductive cycle, Anne Wright (1982a, 1982b) found that Navajo women's attitudes toward menstruation, pregnancy, and menopause differed from those found in American society. At menarche, a Navajo girl is publicly honored with the Kinaaldá ceremony in recognition of her new status as a woman. Subsequent monthly menstrual periods signified "momentary infertility" (1982b, 388), the absence of pregnancy in a society that desired large families. Significantly, no specific word for menopause exists in the Navajo language, which suggests the lack of a preoccupation with menopause as a troublesome period of ill health. Among the forty Navajo women in Wright's study categorized as traditional, only five had ever heard of menopausal symptoms.

Traditional Navajo Pregnancy and Birth

Cultural attitudes, beliefs, and practices relating to pregnancy and childbirth that were prevalent during the early decades of the twentieth century still prevail. Foremost among these attitudes is the understanding that pregnancy is a natural state, not an illness, and that women should remain busy and active during pregnancy (Dempsey and Gesse 1995; Milligan 1984). The understanding that childbirth is natural contributes to a calm approach to labor (Begay 1985). Also basic, not only to pregnancy but to all of Navajo life as well, is the belief that one should think positively and avoid negative thoughts (Carrese and Rhodes 1995; Evans and Fike 1975; Begay 1985). Navajo women often substitute prenatal vitamins for herbal teas before birth (Begay 1985) but continue to drink them after childbirth. Of 479 women questioned in the study reported by Carol Milligan (1984), 86.2 percent indicated that they drank herbs after giving birth. Meanwhile, the avoidance of specific foods during pregnancy has become less prevalent (Evans and Fike 1975; Milligan 1984).

Furthermore, specific prescriptions and proscriptions guide the behavior of both the pregnant woman and her husband during pregnancy. Frequently mentioned taboos are avoidance of any association with the dead and tying knots (Bailey 1948, 1950; Begay 1985; Evans and Fike 1975; Milligan 1984; Schwarz 1997a). Sewing during pregnancy could cause the child to have urinary tract or bowel problems. Sewing, weaving, or crocheting, like tying knots, can affect the baby by causing its umbilical cord to be wrapped around its neck. One midlife mother, Charlene Grey, was weaving a Navajo rug during her pregnancy. When she went into labor, her mother unwove the rug she was working on to ensure that she would give birth easily.

Untying or unraveling a string can act as a preventive measure against having a difficult childbirth. Recalling her first difficult birth, a grandmother, Dorothy Martin, remarked, "I forgot that I was supposed to untie my shoestring" (11/14/97). In fact, to counteract the effects of tying, sewing, weaving, crocheting, or even welding, an unraveling ceremony may be conducted during pregnancy.

When discussing the birth of my nephew with one midlife mother, Carla Harwood, I related that my sister-in-law didn't dilate as expected. Carla responded that with her first child she did not dilate normally, either. "No bigger than a dime. My aunt said that is what happens when you crochet something. I had crocheted something and given it to her." Carla continued: "She went to get it and unraveled it and looped it over me. Then as soon as my husband took her home and came back, she [my baby] was born. I was in labor thirty-six hours" (5/26/88).

In general, it is preferable to concentrate on the present rather than on the future and to delay assembling supplies for the baby. Women do not have baby showers until after a baby's birth (R. Begay 1985). In Crownpoint, baby showers are held after the birth of the baby, making it easier to give appropriate gifts for boys or girls.

Toward the end of a pregnancy, a medicine man may conduct a Blessing Way Ceremony for the mother and child to assure that a mother will give birth without complications and have a healthy baby. Traditional Navajo births occurred in a hogan, attended by experienced female relatives and friends, the woman's husband, a skilled midwife if available, and at times a medicine man (Bailey 1950). When labor began, a midwife first prepared a shallow excavation lined with a sheep skin for the pregnant woman to kneel on. To help with the delivery, another person, either man or woman, also assisted by kneeling behind the woman, and periodically squeezing on the abdomen. The midwife placed herself in front of the laboring woman, placing her hands on her knees. If the labor was long, a diagnostician and medicine man were called in (Lockett 1939).

Loretta Benally described a traditional Navajo birth that she had witnessed:

> When a child is about to be born the Navajo woman hangs on to the sash belt that is connected onto a beam or post in the hogan. The sash belt is used to put around the mother's waist after childbirth, too.
>
> A child is born, and then while it is being washed the after-

birth usually comes. You cannot just throw the afterbirth away, just anywhere.

After the baby is properly cleaned and the placenta is disposed of properly, the baby is bundled in a warm blanket. The baby's head is centered toward a warm fire which is in the center of a hogan. That's how I witnessed a childbirth.

Before the mother breast-feeds the baby, it has to drink a special tea made from tree bark and a broth made out of corn pollen. The baby usually drinks the tea for one day, and then you can breast-feed your child. You can go through all this event, if you want your child to grow up properly. (4/10/89)

For several days, the mother also drank a special tea made from various herbs to promote quick recovery from childbirth.

Loretta stated, "As for the cradleboard, you have to find a wood called *deetsiin* [piñon]. If a boy is born, the wood from the tree is cut from the east side of the tree. If a girl is born, the wood is cut from the west side of the tree." According to Loretta, "You have to gather the materials in order to have a completed cradleboard, like the headpieces, the buckskin pieces, and the padding" (4/10/89).

After the birth of the baby, a medicine man performed a second "two-day prayer ceremony. I think that's why the children were healthier and stronger." Because there was no alternative, all mothers breast-fed their newborns. Loretta observed, "I didn't really hear of anyone bottle feeding their children" (4/10/89).

The Medicalization of Pregnancy and Childbirth

When most of the grandmothers in the Crownpoint sample were giving birth to their children in the 1940s, 1950s, and 1960s, the transition from home to hospital births on the Navajo Reservation was already underway. Prior to the 1930s, almost all Navajo births took place at home, and after 1969 essentially all babies were delivered in hospitals. The decades of the 1940s and 1950s saw the largest change from home to hospital births (Kunitz 1989). Grandmothers in the Crownpoint sample frequently gave birth to their older children at home and to their younger children in the hospital.

The transition from home to hospital births at first proceeded slowly. Navajo women feared the hospital as a place where they were vulnerable to ghost infection because they would be exposed to those who died there. Women feared the hospital as a place to die, as did patients who went to the hospital for emergencies or when death was imminent (Bailey 1948). In his examination of factors that promoted the widespread acceptance of hospital births among Navajo women, Waxman (1990) notes that Navajo women found hospital births a safer, more comfortable way to give birth. The IHS practice of giving mothers free layettes for new babies was an important incentive.

Rather than viewing them as incompatible with each other, Navajos recognized that traditional healing practices and biomedicine could be mutually beneficial. In fact, "medicine men are now frequent attendants at the bedside of ill patients including, on occasion, helping with an unraveling ceremony for a protracted labor" (Waxman 1990, 197–98). During childbirth at the Crownpoint hospital, family members, often the women's mothers, step in to give traditional forms of help during difficult labors. One mother related that during her prolonged delivery her mother braided and unbraided a string. "When my mom did her string trick, he [her son] was born right away" (Juan 2002).

As the rate of Navajo women who gave birth in hospitals approached 100 percent (Boyce et al. 1986), the leading cause of admission to Navajo area IHS hospitals became conditions related to pregnancy and deliveries (Navajo Area Indian Health Service 2002). Due to the availability of obstetricians, use of fetal monitors, and delivery by cesarean section, childbirth at IHS hospitals became indistinguishable from that at other modern American hospitals. The specialized medical care available for high-risk women during pregnancy and for infants in need of intensive care has contributed to sharp declines in rates of infant and maternal mortality, which now approach U.S. rates (Waxman 1990). In a study of pregnancy complications among 968 Navajo women, Boyce and colleagues (1986) found that women who were classed as more traditional had twice as many complications. The reasons for the different complication rates of these traditional and acculturated women are not clear but "may reflect the influences of social isolation on the course and outcomes of pregnancy" (1986, 252). One nurse at the IHS Crownpoint medical center estimated that one-third of the pregnant women were classified as high risk (Fuermann 1990).

Accompanying the transition to hospital births was Western medicine's emphasis on prenatal care, which increasingly replaced a Blessing Way Ceremony before the birth of a child (Begay 1985). An estimated Navajo maternal mortality rate of one thousand maternal deaths per one hundred thousand live births in the early 1940s (Leighton and Kluckhohn 1947) dropped to 19.6 deaths per one hundred thousand deaths in 1985 (Waxman 1990). Just as dramatic, infant mortality decreased from 87.8 Navajo infant deaths in the first year of life per 1,000 live births in 1955 to 9.3 in 1989, a rate lower than that of the U.S. total (Howard 1993).

Grandmothers, who gave birth to their children during a time of high infant mortality rates, frequently told of infants who did not survive. In contrast, among the midlife and young mothers, infant deaths were rare occurrences.

Grandmothers' Pronatal Values

Although affected by Western medicine while giving birth to their children, the grandmothers as a group expressed remarkably uniform pronatal values in their beliefs and attitudes. The grandmothers described their children as a source of wealth and blessings bestowed on them by the Holy People or the Lord, depending on the religious affiliation of the individual woman. They opposed the use of birth control and the practice of abortion. In regard to the Keetso baby case, almost all grandmothers thought that the baby should have stayed on the reservation, if not with the mother, then with other family members.

Grandmothers agreed with the saying that Navajos measure their wealth by the number of children they have. Grandmothers interpreted the saying to mean that Navajos measure their wealth in children as future sources of social and financial support in old age. The major reason for agreement was not the benefits from children's labor but, rather, the help that adult children give to their parents.

The woman who had no children was to be pitied and, in Kluckhohn's (1944) sample, suspected of being a witch. Annie Mitchell reflected on the plight of her childless sister. "I don't think it's good for you to have no children. My sister has no children; she has no one to ask for help. She is just alone. Your children will always help you, will help with money. Especially if they're successful, they will help you back" (4/11/89). Annie's sister's lack of social support from children and grandchildren portended loneliness and lack of financial help in spite of her marriage and her success as a weaver.

Inseparable from grandmothers' pronatal values that favored large families was their disapproval of birth control for Navajos, in spite of the existence of traditional means of contraception (Vestal 1952; Wyman and Harris 1941). All of the grandmothers in the sample disapproved of birth control, but sometimes for different reasons. They felt that the number of children should be up to the Holy People, that birth control could affect the mother or children born later, or that that birth control was simply not for Navajos.

Annie Burnside, who gave birth to eleven children, anticipated the help and resources that adult children can provide. She rejected recommendations that she use birth control after the birth of her younger children.

> It is truth that you measure your wealth by your children because your children will bring you whatever you need. Like if you need things done, if you need food. They will bring it when they grow up.
>
> The advantages of having a large family are you'll never be lonely. The disadvantages of having a large family, I mentioned before, are in their teenage years. They get into marital problems and other problems.
>
> Nowadays my children want to have only two or three children. I was criticized by one of my sisters when I was having my children, and she said I should have only two or three. I feel it was what I was given, and I enjoy having a large family.
>
> I was given birth control before my last four children, and I

> refused. I told the doctor it was up to Mother Nature and the Holy People when I will stop having children. There was a lot of hearsay that birth control will damage you, but it was just hearsay. (11/10/88)

Although Annie disagreed with warnings about negative consequences of using birth control, she nevertheless rejected the idea of family planning. With a reproductive span typical of the grandmothers, Annie gave birth to her oldest child when she was twenty-one and to the youngest when she was forty-one.

Some grandmothers recognized that, although large family size was appropriate when they were having children, conditions have changed. In light of today's changed circumstances, there is a trend toward having fewer children. Loretta Benally cautioned, "I think for younger mothers it is better to have less children. For today's mothers, sometimes they are very young and suffer, and there are drugs. Clothing and everything is high now. I had eight children," she continued. "I really suffered. It's up to the Lord and the Holy People how much children you should get. I think that women who have a lot of children are strong. I always wonder how they did it" (9/27/88).

When asked what she thought about birth control, Loretta responded:

> It's not good. That's a foreign thing that was introduced to us. It's like killing children. It used to be that medicine men treated women with herbs. It was only in two cases—those who conceived very often or those who suffered.
>
> Now birth control is a very foreign substance that I can't accept. A lot of women suffer because of it. There are no prayers for birth control. In the old days, a lot of singing was done with herbs, and it was conducted by medicine men. (9/27/88)

The introduction of family planning methods to the grandmothers fell on deaf ears. Kunitz and Tsianco (1981) hypothesized that older, less-educated, high-parity Navajo women would be less likely to use contraceptives when they were more dependent on kin. Women who "wanted to limit their fertility reported being discouraged from doing so by husbands, mothers, and other family members" (1981, 450). The accounts of Crownpoint grandmothers themselves, however, indicate that large families resulted from women's own beliefs and values about children and motherhood since some lived in and depended on coresident kin groups, and some did not.

Without exception, Navajo grandmothers opposed abortion, a serious transgression against Navajo cultural beliefs. Since I consider abortion a matter of personal choice for women, I struggled to understand the meaning of abortion in the context of Navajo culture. Grandmothers adamantly opposed abortion, typically stating, "Abortion is not for Navajos," or "It's against our religion." Some grandmothers warned of serious consequences that could result from having an abortion. For example, Dorothy Reed declared, "I object strongly to abortion. Some of the young Navajo nurses help perform abortions. Some of these nurses aren't living today," she asserted. "Some of the young Navajo mothers are suffering because they have abortions. If you have an abortion, you will hemorrhage, have back problems, and reproduction problems later on" (4/11/89).

Most grandmothers strongly objected to Patricia Keetso's decision to give her baby to the Pitts family. Some grandmothers warned of the repercussions from giving away her baby. Thelma Curtis insisted: "The natural mother should have kept the baby; it's part of her flesh. If she didn't want the baby, she should have stayed away from men or used preventive measures. The Spirit gave it to her," Thelma said, "and she should have raised it or kept it. She would pay for this later, in her health. It should not have been done. The natural mother will start worrying later on, and the child will grow up and worry, too. There's a lot involved" (12/8/88).

Attitudes toward the Keetso baby case revealed the strength of pronatal values among the grandmothers. Most believed that the baby belonged on the reservation and should be raised as a Navajo, regardless of the young mother's situation. For a mother to give away her child was unthinkable.

Grandmothers spoke of reproduction as holy, a sacred process that demanded reverence and respect for life. Because it is holy, grandmothers rejected family planning methods and abortion as options and deplored the idea of giving away a child to be raised in white society. Despite the possibility that the grandmothers' views may have become more conservative as they aged, their large families attest to consistency in behavior and attitudes over the life span. They gave birth throughout their reproductive years and expressed great pride in their large families.

Midlife Mothers' Adaptation to New Childbearing Practices

Midlife mothers routinely gave birth in hospitals and accepted prenatal care as a means to ensure a healthy pregnancy and baby. However, the prenatal medical practices transformed pregnancy from a natural state to a medical experience that involved tests and procedures. Although they retained the fundamental Navajo values that cherish children, midlife mothers contrasted sharply with the grandmothers in the size of their families and attitudes toward family planning. Most midlife mothers thought the ideal family size should be between three and four children, similar to the number of children they had. If they had only one or two children, midlife mothers regretted that they had not had more. Unlike the grandmothers, they did not consider without question the number of children they had to be a divine gift. Many midlife mothers had used or were using birth control, available through the united tribal and IHS efforts to promote family planning. Midlife mothers agreed that children are wealth, but they considered today's cost of raising children to be a limiting factor.

Sarah Forrestal's experiences with childbirth and pregnancy illustrate the influence of both traditional and Western practices. After two days of labor with her first child, Sarah's mother prayed for her and rubbed corn pollen on her hands. "The doctor told me the baby wasn't moving. It won't go down. She [her mother] put her hands on my belly, and then she went like this," Sarah motioned. "She went like this downward, and I could feel the baby going down. And I had a baby then. That morning. That's why she [my mother] was real special. She helped me out" (4/18/89).

During her second pregnancy, Sarah, whose mother was diabetic, was diagnosed with gestational diabetes. Although Sarah was careful with her diet and monitored her blood glucose level daily during her pregnancy, at one point she was admitted to the hospital to lower her blood sugar level. Sarah deplored the worry and anxiety that she experienced.

> And they used to take my blood for three hours, one hour at a time. I had to go in before I even eat anything. I just drink some kind of a drink. It's real sweet; it tastes awful. Something like Cola. You have to drink the whole bottle, and then every hour for three hours, they take some of my blood and all that.
>
> Especially, the last month they watched me every week. I had to come over every week. But the doctor says since I know how to take care of myself that they just let me go home. But only once about in May, I think it was, I had to be hospitalized for at least two or three days to lower the blood sugar. But I knew that so I was in there for three days, and I was worried about her [my daughter] so I had to tell the doctor, "I got to go home."
>
> So that's why, I guess it's kind of hereditary, if your mom or your dad has some kind of a sickness or something like that. That's why I went through that with my pregnancy with my little boy. I couldn't go through another one like that so I said two is enough for me. That's enough. (4/18/89)

Sarah gave birth to a healthy baby boy, but not wanting to repeat her stressful pregnancy, she made up her mind not to have any more children.

Changing Attitudes toward Family Size

The Navajo fertility transition parallels similar transitions, either completed or in process, throughout the world. The fertility transition, "has a claim to be the most important happening of our time." The reduction in family size "has changed the nature of the family and the relationships between old and young" (Caldwell and Caldwell 1997, 15). No longer sources of labor, the children become investments during long years of growth and education.

Whereas grandmothers followed a pattern of natural fertility (Henry 1982), midlife mothers chose to limit their family size and to end their reproductive years in their late twenties or early thirties. Compared to demographic data from the entire Navajo Nation, Crownpoint women's fertility behavior approximates that of the Navajo Nation as a whole (Howard 1993). Among Crownpoint midlife women, the average family size was 3.4 children (McCloskey 1993). For the entire Navajo Nation, the total fertility rate between 1983 and 1986 was 3.7 children per woman. Navajo family size remains high when compared to the 1990 U.S. rate of 1.8 children per woman (Howard 1993).

The reproductive span, the years between a woman's first and last birth, is a useful measure to compare grandmothers' and midlife mothers' fertility patterns. The grandmothers' average reproductive span of 15.3 years is almost double that of the midlife mothers, which is 7.9 years. Both grandmothers and midlife mothers first gave birth in their early twenties, the grandmothers at a mean age of 21.7 years, and the midlife mothers at 22.8 years. Grandmothers opposed the use of birth control, but midlife mothers embraced birth control in light of the changing role of children in Navajo society (Wright 1982b).

The family planning program offered to Navajo couples represents a unique cooperative agreement between the IHS and the Navajo Nation. The local family planning counselor, a young Navajo woman whose office was located at the Crownpoint IHS hospital and clinic, explained that the Navajo Nation Family Planning Corporation officially sponsored the program. Education focused on spacing children and preventing unwanted births. The counselor provided information on birth control methods and sexually transmitted diseases and responded to requests from the schools to educate students about sexuality and reproduction. A critical point of contact was when mothers were in the hospital after childbirth and at the six weeks postpartum visit. Overwhelmingly, the most popular method of birth control was the pill, the method of choice in 85 percent of Crownpoint outpatient visits in 1988 (Navajo Area Indian Health Service 1988).

Although the majority of midlife mothers favored the use of birth control as a useful way to space children and limit family size, they differed on which form of birth control was safer. Mary Jo Morgan, the mother of four girls, preferred using the pill.

> Mostly that's [the pill] what I've been using. Hopefully, I'm doing okay. I've been doing okay. I've been going to the doctor. They said there's an age limit. Eventually, I have to get off of that. I think it's safe because I've been on it in between when I decided to have a baby. But there are certain kinds I'm afraid of using—the IUD. It could easily hook on.
>
> My one sister says, "I just want two and that's enough." Another had eight, and one sister had one and said that's enough. It's up to the individual. I'd just keep on having girls. I think I'll just wait for my grandkids, 'cause he [my husband] wants a son. Even if I try, it'll be another girl. (5/17/90)

Angie Bahe's childbearing history portrays the clash between traditional views toward childbearing and pressures of Western biomedicine. Over a period of twenty-three years, Angie gave birth to seven children and had three miscarriages. After the birth of her fourth child, she used an IUD because she did not want another baby. When it caused problems, she had it removed and subsequently became pregnant. After her fifth child, a son, was born she had a ceremony to restore harmony. "And then that's when I got pregnant with Michael. At the time I was working, too. I just didn't want to be pregnant again. I tried just everything under the sun to lose it, but I never did. After we came down over here," she remembered, "I had to straighten up in the ceremony. It's very hard to do. He used to cry all the time. I guess he feels that I didn't want him. A kid, a baby can tell that way. So I really had a hard time. We both had a hard time straightening up" (1/19/89).

After having three miscarriages over the next few years, Angie again sought the help of a medicine man. "But I love my three babies [that she lost]. I don't know how it happened, and somehow I got help with the Navajo Way. That's how I had the two girls. I'm grateful for it" (1/19/89).

When her youngest daughter was born, Angie had a difficult delivery. Because she was still having health problems six months later, the doctor recommended a hysterectomy. Angie went ahead with the operation in spite of her husband's opposition. "So my husband didn't agree to it, but I just have to do it. And I started to bleed. My husband was against it, but I had to go in there and have it done. On my own" (12/15/88).

Angie reflected on the large family she has in comparison to the smaller families she observes.

> Well, I have seven. I would have had ten [if I hadn't had three miscarriages]. I think the more kids you have because that way when you get older, they'll care for you, and they'll come see you.
>
> I see, going somewhere, I see the white people, a white man and a white woman, they only have maybe two or three kids. Maybe that's all they want, I don't know. I just see them on the high road, on the highway somewhere. Like if we go to Grants, we stop at the Pizza Hut. They'll be just sitting, maybe just the two, the couple, two kids with them. And I'll be sitting there thinking, "I wonder if that's all they have." So I guess it's up to the person. (1/19/89)

Ellen Mitchell sought traditional help to have a second child. Unable to conceive again after having a daughter, she asked her mother about a Navajo medicine for infertility. Ellen recalled:

> It is really hard for me to conceive. You know the gap between my daughter and son? It is twelve years between my daughter and son. I wanted a baby.
>
> I asked my mom if there was any Navajo medicine I could take. She said there was. I'm more open to a medicine woman than a medicine man; I went to a medicine woman. I guarantee that it works.
>
> "It's up to you," [the medicine woman] said. "It depends on how much respect do you have for yourself and your family." She asked me if I wanted a girl or a boy. I said that I already had a girl so I wanted a boy. She said, "I have to go to the mountains and pray for you, and it has to be the special herb."
>
> It didn't take more than thirty minutes. I thought, "Will that work?" She ground it up. I kind of forgot about it, and then I

> missed a period. I took an EPT [early pregnancy test], and I went to doctor, and I was pregnant. My mom couldn't believe it. I have told my daughter about it. I haven't told my son, but I will when he's older. . . .
>
> [The herb was] water, just like tea, that's all I drank. (3/21/88)

Although she still wanted more children, Ellen became resigned to the two she already had after she had a miscarriage in her early forties.

The Value of Children

When questioned about the saying that Navajos measure their wealth by their children, midlife mothers were more likely to associate it with Navajo beliefs about the continuity of generations. For them, the saying represents a philosophical statement about the value of children and does not warrant a literal interpretation. Ellen Mitchell succinctly summed up the philosophy underlying the maxim that children assure the continuity of generations and can be equated with wealth. "If you have children, never say that you are poor. Children will give you children, grandchildren. You live through the generations—that's what they tell us. Based on that, I try to give everything to my kids" (2/26/88).

The influence of family members may lead to a difference of opinion between husband and wife. Carla Harwood's husband and his family equated wealth with children. "My husband's grandmother is that way. That's where I first heard that. His aunts and uncles had lots of kids. You have wealth when one kid herds sheep," said Carla, "one kid is working with the corn, and one with the horses. I think that's why he wanted more kids. But I think they're expensive" (5/26/88). Carla prevailed in her ideas about family size, choosing to limit their family to three children. No longer did Navajos depend on the land-based economy when children worked at a myriad of labor-intensive tasks.

The midlife mothers were polarized in their opinions about the young mother, Patricia Keetso, who gave her baby, Alyssa Keetso, to the Pitts family in California. Bonnie Yazzie, mother of four children, talked over the Keetso baby case with friends and acquaintances, sometimes while

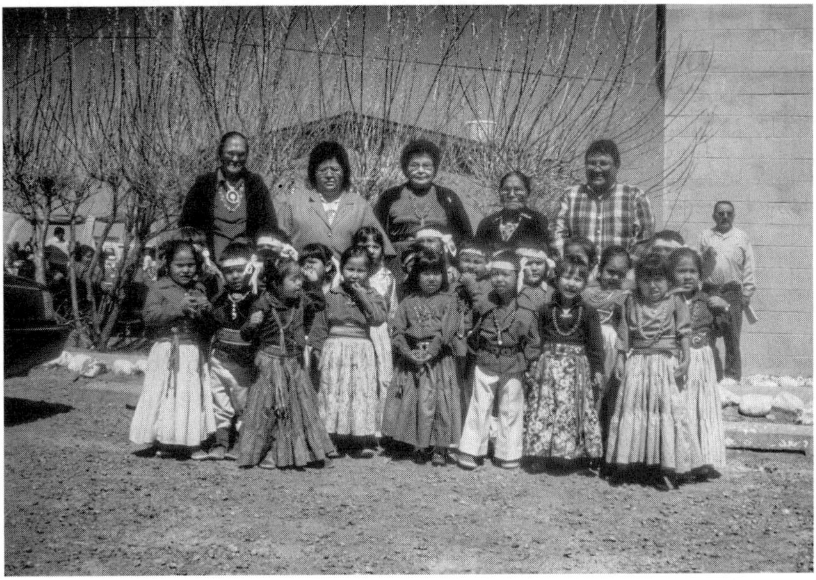

Crownpoint Headstart children in traditional dress, performing on Justice Day 1989.

waiting for doctors' appointments. Opinions about the case tended to divide along generational lines. Bonnie heard differing opinions for and against the mother's decision to give the baby up and about the Navajo Nation's interference when tribal social workers grabbed the baby from the adoptive and natural mother at the Phoenix airport.

> I'd say it was about 50–50. Elders were more for Baby Keetso [growing up] on the reservation. And these working mothers and educated parents were more for the Pitts. Like my mother, she vouched for the Navajo Tribe even though they shouldn't have run with the baby and made themselves look bad.
>
> We discussed it a lot at the hospital. My other friends, we even say, "Did you hear about that Keetso baby case?" A lot of people didn't agree, and a lot of them agreed. Except me, I was mixed up. I thought the Navajo Tribe acted unfairly. I thought that way. They shouldn't have taken the baby and run with it. I thought

> that since the mother gave her consent, too, I thought the baby should stay with the Pitts.
>
> I thought it was the mother's problem. She wanted that life for her baby. Maybe the mother had some kind of a childhood. She didn't want her baby to go through that. I thought that way even though our culture is very important. I thought maybe she'll learn that when she grows up. She'll make her own decisions when she becomes a big girl. (5/24/88)

One question raised by Ellen Mitchell was, "Where was the grandmother?" She felt that responsibility for the child rested with the maternal grandmother, who should have exercised her authority in the matrilineal family to determine where the baby belonged. For Edna Tsosie, the major issue in the Keetso baby case was tribal sovereignty and the right to invoke the Indian Child Welfare Act.

> We were really happy that that law came into effect. I think it's good that the tribe did that. I think we can do just as well raising the child. I really supported what the tribe did even though there was a lot the family did to help. She had to remember she was Navajo; she had to go by the tribal rules. I was for the tribe and bringing the case back and hearing it on the reservation. We have our own courts, our own government. Instead of dealing with those cases outside the reservation, we have our own courts, our own advocates, who can handle these cases. (10/16/90)

In contrast, Carla Harwood sympathized with the mother's decision to give her baby up for adoption. "I think she did right for the child. I think she was thinking of the future of the child," said Carla. "If she was at home, she would be in poverty. I think a child could always come back to their heritage. I don't know why they had to make a big issue of that." Carla went on: "In my case, if I were going through something like that, I don't think I would give up my child. She made a decision for the benefit of the child, and I can see that, too" (5/26/88).

Issues of tribal sovereignty, cultural identity, and economic stability surfaced in opinions of the Keetso baby case. Whereas some midlife mothers prioritized being raised as a Navajo, others felt that the opportunities the child would have if raised by a white family took precedence.

Like the grandmothers, midlife mothers uniformly disapproved of abortion. While interviewing women in the Crownpoint area, the only time I was asked not to write something down was when a woman told me about her sister's abortion. Midlife mothers often referred to their own parents' influence on their own beliefs. Sadie Goodluck explained how her mother's ideas about abortion had an impact on her.

> That's a very sensitive question. I often think about it myself, and it rings in my mind just about every day. To me it would be murder. To me, it would be killing, and that's the way I've always been taught, too. Back again to my parents. My parents have always said that you don't.
>
> And my mother was saying at one time, I asked her, "What do you mean by talking about this person? What happened? What were you talking about?" Well, she says your cousin's mother came over, her [my mother's] sister, and said that her daughter was pregnant. I guess she was in Gallup for some time, and she came back pregnant. And the unborn child was not being accepted among the family, and they were saying, "Who's the father? What's going to happen?" And all this. And, "You brought shame to our family. This shouldn't have happened. You should have had a proper marriage and have children." All this kind of thing.
>
> And my mother told the family that you don't say that. It's a human life, and we should just all accept this child. And this child is now like about close to fifty years old, alive, born. And my mother used to say that whenever she sees him around, that unwanted man, that unwanted baby.
>
> Don't ever, don't ever let that happen. That shouldn't even be practiced among the Navajo. And no matter how hard that would be, that child has a right to be born. (10/5/89)

Despite a dramatic reduction in family size, the midlife mothers maintain Navajo pronatal values as they adhere to pregnancy taboos, count their children as blessings, oppose abortion, and fervently desire more children if they have only one or two. Midlife mothers had families one-half the size of their grandmothers' and favored birth control as a useful innovation for spacing children and limiting family size.

Young Mothers' Early Childbearing Years

Either beginning or in the midst of their reproductive years, young Navajo mothers demonstrated the influence of Navajo culture and their own families on their childbearing patterns. Young mothers welcomed the birth of a child regardless of their age or marital status, desired between three and four children as an ideal family size, and most opposed abortion. However, two young mothers had had abortions. Like the midlife mothers, the young mothers favored birth control. Among adolescent mothers, the most striking departure from the reproductive patterns of the grandmothers and midlife mothers was the frequency of births. Young Navajo mothers were often unfamiliar with the Navajo saying that wealth can be counted in children. Many of the young mothers tended to sympathize with the young mother's decision to allow the Pitts family to adopt her baby because they believed she was unable to support the child. Overall, economic considerations in raising children were a persistent concern among the young mothers.

Adolescent Childbearing

Although some grandmothers and midlife mothers in the Crownpoint sample gave birth to their first child in their teens, far more young mothers give birth to their first child as adolescents. In a series of articles on Navajo adolescent childbearing, Rochelle Dalla and Wendy Gamble (1997, 1998, 2000, 2001) examine patterns of Navajo adolescent childbearing in a small northeastern Arizona community. These patterns often coincide with those of Crownpoint mothers who gave birth as teens. Most teen mothers received financial, emotional, and child care support from an extended family network (Dalla and Gamble 1998). Mothers and fathers of their children were most important in providing financial help (Dalla and Gamble 1997). However, some relationships ended in separation because of fathers' alcohol abuse or lack of emotional and financial support. Teen mothers preferred to be single rather than maintain an unpromising relationship or marriage, a position supported by the teens' mothers (Dalla and Gamble 2001). These authors insist that adolescent childbearing must be considered in light of the Navajo worldview, in which "Motherhood, fertility, and procreation are highly valued within the Navajo belief system" (Dalla and Gamble 2000, 227).

One young Crownpoint woman who gave birth to her first child as a teenager illustrates the reliance on boyfriends and family as sources of financial and emotional support. Tracy Begay gave birth to her son at the very end of her senior year at Crownpoint High School. She hid her pregnancy as long as she could.

> When I was pregnant with Darren, I was scared, and I wasn't sure. She [my mother] saw I was eating a lot. I was playing volleyball up until the third month and basketball 'til four months. I quit. They were all wondering why I quit.
>
> She [my mother] heard from a lady at school. I was scared. I didn't tell anyone.
>
> It was prom night, on a Friday. My water bag broke. Jeremy was at school. His sister went to school to get him out of school to go to Gallup [to the hospital] with me. They wouldn't let him out of school [at first]. She said, "Tracy's in labor." He stayed with me.
>
> That Monday I got out [of the hospital] and was at the mall, looking for a dress. It didn't bother me. Well, maybe—I got sick a week later. I wasn't sore. It didn't bother me to walk. I was there for graduation practice Tuesday. (9/27/88)

The young couple has the support of both Tracy's and Jeremy's families. Since the birth of their son, Tracy and Jeremy have lived at different times with Tracy's mother and Jeremy's parents, and on their own. When their son was five months old, Tracy went to work at a local convenience store. During the sixteen months she worked there, her mother, her grandmother, her sister, or her aunt took care of the baby. Tracy's mother, Jeremy, and Jeremy's parents all contribute financially to the support of the young family. Tracy received training at the International Business School in Albuquerque, and Jeremy attended the University of New Mexico. The couple later married and had a second child.

Not expecting the immediate independence of young parents, the senior generation offers a place to live, child care, and emotional and financial support. However, the meaning of Navajo adolescent childbearing has implications far beyond those that involve kin support for the young family.

The prevailing view maintains that adolescent pregnancy severely hampers a young mother's life chances. Research indicates that teen mothers complete fewer years of schooling (Hofferth et al. 2001), are more likely to be poor, and are less likely to be married (Hoffman 1998). However, challenges to this view assert that the negative impact of teen births has been overstated (Coley and Chase-Lansdale 1998; Geronimus 1997; Geronimus and Korenman 1992; Hoffman 1998; Smith-Battle 2000). For Navajo young people, who face formidable obstacles while pursuing educations and obtaining employment, parenthood becomes a more attainable marker of adult status (Ginsburg and Rapp 1991; Konner and Shostak 1986). As in other cultures, motherhood offers young Navajo women "a readily available route to adult status, given the lack of viable education and job opportunities" (Ginsburg and Rapp 1991, 320).

Rather than label adolescent pregnancy a serious social problem—along with teenage substance abuse, gangs, crime, and dropping out from high school—I argue that early pregnancy becomes a reasonable choice for Navajo youths who face daunting barriers to adulthood. According to Ginsburg and Rapp, "this 'problem' is as much a reflection of our own society's marking off and prolongation of adolescence, reduced value placed on fertility, and lack of cultural and social supports" (1991, 320). Western middle-class perceptions of adolescent pregnancy as a social problem promote a view of early parenthood as a threat to young people's life chances, interfering with education, employment, and financial security. An optimal life course consists of a series of progressive fixed steps during the transition to adulthood that proceed from completing an education, to finding employment, to getting married, and then to having children. Associated with this trajectory is the assumption that on-time life events assist in the development of a favorable life course, whereas off-time life events detract from it (Brim and Ryff 1980). For Navajo youths, the more elusive goals of education and employment preclude a sequence of on-time life events.

The Value of Children

The young mothers were less likely to have heard or to agree with the saying that wealth is measured in children. Young mothers who grew up in large families enjoyed having many siblings but observed that conditions had changed. About the viewpoint that children are wealth, Sandy Etictty, who has eight siblings, observed, "I guess it's true, but my mom had a hard time raising us, and we're not helping her back, keeping the house clean, helping her financially, and all that. And that's just how it is financially." Sandy continued: "My brother's the only one that pays for the water bill and all that. We have a hard time helping my mom so we decided to go back to school and try to help out" (5/3/1989).

Judging from the young mothers in the Crownpoint sample, the family planning program at IHS in Crownpoint has been successful in convincing young mothers to use birth control. The majority of young mothers were present or past users of birth control.

They approved of family planning methods to avoid unwanted pregnancies and to plan for and space their children. With one exception, the young mothers assumed responsibility for contraception. In that case, a young mother's husband had had a vasectomy.

The young Navajo mothers who had heard about the Keetso baby case were divided in their opinions. They identified with her dilemma, but disagreed about whether or not she had made the right decision. Michelle Jimmie, who gave birth to a son as a teenager, identified with Patricia Keetso's situation because she also feared that she could not have taken care of her son. She was thankful that her sister wanted to raise him.

Michelle stated,

> Because I couldn't take care of him at the time. I was in school, and I couldn't financially, I just couldn't take care of him. So I

> decided to put him up for adoption to a good home. . . . I almost gave him to a white lady. I called my older sister, and she couldn't have no more kids.
>
> She said, "I'll take him."
>
> I got in trouble. My sister chewed me out and said, "You got to keep him in the family!"
>
> And so I said, "Okay. You want him?" (9/19/89)

If a woman's circumstances prevent her from raising a child, the preferred alternative is to have a relative do so, preferably a matrilineal clan relative.

Influenced by cultural teachings that cherish life, most young mothers opposed abortion as an option. A first in the Crownpoint sample, two of the young mothers had had abortions. Margaret Hoskie had an abortion when she was a pregnant teen facing a visit to the New Mexico School for Girls, a state correctional institution. She recalled, "I had an abortion when I was fifteen. I didn't know who the father was. At that time, I didn't know about abortion. They say it's not right," said Margaret. "It's killing a child. Now, I know it's wrong. At the time, I was heading to the Girls' School, and I would have had it there" (6/5/89).

The discovery that she was pregnant when the younger of her two children was only six months old motivated Cathy Howard to have an abortion. Cathy stayed with me the night before she had her abortion in Albuquerque. She realized that she was not ready to have a third child while in a new, uncertain relationship with a boyfriend who was also the father of her second child. For Cathy, the pragmatic decision to abort rested on her current situation rather than traditional Navajo values and attitudes toward abortion.

The childbearing patterns of young mothers in Crownpoint differed from those of the grandmothers and midlife mothers in the fact that many gave birth as teenagers. Yet these young mothers opposed abortion as an alternative to early motherhood. The birth of a baby acted as a magnet for resources, and both the mother's and father's extended family members rallied to support the young family. Like the midlife mothers, many young mothers accepted birth control as a useful way to plan their families. Also, like the midlife mothers, they were divided in their attitudes toward the Keetso baby case.

Conclusion

When the grandmothers gave birth to their children in the first half of the twentieth century, they followed a pattern of natural fertility, giving birth to children throughout their reproductive years. Values and attitudes that supported their reproductive patterns equated wealth with children and welcomed children as gifts from the Holy People. With the increasing presence of Western medicine came the transition from home to hospital births and an emphasis on prenatal care. When medical personnel suggested they use birth control, grandmothers firmly resisted. Their staunch opposition to abortion reflected their reverence for all life. Grandmothers opposed the adoption of the Keetso baby by a California couple, insisting that the baby should be raised by Navajo family members, if not the mother, and that she should learn about her Navajo heritage and culture.

For the midlife mothers, pronatal values and attitudes held sway despite the medicalization of childbirth and the adoption of birth control as a way to limit family size. Propelling these changes in childbearing patterns among Navajo women in the latter half of the twentieth century were modified values and attitudes toward children and family size; they valued children highly yet acknowledged the demands of the cash economy. Although midlife mothers had families that were half the size of the grandmothers', they nevertheless gave birth to larger families than the two-child family norm in the United States. They remained strongly opposed to abortion. In regard to the Keetso baby case, midlife mothers were divided among those who opposed the adoption of the baby by a white family and those who favored it because of the increased opportunities for the child.

The young mothers demonstrated both continuity and change in their childbearing patterns. The majority of young mothers' values and attitudes toward children led them to welcome pregnancy regardless of their own age and the status of their relationship with the father of their children. Young mothers more often gave birth during their teen years and relied on their extended family for help with housing, as well as for emotional and financial support. Young mothers accepted birth control as a way to plan and space their children.

Despite the significant changes in Navajo women's reproductive patterns, cultural strategies related to childbearing and raising children maintain fundamental values. Regardless of the age of the mother, children are welcomed as blessings. For the vast majority of Navajo women, abortion is unthinkable. Children ensure the continuity of generations and symbolize growth, increase, and renewal in the family, clan, and tribe.

8

Motherhood in Navajo Society

Sarah Forrestal's model for motherhood comes directly from her own mother, who inspired great respect because of her skills, wisdom, and nurturance. A thirty-nine-year-old midlife mother of two children, Sarah grew up in a rural area north of Crownpoint. She venerated her mother, a monolingual Navajo speaker who managed on her own while her father worked on the railroad. Sarah's mother supported the family economically and emotionally, providing for them by caring for the sheep, weaving rugs, and teaching her children.

> But we were happy with our mom, especially. 'Cause my dad was hardly with us all through our childhood. He used to be away all the time, but my mom was there for us all the time. And she taught us a lot of things I think to better ourselves in the long run. And she used to let us do a lot of things ourselves, just to learn. And I think that was a good idea because I've been doing that all my life just to try myself to do things, not to depend on anybody to do something for me.
>
> Like I said, we were happy with our lives during childhood. Even when we get sick, we didn't even know what's wrong with us. She used to help us with a lot of different kinds of herbs and stuff like that. As far as I know, I remember that she used to get a lot of different medicine men to help us out, and I didn't even know what was going on. I guess she knew it would help us for a little while or something like that.
>
> And she always tells about in the long run if you have children, you have to do the same thing for them, she says. She talked

> to us like she used to know everything. Like what's best for us and what's not best for us. And sometimes I think about it, and I think it was just for me to do good on my own life. And she was right. So I try to teach my little girl the same things.
>
> My mom used to make a rug, and then she sells it, and she buys some groceries. We never had new clothes, but we were just satisfied with what we had.
>
> Most of all we had our mom with us. She loves us and stuff like that. And then once in a while my dad comes home from wherever he is—like he goes out to Idaho or Colorado to work on the railroad.
>
> So that's how my mom was. People used to tell us that she's a wonderful person. She was kind. We knew that. I never met anybody like her before. Like someone really cares for some other people even if they're not a relative. Just when they come to the house, she will just cook for them, invite them in, and stuff like that. She was that kind of person. It's real hard. It was real hard for me when we lost her. (4/18/89)

With her mother's legacy in mind, Sarah demonstrates resourcefulness and responsibility.

> You know, I'm married to a white guy, and he couldn't believe what I can do. One time, he watched me work on the tire. He said he was going to bring it to Crownpoint, and I said, "No, I don't think so."
>
> And he went outside to another shed, and I just started working on it, and then when everything was just all ready, and then he says, "I'm surprised."
>
> I said, "That's what I've been doing, mostly [since] when I was big enough to do things." (4/18/89)
>
> I like to do things for myself. I like to go out and do things. I help out a lot at church and at school, just try to do things, what I can do to help out. I always like to help out with something, somewhere. So then my husband always says, "You always help out with something!"

> I says, "I don't know, I guess that's the way I've been taught to do, to help out." (5/2/89)

To Sarah, Navajo women are important because they are mothers.

> The women are important. They're mothers, and they teach their kids a lot of what they went through in their childhood. Some of them, they want their kids to learn more and do good for themselves and all that. I think that's a good idea. To me they're important that way.
>
> And they care about their children, and they take good care of them even though they're going through a lot of financial difficulties and stuff like that.
>
> It was always my mom that came out with some kind of a plan, or what we should do, and when we should do it. It's always her. Her way of trying to do things for us and other people. (5/2/89)

Sarah's mother taught her daughters to be economically self-sufficient, encouraged them to learn skills that ignored a rigid division of labor, and took a lead role in making decisions for the family.

The cultural constellation of ideas and values related to children, family, kinship, and home invoke motherhood in ways unique to Navajo society. "The concept of 'mother' is not merely given in natural processes [pregnancy, birth, lactation, nurturance]," states Henrietta Moore, "but is a cultural construction which different societies build up and elaborate in different ways" (1988, 25). The cultural construction of Navajo motherhood begins with universals of biological reproduction and builds on gendered meanings of women's roles and behavior.

Navajo motherhood is uniquely shaped by Navajo social organization, a worldview that venerates procreation, and conjugal relationships based on the economic partnership of men and women (Denetdale 2001; Frisbie 1982; McCloskey 1998). Women's roles as childbearers and caretakers are pivotal in assigning women's status and power within a society and their position in relationship to men. As summarized by Navajo historian, Jennifer Denetdale, "Navajo women had and continue to have voices in economic, political, and social realms. Navajo women continue to find significant their roles as mothers, wives, daughters, and sisters.

As grandmothers, mothers, and daughters," writes Denetdale, "Navajo women claim authority, dictating, in many cases, land use. They retain primary care of children and seek formal education for the purpose of sustaining family and community" (2001, 19).

Esteem for women as mothers combines with a worldview that honors reproduction and nurturance in all of earth's plant and animal life. The reproductive activities of women, as life givers and life sustainers, garner respect. Likewise, Navajo women's centrality elevates the home as the source of the bonds that nurture all of society, preventing the domestic sphere from being relegated to a relatively insignificant private realm. The central concept of motherhood acts as a powerful cultural symbol that enhances rather than detracts from women's value in Navajo society.

As their own mothers did, Navajo mothers expect to combine work and motherhood, whether that work is in the labor force or in the informal economy. Navajo mothers, like other American Indian women, seek employment because it allows them to provide economically for their families (Ackerman 2003; Berman 2003; Fast 2002; Powers 1986). As Linda Begay, an employed Navajo mother, stated, "Most women today work to survive, and then we're mothers after five o'clock" (5/17/90).

Sarah Forrestal preferred to be employed but was unable to find steady employment since the mine where she used to work closed. "Once in a while, I go to work, but it makes me feel a lot better just working," said Sarah. "I'm not saying that I'm not happy with only taking care of them [her children] right now. I think I'll be content with being both, just working and just being a mother. So I guess it's not hard for me. I've been doing that." Sarah continues: "I was working for a whole month, and then I took care of my kids when I got home. So it's okay. Even though it's a lot of work, but it's worth it" (5/2/89).

In an environment of scarce economic resources, Navajo women welcome employment as an endeavor compatible with mothering. Mothers in the labor force often find babysitters among unemployed members of the extended family. Furthermore, a concept of shared mothering survives, despite the dispersal of rural extended family residence groups that supported the pastoral economy.

Women's economic autonomy began in childhood when parents gave children of both sexes lambs and kids, which formed the nucleus of later herds. Most often, Navajos chose matrilocal residence patterns at marriage, in which the husband came to live with the wife's family. Navajo women entered a marriage owning her own sheep and surrounded by supportive kin. Despite the replacement of the land-based economy with the cash economy and wage labor, Navajo women have maintained the legacy of female economic productivity by holding jobs while raising their children.

Reproduction and the Life Cycle

The fundamental importance of women's fertility in Navajo society is reflected in the meaning associated with life cycle events that herald the biological markers of reproduction: menarche, pregnancy, and childbirth. As cultural transitions, these reproductive life events assume profound meaning and power in Navajo women's lives. A girl's first and second menstrual period and the birth of a baby are celebrated as joyful events within a wide circle of kin and friends. In contrast, although menopause may go unmarked as a life cycle event, the advent of grandmotherhood is invariably a significant, positive event. As the new head of a local clan segment, a grandmother strengthens her position within the family when her daughters give birth to members of the youngest generation.

Menarche, pregnancy, and childbirth assume distinctive meanings in Navajo women's lives that transcend the twentieth-century historical, economic, and sociocultural changes contributing to dependence on the cash economy and a bicultural lifestyle. These universal biological events transmit culturally constructed shared values. At menarche, Navajo girls celebrate their potential for motherhood with a Kinaaldá, a four-day puberty ceremony that culminates in an all-night sing. With the birth of her first child, a Navajo woman becomes a mother, which confers on her adult status, and a multifaceted symbol of fertility, productivity, and sustenance. The transition to menopause in a Navajo woman's life recedes into the background, whereas achieving the honored status of grandmotherhood signals matrilineal clan continuity across the generations as a woman's daughters and granddaughters, in turn, fulfill their reproductive potential.

For medicine women and other Navajo women, menopause ends monthly periods during which ceremonies must be avoided (Schwarz 2003).

For a Navajo girl, the Kinaaldá ceremony honors the arrival of womanhood; it is a recognition of her future reproductive potential. By reenacting the first Kinaaldá conducted for Changing Woman, young Navajo girls identify with the respected female deity. "In the Kinaaldá, the girl herself is a symbol, not only of the major Navajo deity, Changing Woman (and her counterparts: White Shell Woman, Turquoise Woman, and others) and the concepts with which she is associated, such as Earth and Life, but also of the power of reproduction" (Frisbie 1993, 373). The Kinaaldá is part of the Blessing Way Ceremony, and as such ensures a favorable future for the girl it honors.

The Kinaaldá "ushers the girl into society, invokes positive blessing on her, insures her health, prosperity, and well-being, and protects her from potential misfortune" (Frisbie 1993, 9).

"One cannot overestimate the importance of this rite in creating a positive self-image in a young girl," asserts Mary Shepardson (1995, 164). As part of a Navajo girl's ethnic socialization, the Kinaaldá contributes to her adolescent identity formation. Besides facilitating identification with Changing Woman, the Kinaaldá imparts the values associated with ideal Navajo behaviors such as generosity, exhibition of endurance and strength, and maintenance of harmony in a Navajo girl's life (Markstrom and Iborra 2003).

For Navajo women in Crownpoint, the Kinaaldá continues to be an all important ceremony for their daughters and granddaughters. The resurgence of the Kinaaldá testifies to the persistent high value placed on women, reproduction, and motherhood in Navajo society. The announcement that a girl has started menstruating initiates arrangements for the Kinaaldá, for which family members often have been planning for years by gathering necessary materials such as grass for the hairbrush and cornmeal for the cake. Major events in the ceremony are daily runs to the east; ritual washing of the girl's hair in yucca suds; baking an alkaan, a large corn cake, in an outdoor circular pit; and the all-night sing conducted by a medicine man on the final night of the four-day ceremony.

One Navajo grandmother, Sarah McCray, who had a Kinaaldá for each of her four daughters, stated that she did so because "That's what's called being a Navajo. When you have respect for yourself and your Navajo religion, that's what's called being a Navajo" (7/16/97).

Dorothy Martin described her own Kinaaldá, which took place after her first and second menstrual periods.

> I remember I was around fourteen years old when I had my first period. I used to sleep under the table. I woke up in the morning, and I felt wetness on myself, and I saw spots of blood, and it scared me. I put a blanket around myself and went to my paternal aunt. She said, "What's wrong with you? You became a woman right there." My aunt told me how to care of myself and make a belt and a pad out of an old mattress.
>
> The news was given to my mother, who was living in Crownpoint. My grandmother gathered up her goods and drove her wagon from south of here where she lived in the canyon to the north of here over a hill to a small hogan. It was here she prepared for the Kinaaldá.
>
> My hair was brushed back and tied with a buckskin, and my bangs were left hanging. The buckskin was from the skin of a deer that was not killed by a shot but died naturally.
>
> They dressed me up in my best clothing, a red sash belt, a concho belt, and a necklace of several strings, and bracelets up my arm. I was told to herd sheep while wearing the jewelry. While I was herding sheep, they were gathering the corn. It was very hard work to grind the corn on the mano and metate, which were placed on a nice goat skin.
>
> Others were helping me grind the corn in a grinder. I had to fill two flour sacks of corn. (1/19/96)

Dorothy's maternal aunt was chosen to play the role of ideal woman to help her throughout the ceremony and to figuratively "mold" her into a strong, shapely woman.

> My mother's sister was told to come over and mold me. The grandson of Chief Manuelito, Black Moustache Man, Manuelito

Begay, was the medicine man that was hired. He was my maternal grandfather.

I was running for four days. On the fourth day, my period was going down. On the fourth day, a ceremony was held. During the four days before the ceremony, starting when my hair was tied back, I ran four times to the east each day. Even on the morning of the ceremony.

My maternal grandmother would grind a holy stone on the metate and what would fall off she would rub it on her hands and put it in the four directions to bless it. It was to make food always be present, everlasting. The two bags of corn that I ground were put on a sheet. Water was boiling, and the corn was put in and stirred with the stirring sticks. Then they let it cool. On another sheet, they placed the corn husks, and I sewed them together, one layer for the bottom of the corn cake and one layer for the top of the corn cake. The fire was burning outside for one day and one night.

After they cleaned out the pit and put in the corn husks, the strong men would take out the corn meal. They poured the corn meal and smoothed it around. Women were sitting around. Before the corn husks were put on top, I put on the cornmeal from four directions and then around in a circle. The women directed me. Anyone who wanted to bless it put on corn meal. Then the corn husks were put on and wood coals over them, and then logs were put on until it cooked and hardened.

About eleven o'clock, women brought the sheet in the Hogan and placed goods and jewelry in front of me. Then the songs are started, the hogan songs, the four mountain songs.

In the morning, my hair was washed with yucca suds. While my hair was still wet, I ran to the east four times. The sheet was taken outside to the east, and the things were put out there. I was molded by my aunt while the medicine man was singing the special song inside. Anyone who wanted to be tall or be skinny would line up to be molded.

After the molding was completed, the cake was cooling. I came back in the hogan, and the buckskin tie was removed, and my hair was tied back with my own tie. White clay, *gliish*, was put on my cheeks to keep my face from drooping when I got older. Red mineral, *chee*, was put on my upper cheeks and forehead.

The medicine man was fed first. The Navajo ceremonial basket that was used to wash my hair was cleaned up, and the pieces of Navajo cake were put in there. They cut up the cake—four pieces in the middle were cut into fourths. The heart of the cake is left to feed mother earth. One is for the medicine man, and one for the woman who sang the most. The rest of the cake is cut up and put on the back of the truck. I passed out the cake, to be really kind and generous, and not stingy. To be helpful.

During the time they were passing out the Navajo cake and treats, popcorn balls, I was told not to eat it. I was told to herd sheep. I kept the jewelry and clothes on for four days.

I had a second Kinaaldá after my second period, [referred to as] "she completed her run." The second ceremony was held at my paternal grandmother's. I was herding sheep when I got my second period. I was not scared; I knew what it was. After the ceremony, I was told, "You know how to take care of yourself. You know what your period is." (1/19/96)

Planning and carrying out the four-day ceremony depends on help from members of social networks that the girl will interact with throughout her life. In the words of Ruth Roessel, the Navajo educator, "it is only through the help of other women in the community and clan that such a ceremony can be possible and successful." Furthermore, "Sharing is the cornerstone of this experience because no family could have enough food to carry out all of the responsibilities that revolve around and with the ceremony" (1981, 82). While honoring a girl's fecundity, the Kinaaldá at the same time anchors her in the web of social relationships and patterns of reciprocity that she will participate in throughout her life.

Pregnancy and Childbirth

Crownpoint women's identity is intimately tied to their role as mothers, actualized by giving birth to their children. Grandmothers referred to childbearing and reproduction as holy or sacred and associated it with strength. Both the mother and father of the baby show respect for the creation of new life by observing taboos during pregnancy. Loretta Benally, who herself gave birth to eight children, stated, "I think that women who have a lot of children are strong. I always wonder how they did it" (9/27/88). In their study of Navajo teenage pregnancy, Dalla and Gamble confirmed that motherhood is greatly esteemed. As one community member explained, "the role of the woman is exalted because she has babies" (2001, 9). Overall, "participants described Navajo women, and mothers specifically, as powerful, strong, and family-oriented" (2001, 10).

In contrast to the persistence and even resurgence of the Kinaaldá ceremony celebrated at the time of a girl's first menstrual period, a Blessing Way Ceremony for the pregnant mother is now conducted far less frequently (Hartle-Schutte 1988). Dorothy Martin recalled that the pregnant woman's mother often made the arrangements to have a medicine person conduct a Blessing Way Ceremony during pregnancy. "Yes, there is usually a time they set, usually the grandmother does it, usually a month before the baby was born," said Dorothy. "Now is the time for the mother to have the corn pollen put in her mouth because the baby is coming soon" (5/9/96). Prenatal care at the IHS clinic has replaced a Blessing Way Ceremony as the way to promote the birth of a healthy baby.

One indication of the importance of reproduction and motherhood is the concern shown for women who do not have children and for women who have problems during pregnancy. Medicine men are consulted in both instances. Dorothy Martin told about her daughter, who did not have any children until after she was thirty years old. Her daughter was concerned that she didn't have any children, in contrast to her mother's nine. One problem was that her husband had kidney failure and had to have dialysis. The couple went both to a Navajo diagnostician and to a medical doctor. "Sometime during the treatment, a baby was conceived." In reference to her daughter, Dorothy stated, "She was thinking about being alone. Who would help her when she got older? She realized that children bring wealth in a lot of ways—not being alone, helping you, carrying on after you are gone. Like Alice McCauley," Dorothy continued, "she never had any children, and she accumulated a lot of things in her life and had no one to carry on. This baby was born just last summer when school was out" (11/14/97). To ensure a healthy baby, Dorothy's daughter had a Blessing Way Ceremony during her pregnancy.

A woman who has problems during her pregnancy may have an *'ooltáád*, an unraveling ceremony, conducted as a variant of the Blessing Way. Also referred to as the unbraiding ceremony, the 'ooltáád counteracts any inadvertent behavior on the part of either parent that might figuratively tie the baby up. Dorothy Martin described the fabric to be unraveled. "The piece of fiber they would use, they would unravel it, a piece of material that belongs to the pregnant woman. Or the hair tie, now they might use a shoestring" (5/9/96).

When Dorothy's daughter had an unbraiding ceremony, the medicine man used both yucca and a knotted shoestring. Dorothy described the ceremony for her pregnant daughter, which took place in the very same hogan where we were talking.

> My daughter couldn't sleep at night. They call that "when the baby is standing up in you." They performed a Blessing Way for her in this hogan. They prayed and chanted about where the baby traveled from. The medicine man gave her strands of yucca that was braided and a shoestring in knots. The medicine man said to unbraid it, and the father unbraided the shoestring. She walked up and back to the mesa and then went to the hospital. They found that the baby's head was showing, and a baby came walking into her life. (11/14/97)

Motherhood and reproduction convey multiple cultural meanings associated with a Navajo worldview that honors women's powers of regeneration. The birth of a baby is a significant life event not only for the family but also for a network of friends and relatives, as a sign of ongoing procreative power, fertility, and renewal.

Menopause

Navajo women's experience with menopause disputes an interpretation that sees it as a life course transition plagued by physical discomfort and depression. Researchers from the University of New Mexico School of Medicine recently questioned Navajo women about their experiences with menopause. They found that women characterized as both more and less traditional who had a Kinaaldá ceremony as girls reported few or no symptoms of menopause, even after a hysterectomy. The less-traditional women, who did not have a Kinaaldá, experienced menopausal symptoms much like non-Navajo women (Mingo, Herman, and Jasperse 2000). In general, menopause "was not a significant thing. It's something that happens" (Manuelito 1999). Rather than losing a youthful identity when reproductive capacity ends, Navajo women, as they age, are venerated for their personal wisdom and cultural knowledge.

Women's variable experiences with menopause suggest that attitudes toward this life course transition and the cultural context in which it occurs are crucial. Epidemiological studies indicate that many women experience minimal symptoms (Lewis and Bernstein 1996). However, the more than seven million American women who receive hormone replacement therapy each year make it evident that many American women view menopause as an estrogen deficiency disease with long-term health sequelae.

In a study of menopause among Japanese women, Lock (1993) found that these women had shoulder stiffness and headaches but not hot flashes or night sweats. Theorizing that the different responses to menopause among American and Japanese women are associated with cultural understandings about the relation of the individual to society, Lock pointed out that the Japanese focus is on the social network, the perpetuation of the family across generations. Similar Navajo cultural values focus on the family and clan, instead of the individual, as the fundamental unit of society. Rather than paying attention to losing childbearing capacities at menopause, Navajo women anticipate gaining the status of grandmother, the head of a matrilineal clan segment.

The Navajo creation story, ceremonial system, and matrilineal social organization transform Navajo women's reproductive life course events into cultural transitions that enhance women's position in Navajo society. Like Changing Woman, the beloved Navajo deity, a Navajo girl undergoes a Kinaaldá at the onset of puberty to celebrate her potential for procreation. Based on the way she cared for and nurtured her sons, Changing Woman also serves as a model for motherhood. The source of clan membership, mothers perpetuate the matrilineage. Attainment of the status of grandmother signifies clan continuity rather than the end of a woman's reproductive years. The cultural meanings assigned to Kinaaldá, motherhood, and grandmotherhood symbolize the ongoing cycle of Navajo life through past, present, and future generations.

Grandmothers as Mothers

The overarching significance of Navajo motherhood as a cultural strategy derives from a combination of traditional and contemporary factors. In cultural context, the multiple meanings of Navajo motherhood, stemming from Changing Woman, matrilineal clans, and women's egalitarian roles have been reinforced by current socioeconomic conditions. In addition, Native American mothers share some characteristics with African-American, Hispanic, and Asian-American women in their endeavors to ensure physical survival of their children, empower children in a bicultural world, and transmit racial and cultural identity while fostering a positive self-identity (Collins 1994). These themes ring true for Navajo mothers who encounter issues of survival, power, and identity while raising their children. For the grandmothers, the role of motherhood was inseparable from that of being a woman (Wright 1982a, 1982b). As mothers of large families, grandmothers recalled the hard work and challenges of mothering, as well as the importance of their role in shaping their children.

Marie Tsosie gave birth to nine children, one of whom died in an epidemic. With the support of her parents, she finished raising her large family after her husband left. As she reflected on motherhood, she emphasized the role of teacher.

> I always emphasized motherhood, and the way a mother should teach her children to behave and to work and to lead healthy lives and be independent.
>
> I've always stressed that to my kids, and now I'm proud of the fact most of my kids listened to me and took my word for it, and

> now they're teaching their young ones the exact things I taught my kids. And I'm very proud of most of my grandkids because they're making out good now.
>
> I feel like what I've always stressed and taught has taken hold. They listened and they learned. They themselves turned out to be good parents, and now my grandkids I hope are being brought up in the same manner. I feel like something is being passed on. Generation to generation.
>
> To me, the most important and effective manner in which you can influence your children as a Navajo and as a mother in general is to just continuously talk to them. Tell them what's important in their lives, what's important for their future, how they live, what they should avoid and shun, and your children will eventually catch on to that. (6/10/88)

Although she never attended school herself, Marie encouraged her children to stay in school even though they were sent away to boarding school in Oklahoma. She warned them about negative influences that would interfere with their success. "They had to try to make good lives for themselves. Most of them listened to me, and they turned out real well" (6/10/88). She expressed pride in her children, who have taught the same principles to her grandchildren and great-grandchildren.

Grandmothers were keenly aware of the vast difference between the way they raised their children and the way children are being raised today. Loretta Benally recalled:

> All my children grew up on the cradleboard. I used to carry the baby to the sheep. When the baby was asleep, I covered it up while I was with the sheep. I used flour sacks for diapers. I didn't have Pampers like mothers have now.
>
> It is very different. We were very involved with our children. We were involved with survival. Children now have everything for them. That is why there is violence.
>
> Younger parents don't lecture to children about rights and wrongs. Old tradition is dying out. Everything is ready for them now. They don't have to work for it. (9/19/88)

Loretta used verbal instruction to discipline and instill values in her children. While growing up, children worked at the numerous chores necessary for maintaining the sheep herds and gardens in the land-based economy. Loretta bemoaned the disappearance of the traditional methods of child rearing centered on work and instruction from the parental generation because she felt that children's less demanding lives led to problems. Rather than contributing to the subsistence economy, children were now dependent on parents' work.

When June Kalleco was raising her children, she adhered to traditional patterns of child rearing. June recalled, "I didn't have anybody to help me. I didn't need to ask. I could breastfeed while weaving or cooking, and the baby was in a cradleboard. Back then," she continued, "the babies weren't very demanding and didn't cry a lot. You put the baby in a cradleboard, and the baby would be watching you. The cradleboard would be laying against you, and you could weave or cook" (9/27/88).

June advises her children about living a good life, based on her own experiences. "I talk to them about growing up days, and I talk to them about the future, step-by-step, because I want them to have a good life," said June. "My children and my grandchildren, I think of them as part of my heart. I want only good things for them." June considers both the past and the future when counseling her children and grandchildren (9/27/88).

Comparing today's children with herself as a child, June remembered that she was very obedient. "Now children do what they want and don't listen," she said.

When June was asked, "In what ways are women important in Navajo life?" the question initiated a discussion between June and the interpreter about how the word *important* is hard to translate into Navajo. Nevertheless, June responded, "A woman is very important because she is the strength and the backbone of the family, like a hogan. If there isn't a woman," she asked, "where is the strength? The woman does a lot of planning and says this will be done and that will be done" (9/27/88).

June's comments about the Keetso baby case reveal her views on motherhood. She stated, "A long time ago Navajo mothers were told that it's your baby, it's part of your body, your heart, and your soul. You should never give it up. Now when I look around," she continued, "I see other people raising someone's kids a lot. I wonder why do they have babies if they can't raise their kids?" (9/27/88).

Besides her sheepherding, weaving, and participation in ceremonies, June initiates both traditional and contemporary activities for her extended family. She sponsors ceremonies, baseball games, and turkey shoots.

With one exception, all of the grandmothers were the senior female members of their families, the progenitors of their clan segment, with grown children, numerous grandchildren, and sometimes great-grandchildren. The one grandmother whose own mother was still alive essentially filled the position of senior female because of the advanced age and frailty of her eighty-one-year-old mother. In their position as "head mother" (Witherspoon 1975), grandmothers took pride in their roles as teacher and "keepers of the culture" (Billson 1995) who assumed responsibility for passing on knowledge, traditions, and customs. They wished to pass on knowledge of ceremonies, clans, traditional foods, and practices such as burying the umbilical cord. A major dilemma for monolingual grandmothers was their inability to communicate with grandchildren who could not speak Navajo. Concerned grandmothers fervently advocated teaching children the Navajo language.

Midlife Mothers

In contrast to the grandmothers, the midlife mothers had grown up with an awareness of Euroamerican conceptions of women as subordinate and of motherhood as a role less valued than those of men. When comparing these conceptions, Navajo midlife mothers recognized the respect for motherhood and primacy of women's role in the home. Marilyn Gilmore, a professional woman who worked in a Crownpoint agency and was also a midlife mother, stated:

> I have heard about liberated women. To me there is no such thing as a liberated woman. The Navajo woman has already been the primary decision maker in the home. The man relies on the women to make the decision. Like First Man and First Woman. First Man would turn to First Woman and say, "What do you

> think?" They're the primary person in the home. Not because they cook, but because they nurture. Like a mother hen, the strength, you can feel the wings spreading out to protect the family. The mother is always the person who makes the decision. When we say prayers, we pray to Mother Earth. (5/24/88)

As nurturers and primary decision makers in the home, Navajo women carried on the legacy of the Holy People.

Like Sarah Forrestal, other midlife mothers respect their own mothers for their strength, patience, and wisdom. Midlife mothers looked to the older generations when speaking of their own roles as mothers. They spoke of their admiration and respect for their own mothers and grandmothers, who had been important influences in their lives. Although Rachel Morgan is a devoted and attentive mother, she feels that she lacks her mother's patience. When asked about differences between the times in which her mother raised her and those in which she is raising her own children, she replied:

> Yeh, I think it's different because I would do anything to be my mom. Because she has patience. She did things a lot different than I did. She hardly ever spanked us. She was more the person that talks to you and reasons with you.
>
> I try to do that. I have very little patience, and there are occasions when I have to spank them.
>
> And she was always concerned about feeding us the three meals a day if we weren't in school. And see, I'm not. Well, I am, but the kids have cold cereal in the morning, and then they get fed at lunch.
>
> Everything's the mothers, the grandmothers, and their decisions are what stands. And, it seems to me that they're the ones that are the head of the family. (9/14/88)

In her own nuclear family, Rachel and her husband have a more egalitarian relationship, making decisions together. "But I think this is more with older Navajos. Like with me, in our immediate family, I don't make all the choices. I don't make all the decisions. It's my husband and I together. Even there," continued Rachel, "I guess they didn't have that in years past.

But really, the majority of the Navajo people it seems like the mother usually is the person that runs the household. And I'm sure there are exceptions, like with my folks" (9/14/88).

A divorced midlife mother of five children, Edna Tsosie lives with her mother in a rural area and works in Crownpoint. Her former husband's drinking problem and sporadic employment led to their separation.

> My kids up to now have been keeping me busy. In spite of my problems with my kids and my husband, I feel like I'm better off with just me and my kids. So we're doing pretty good. I still live with my mom. I guess one thing I look forward to is living with my kids.
>
> I just gave you some information and the struggles in my life. I compare that with my husband. He's just hit bottom. He's lost his job, his vehicle, he's put in jail, lost his driver's license. In the problems I went through in my marriage, I was stronger. I just kept going forward.
>
> My mother is another example. She was stronger than he [her father] was. Looking back on my sisters, the problems they've had, they're stronger than their husbands. I'm basing that on what I went through and what my sisters went through. (10/16/90)

Edna exhibits strength in caring for her children on her own. Since her return home, Edna is learning about traditional religion from her mother, who cares for the family's *jish,* or medicine bundle, because she is "the only one who knows how to use it." She questions her mother about traditional practices in order to carry on her family's ceremonial customs.

Ellen Mitchell relies on traditional prayers and ceremonies for herself and for her children. Although Ellen did not have a Kinaaldá as a girl, she had one for her daughter and is now planning for her granddaughter's. She also has prayers or ceremonies done when her children need them. When her rebellious teenage daughter was in high school, she had a medicine man perform ceremonies for her. Ellen recalled, "My daughter didn't come home, ran around, smoked. When she wasn't at home, I had a medicine man come to the house and perform a ceremony for her. And then when she was there," Ellen continued, "I had a medicine man come back and perform a ceremony for her. I don't tell everyone that, but that's what I did. My daughter tells me that she was glad that I did it" (2/26/88).

For Ellen as well as other midlife mothers, the high value placed on giving birth and raising children prevailed regardless of marital status. After her divorce, she worried about the opinion of others when she was pregnant with her son. "I wanted that baby. I was worried what so-and-so would say. I told you what I went through to get him. I wondered what my mother was thinking, what my brothers and sisters were thinking. Where's the man?" they asked. "I talked to some of my friends about it. They said that they would still be my friends. It's not like you're sleeping around" (4/19/88). Although her son's father wanted to get married, Ellen did not, preferring to be independent.

Even when her pregnancy resulted from forced sexual contact, one midlife mother chose to give birth to the child. Evangeline Benally explained that she became pregnant with her daughter when she was raped.

> And it was in my mind for a long time, and finally I got rid of it. Then my little girl, the one that's staying home, that's her father. And it's her dad that raped me, and I got her. That's how it happened. And they told me to turn him in, but I didn't. I didn't want to. So even though I went to work, and I was working at that time over here at the hospital. After that, in nine months I got her. So they told me to quit my job. So I quit. So I stayed home with my little girl. And I took care of her. My mom and my dad helped me out with the diapers and the things I needed. They helped me out to raise her. (5/25/89)

Children are welcomed into the extended family, regardless of the circumstances that surround their birth.

Young Mothers

Young mothers exhibited remarkable determination and maturity in their roles as mothers. For example, when Julie Etcitty became pregnant at fourteen, she resisted the pressure from Indian Health Service personnel who suggested that she have an abortion or put the baby up for adoption. "I don't want to have an abortion 'cause I don't think it's the Navajo traditional way. That's what they were saying at PHS [Public Health Service, or IHS] when I had my little boy, and I said, 'No.' And they were trying to have an adoption, and I said, 'I'll raise him myself,' and I did" (6/5/89).

For many young mothers in the Crownpoint sample, the transition from daughter to mother is still in process. When younger adolescents became mothers, they often depended on their own mothers to help care for the baby. When Rosie Slim, a young single mother, began working in Albuquerque and later transferred to Colorado Springs, her parents started caring for her daughter.

> With my work, I hardly spent time with her, so my parents wanted to watch her one week, and one week turned to two weeks. She stayed with my parents, maybe about a year or so. My mom and dad took care of her to where I could see her. I came back out here on my days off, and stuff, or Saturdays and Sundays they would take her up there and stuff like that. I didn't want her to stay with my parents; I thought after a while she would start calling my mom, Mommy, and my dad, Daddy, and not know who I was. So that bothered me a lot. But she doesn't do that.
>
> Then after I went to Colorado Springs, it was like I was coming back almost every weekend, too. It was like a six-hundred-mile drive. So I was going back and forth round-trip. I would leave like a Saturday evening about five, and I'd get here about midnight or something. And I kept doing that. I'd leave Monday night, and I'd get back there about Monday night and go to work the next day. So I kind of got tired of that, too.
>
> I really didn't have that much to do with raising my daughter. I always had my parents there for me. They're always there for me if I had any kind of money problems or anything. I'm not financially settled. I don't have a house.
>
> I don't want to depend on my parents. If I have another child, I don't want them to be the one there again. Depending on them. I want to get independent as soon as possible. I pretty much had my independence from them until after I had her. And I lived in Albuquerque, and she came back out here and all that, and I just

> ended up coming back, too. And I want to go back to school. I said, "I don't want to have any kids in the near future. For right now, that's enough." (11/2/88)

Anticipating that her current reliance on her parents will be temporary, Rosie plans to continue her education and work toward independence.

Young women who spent their teenage years "partying" credit the birth of a child and their responsibilities as mothers to the change in their lives. The allure of drinking with friends lost its attraction. The birth of Margaret Hoskie's daughter likewise changed her priorities. She stated, "Me, going out to party and drink, it won't prove nothing. Since I had her, I just started settling down. I just stay home." Margaret and her two-and-a-half-year-old daughter live with her mother, but in order to earn money for diapers and clothes, Margaret sells baked goods. "My mom told me, 'If you want something, you have to work for it' " (6/5/89).

In the Crownpoint sample, some young mothers cared for their children while enduring turbulent relationships with men. Cathy Howard recalled her abusive relationship with the father of her three children, two of whom died as infants and the third when he was five years old. Their third child had severe health problems as a result of infant meningitis, which affects Navajo infants at a higher rate than U.S. infants as a whole (Williams 1987).

> And then I had another one. It was a boy also. And then he had meningitis. Boy, did I have a rough time with him! With that meningitis. He had that meningitis for about five years. And right on his birthday I lost him. He was going to be five.
>
> With that other guy, he had a dope problem, a drinking problem. He used to always go out and party, and then he'd come in 'til about three or four in the morning.
>
> And I would stay home with the kid. So I had to pump his shunt every morning, afternoon, and evening. And he used to get seizures a lot, too. I think he spent most of his time in the hospital. We used to be down in Phoenix and then Albuquerque, and then Tucson.
>
> Anyway, I left that guy. I just walked out, just like this. And

> he tried to apologize and what not. I said, "Sorry. I must have been so stupid. I went and took your word so many times."
>
> He even abused me. He used to tie me up with the speaker wire and throw me in the closet. Leave me there for half of the day. Because I was bad-mouthing off, and he doesn't want to be told what to do. (1/19/89 and 3/22/89)

After her son's death, Cathy left his father and went back to school. At the time I interviewed Cathy, she had married and had a two-and-a-half-year-old son, whom she was still breastfeeding. "Everybody says he's too big to be breastfeeding, but then I always tell them he's a special baby to me" (3/22/89). Because of her tragic experiences with other children, Cathy is doing all she can to protect the health of her son.

For the young mothers, the responsibilities of motherhood marked the transition to adulthood and sometimes led them in a different direction, away from a lifestyle that included substance abuse. Female members of their extended families, primarily their own mothers, imparted values and beliefs associated with motherhood. Despite the extensive influences of Western society, young Navajo mothers assumed the role of mother with pride and with the support of kin networks.

Conclusion

For the three generations of Navajo women, motherhood is revered, an honored status reminiscent of female deities such as Changing Woman. The intergenerational relationship of grandmother, mother, and daughter assures clan continuity. For the grandmothers, the role of mother was inseparable from other roles. They enlisted the help of their children in the land-based economy and prepared them for adulthood by talking with them about the right way to behave.

Midlife mothers lived in a bicultural world affected by inescapable Euroamerican influences but nevertheless maintained their pivotal role in Navajo culture. When the need arose, they at times relied on traditional ceremonies for help with their children. In an era of more tenuous relationships with men and fragile marriages, midlife mothers more often became single mothers. Young mothers, still in the process of completing their families, often saw motherhood as a viable route to adulthood. Although they often became mothers at an early age, extended families welcomed their children and provided assistance for the young mothers.

Navajo motherhood becomes a cultural strategy derived from the beliefs, practices, and values embedded in Navajo traditional religion, matrilineal social organization, and the pastoral economy. Navajo motherhood gives rise to multiple connotations such as nurturance, strength, fertility, and regeneration. The associations, in turn, extend to several domains: actual mothers and children who are part of an extended family; the earth, crops, and livestock, which sustain humans; and Changing Woman, who, along with other Holy People, taught the Navajo how to live. The cultural, social, and economic context of Navajo motherhood reveals an ideology that continues to elevate and empower Navajo women.

9
Guardians of Cultural Knowledge

Eighty-one-year-old Ruth Sanchez relished the opportunity to talk about her life, stating, "I have a lot of stories to tell, but it will take a lot of time. There is no one to listen." After answering some questions about her childhood and young adult years, she declared, "I want to talk about traditional foods."

> I used to cook a lot of traditional foods. We used to bake a corn bread, like a loaf of bread. We used a lot of local vegetation for food. We used sheep and goats for food.
>
> The plant with horns. About three feet high. We would lay a cloth on the ground and gather it up and tie it up. We would take it home and put it on a tarp. We would beat it and grind it to get the shell off to get the dark part of the seed.
>
> We ground it lightly. My mother would store it in a big bag. I loved it. I would put it in a big bowl and eat it. I used to sprinkle it with milk.
>
> The banana yucca fruit. We would harvest it and cook it and boil it and make it like a fruit roll up. [Some of it] we would make it into a paste and eat it then. Then part we saved for the long, long term. We made a hole in the middle with a stick, put a rope on it, and let it dry on a line. The part that will be used, we would slice it off and add it to cornmeal mush, pudding, and breads.
>
> In the fall, we would kill only the old sheep that wouldn't make it through the winter. We would save the sheep fat in the sheep's stomach and even the crispy part and use it in the winter.
>
> A horse is usually butchered, and we would slice it thin into

> jerky and dry it. We would dry it so much it would make it dark, like night. Then we'd chop it up and heat it up with the fat. Now people don't want it; they say it stinks. When people had colds they would say, "Let's butcher a horse." . . .
>
> [My favorite foods are] the horse jerky cooked with fat. Banana [yucca] fruit. The berry with clay. (6/23/96)

In this chapter, I focus on Navajo grandmothers as valuable repositories of cultural knowledge who bridge the gulf between a traditional heritage and contemporary Westernized patterns of life. They consciously act as mentors for younger generations. Grandmothers share a desire to pass on the Navajo language, customs, and traditions to the younger generations.

When they reflected on the vast differences between the way they were raised and the way that their grandchildren are being raised today, the grandmothers expressed their regrets about the loss of the Navajo traditional way of life. Maureen Bitsuie misses the spiritual practices of daily life. She recalled, "Back then, everything was mostly done in a holy way, a spiritual way. When you were going to cook, there would be a prayer. Nowadays, they don't care" (12/5/95).

Annie Burnside remembered the never-ending hard work necessary for survival.

> I knew how to milk goats. I raised my little brothers. My older sisters went to school, and my younger brothers went to school, but I never did. I think it was because I was trying my best to be a sheepherder.
>
> When I was growing up, you had to travel a great distance for water. I often wondered where my older sisters and younger brothers were. I wondered where Crownpoint was. I didn't know it was a short distance.
>
> You had to struggle for the food. Now you go to the store and buy it. (12/12/95)

When she compared her childhood with that of today's children, Loretta Benally drew attention to the constant work expected of all family members. She declared:

> Today, people just all come into town and sit in front of TV. Back then, we used to work in the garden, herd sheep, go into the hogan to hear stories. They used to get us together to tell us what to do, what not to do.
>
> In the evening, we would be fixing the wool. Someone would be pulling the wool apart, someone will be carding, someone will be spinning, someone will be preparing the food for the next day. At the same time someone would be telling winter stories, or what you should do and give examples.
>
> We would get a whack by a rope or a fire poker stick if we slowed down working with the wool. I was whipped a lot by my father and aunt but not my mother. We got up at the white dawn and ran to the east. I remember grinding corn with the stone. My hands would hurt and I would cry, but we would keep on.
>
> It's really difficult to talk to my grandkids these days because they don't understand Navajo. (12/5/95)

Annie Mitchell also acknowledged the great effort expended to have enough food to eat. "We had to hunt and gather our food from the local vegetation. We had to cook our food in a fire in the ground and get water from a rock basin" (6/13/96).

Common Themes in Studies of Navajo Grandmothers

Two recent autobiographies, *Tall Woman: The Life Story of Rose Mitchell, a Navajo Woman, c. 1874–1977* (Mitchell 2001) and *The Scalpel and the Silver Bear* (Alvord and Van Pelt 1999), and one biography, *I'll Go and Do More: Annie Dodge Wauneka, Navajo Leader and Activist* (Niethammer 2001), highlight outstanding characteristics of Navajo grandmothers. Family members remembered Tall Woman as hard working, kind, strong, quiet, patient, devoted to her family, and generous both with material help and in sharing her knowledge. Her knowledge and skills of midwifery, livestock, traditional foods, weaving, herbal medicines, and traditional practices and religion verify that she was an encyclopedia of cultural knowledge. Tall Woman's preeminence in the family was demonstrated by her major economic contribution to the family, the sale of her weavings, and her daily direction of family activities (Mitchell 2001).

In contrast to Tall Woman, whose life centered on her home and family, Annie Dodge Wauneka, the daughter of the former Navajo tribal chairman, Chee Dodge, had an impact on the entire Navajo Tribe as well as American Indian policy. Her political activism often took her to Washington, D.C., to testify before Congress. During her twenty-seven-year tenure on the tribal council, Annie spearheaded the campaign to eradicate tuberculosis by persuading medicine men to refer tuberculosis patients to doctors, tracking down Navajos with tuberculosis to convince them to seek treatment, and visiting patients in sanatoriums, where she showed them the tubercle bacillus under the microscope and used a tape recorder to record messages to take back home to relatives. Annie was firmly rooted in Navajo culture, traditions, and religion, which were represented by her advice to Navajo women to follow the teachings of Chạnging Woman, the creator of the Navajo people (Niethammer 2001).

In her autobiography, Lori Arviso Alvord, the first Navajo woman surgeon, acknowledged her awakening respect for and identification with her Navajo heritage. After Lori finished medical school and moved to Gallup to take a job as a surgeon at the Gallup Indian Medical Center, her grandmother, Grace Cupp, lived with her until her death at age ninety. Lori's grandmother as well as her Navajo patients instilled a desire to integrate the Navajo concept of *hózhǫ́*, which is fundamental to traditional healing, into Western medical practices in her surgical practice and in her own life.

Navajo Grandmothers and Cultural Transmission

Grandparents' legacy to younger generations constitutes a unique resource for future generations. Erik Erickson (1963) labeled the transfer of this legacy from an older generation to a younger one as generativity. Generativity is "primarily the concern in establishing and guiding the next generation" (Erickson 1963, 267): Generativity has become a cross-cultural theme in adult lives. Adults, in roles as parents, teachers, mentors, and leaders, take responsibility for passing on knowledge and traditions to the next generations (McAdams and de St. Aubin 1992).

Kotre (1984) identified four types of generativity, all of which involve cultural transmission. First, biological generativity concerns begetting, bearing, and nursing offspring. Second, parental generativity involves nurturing and disciplining offspring, initiating them in a family's traditions. Third, in the area of technical generativity, adults employ teaching skills to pass on the body of a culture to successors, implicitly transmitting the symbol system in which the skills are embedded. And fourth, in the domain of cultural generativity, adults create, renovate, and conserve a symbol system, the mind of a culture, and pass it on to successors.

In their mothering and teaching activities, the grandmothers demonstrate the four types of generativity. During their childbearing years, the grandmothers exhibited biological generativity by giving birth to children who assure continuity among the generations. Grandmothers maintain parental generativity by participating in children's lives and caring for grandchildren, whether or not the extended family lives together in a cooperating residence unit as they did in the past. Grandmothers pass on technical knowledge by teaching skills such as how to care for sheep; how to clean, card, spin, dye, and weave wool; and how to prepare traditional foods. Also, grandmothers transfer cultural knowledge associated with ceremonies; with traditions such as a baby's First Laugh ceremony, saving a baby's umbilical cord, and the shoe game, played in the winter; with knowledge of relationships among matrilineal kin; and with traditional teachings about how to live a productive life.

In this chapter, I focus on technical and cultural generativity, topics not discussed in previous chapters. Convinced that Navajo young people need to be informed about the traditional lifestyle, customs, and beliefs as a guide to responsible adulthood, the grandmothers wished to share their knowledge of "the Navajo way." As an example of grandmothers' attitudes toward their stories, Dorothy Martin stated, "I'm hoping that they will be used for the Navajo youth. I'm hoping they will relearn" (5/9/96). Maureen Bitsuie asked about the purpose of her interview, "Is this going to be for future use for young Navajos to learn?" When I responded that I hoped it would benefit Navajo youth, she approvingly stated, "As long as other people are going to benefit from it, my Navajo people" (12/5/95).

Sarah McCray worried about the loss of Navajo ceremonies. "I think

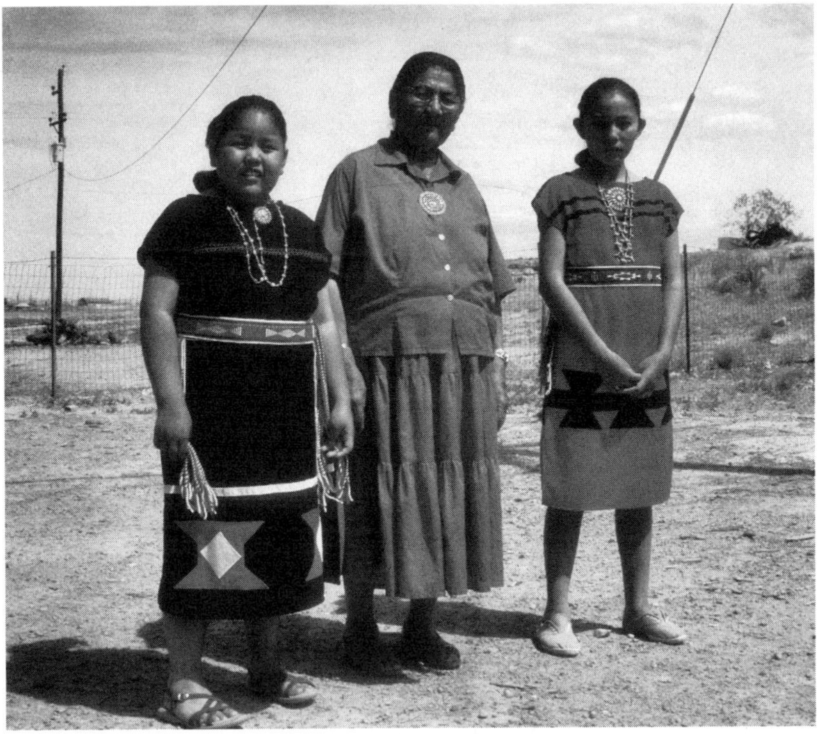

Loretta Benally, center, with her two granddaughters (Bonnie Benally Yazzie's daughters), Rondelle Yazzie (in red) and Roxanne Yazzie (in black), dressed in *biils*, traditional women's dress that predates Navajo incarceration at Fort Sumner.

what you are doing is really good. I stay awake at night wondering what will happen. There are too many Christians; people want to push away Navajo traditions. What will their children do?" she asked. "Their children will wonder how it was done. What will happen to their children? Who will perform the ceremonies? People should get together more and talk about doings and write it down and put it in books" (9/7/97).

Grandmothers care deeply about transmitting their skills and cultural knowledge to the younger generations. They are fully aware of their role as teachers, cultural guardians, and cultural bridges for a way of life that has undergone fundamental, irreversible changes during the twenti-

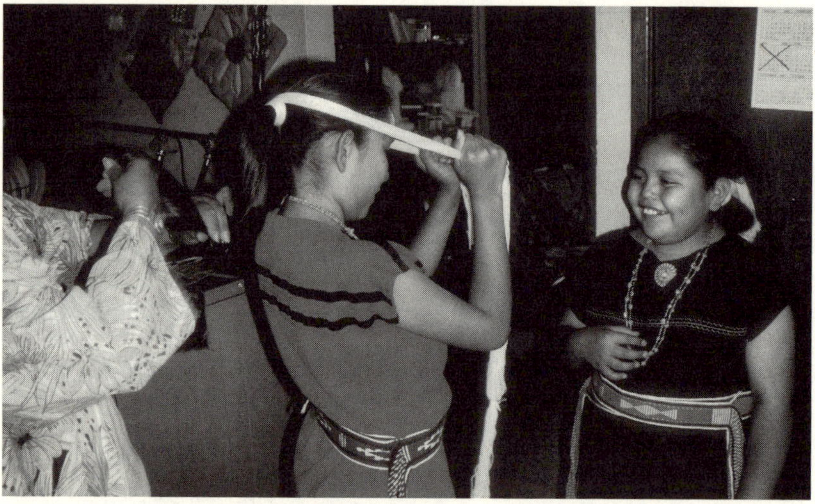

Rondelle Yazzie holding the tie for her hair knot while Roxanne Yazzie looks on.

eth century. Because of this passionate concern for preserving and passing on traditional knowledge, many grandmothers wished to be identified rather than have their identity concealed. Thus, many grandmothers in this chapter are identified by their own names instead of pseudonyms.

Traditional Subsistence Patterns

As a group, the grandmothers include elders categorized as both the Third Age, "the young old," and the Fourth Age, "the old old" (Laslett 1996). Among the young old grandmothers were those who did not have health problems that interfered with their mobility, who lived either in rural areas or had easy access to a rural home, and who still herded sheep and goats. Some herded sheep daily, whereas others shared responsibilities with husbands, children or grandchildren, clan relatives, or someone hired to take the sheep out. These grandmothers with herds also prepared the wool for weaving by washing, carding, spinning, and dyeing it. Some prepared natural dyes from vegetation and minerals and wove traditional designs in their rugs-twills, double face, and even the red and black design for the very old *biil*, the Navajo women's dress worn before incarceration at Fort Sumner. Grandmothers loved to reminisce about traditional foods such as mutton stew, fry bread, blood sausage, corn dishes, and dishes prepared with ingredients that grew wild in the surrounding countryside. Except for the grandmothers who belonged to fundamentalist Christian churches and attended Navajo revivals, grandmothers who frequented traditional ceremonies were called upon to prepare ceremonial dishes needed for specific ceremonies. Grandmothers who cared for herds of sheep and goats adjusted their lives to the seasonal cycle of lambing and shearing.

Sheep and Goat Herding

Grandmothers who continue to herd sheep employ knowledge and skills gained from a lifetime of caring for livestock. On a cold April day during a drought on the Navajo Reservation, I visited Rose Freeland, a grandmother who had brought three baby lambs into her house to keep them warm. One was standing up in a box by the stove. Sleeping in another box were twin lambs only two days old. Because the lambs' mothers did not have enough milk to feed them after a very dry winter and spring that produced very little grass, she was feeding the lambs herself with powdered milk that she mixed with water.

Annie James, a fifty-eight-year-old grandmother, has a sheep herd that she and her husband care for. Lambing season is a demanding time. "When the lambs and kids are coming you have to feed some of them. You have to give them to another ewe who has a lot of milk. For some reason they will abandon them;" said Annie, "you have to hold the ewe morning and evening while the lamb feeds. For me, in more than half of these situations, they will readopt their baby" (3/14/96).

When I jokingly volunteered to herd sheep for her, Annie responded, "They'll take off towards the mountains. They sense when you're confused and don't know what you're doing" (3/14/96).

Like most grandmothers who have sheep and goats, Annie weaves traditional rugs, using a mixture of handspun and commercial yarns. In addition to the wool that she has carded, spun, and dyed in preparation for weaving, Annie also purchases commercial wool. When we visited Annie's hogan, she had started a weaving with a purple commercial yarn.

Depending on where they lived, the grandmothers had different relationships to their land. Because the actual border of the Navajo Reservation lies east of Crownpoint, land on the reservation differs from off-reservation land in the checkerboard area. Within the reservation, residents have land use permits and grazing rights, whereas residents in the checkerboard area hold title to the land allotted to them. Regardless of the legal status of the land and the marital status of the grandmother, a grandmother often exercises control of the land she lives on. For example, Mary Cayaditto lived on land that her grandmother had given to her after she cared for her grandmother during "her golden years." Another grandmother, Theresa Bia, owned land that her mother had given to her when she died.

Against doctors' orders and the cautions of her children, seventy-eight-year-old Rose Freeland still rides a horse when working with her sheep. With a smile on her face, she told how she defies them. "The doctor told me not to ride horses. The doctors aren't here. They can't see me! I get on the horse and herd sheep. My kids tell me not to ride horses," continued. "They just all leave so I saddle up the horses to herd sheep. They're all getting lost" (4/21/96).

Although Rose's children's jobs prevent them from helping her on a daily basis, on weekends they help her with such demanding tasks as castrating male lambs and shearing the sheep. They tried electric shears but found that they got too hot during use. They experiment with new breeds of sheep and give the sheep vaccinations against diseases. In the past, Rose gathered an herb to apply after castrating lambs, but her children have substituted a medicinal spray.

Traditional Plants Used for Food and Medicine

The nostalgia associated with traditional foods, both cultivated and wild, aroused fond memories of family members and good times in the past. Corn dishes, in particular, brought back memories of the years when mothers were raising their children, with corn as the mainstay of the diet.

Jane Jim reminisced about some of the corn dishes they prepared.

> We did a lot of cooking with corn. We made a small loaf cooked in hot ashes, burritos, Navajo cake, cornmeal mush, blue corn tortillas. We used to grind a lot of corn into a real fine powdery consistency. Then we used to grind the wheat sprouts, too, and make a Navajo cake. My mother made kneel down bread. The blue mush, then you roll it into balls, mash them. You don't leave them round, because if you throw them in like that, it will cause it to hail.
>
> We did have a lot of gardens back then. We used to plant a lot of seeds and grow a lot of corn. We used to live a lot on the corn dishes from the corn that we grew. (9/18/96)

Examples of knowledge of native foods and medicinal plants will be limited to common plants whose uses have been detailed in published sources. In accordance with the Navajo respect for plants as a gift from the Holy People and the desire to protect ethnobotanical knowledge as culturally sensitive information, I will follow Charlotte Frisbie and Tall Woman's children's (Mitchell 2001) editorial decision about discussing wild plants used for food and medicine. They limit their discussion to those plants that are used for "everyday" food and medicine. Thus, this discussion will include only information about common plants that are confirmed in other published sources and will exclude references to ceremonial foods and medicines.

The most informative and reliable sources for identifying plant foods were Francis H. Elmore's *Ethnobotany of the Navajo* (1943) and Carolyn Niethammer's *American Indian Food and Lore* (1974). Additional sources that confirmed medicinal uses of plants were Vernon O. Mayes and Barbara Bayless Lacy's *Nanise', A Navajo Herbal: One Hundred Plants from the Navajo Reservation* (1989) and M. Walter Pesman's *Meet the Natives* (1967). The source for the Navajo names of plants was Martha Austin and Regina Lynch, *Saad Ahąąh Sinil: Dual Language, A Navajo-English Dictionary* (1983). Because of my own longstanding interest in plants native to the Southwest, I am familiar with many of the plants the grandmothers discussed.

Mary Cayaditto fondly remembered some of the wild foods that she and her family regularly gathered and ate. *Waa'*, Rocky Mountain bee plant, was harvested early in the season because the plants became bitter as they aged. According to Niethammer (1974), a Navajo stew prepared with the bee plant also included wild onions, *tł'ohchin*, and wild celery, *haza'aleehtsoh*, and tallow or bits of meat (Austin and Lynch 1983). Wild onions and wild celery were also used to flavor corn. Mary referred to wild onions as crows' onions because crows liked to eat them. *Tło des kiidi*, wild spinach, was dried and then boiled in the winter (Niethammer 1974). One favorite food was the banana yucca fruit, the fruit of the wide leaf or Datil yucca, *tsá'ászi'niteelí*, which looks like a short green banana (Austin and Lynch 1983; Niethammer 1974). Mary's grandmother boiled the fruit until it reached the consistency of jam, then rolled it into logs that were sliced off to flavor cornmeal dishes.

Reflecting on the availability of some wild plants, Mary said, "The earth is changing. Some plants are no longer here for us. It was two years ago that we collected the wild spinach" (4/30/97).

Corn dishes, the mainstay of the diet, inspired much eager discussion among the grandmothers. Many grandmothers mentioned corn meal mush, a Navajo version of the Spanish *atole*, or gruel. Other dishes prepared with yellow and blue cornmeal were corn bread, dumplings, noodles, and mutton stew. Kneel down bread was a favorite dish made from green corn, in which the kernels are ground up and roasted in corn husks. A staple in the diet was corn tortillas, eaten before the introduction of wheat flour. Mary Cayaditto noted that when corn dishes were eaten, "There wasn't diabetes back then" (12/11/96).

During two summer field trips to sites in a piñon-juniper vegetation life zone on the slopes of Mount Powell, Nancy Pinto, a sixty-six-year-old herbalist, identified plants used for dyeing wool; for ceremonies; for household remedies; for personal hygiene; for pregnancy, childbirth, and contraception; and for healing illness, wounds, and sores. A commonly used plant was sagebrush (*Artemisia*), in Navajo *ts'ah*. Nancy recommended smelling sage for a headache. A tea brewed with sage is used to treat a cold (Mayes and Lacy 1989).

Another use for *Waa'* is as a deodorant when the leaves are soaked in water (Mayes and Lacy 1989). The gumweed plant (*Grindelia*), translates from the Navajo name *wóláchíí' beeyigá* as "red ant killer." When mixed with water and poured on an anthill, it will get rid of ants (Mayes and Lacy 1989). Velvet weed (*Gaura parviflora*) translates from the Navajo as "plant that cools." The plant is used to relieve inflammation and burns (Elmore 1943). Interestingly, these three plants, Rocky Mountain bee plant, gumweed, and velvet weed are all labeled as "common weeds" in one plant identification book, *Meet the Natives* (Pesman 1967).

Weaving and Other Crafts

Grandmothers' expertise with crafts demands respect for their knowledge of complex techniques. The transmission of these skills to the younger generations is crucial to the survival of traditional weaving, potting, basketry, silversmithing, and hide tanning. For the most part, it is the younger grandmothers who still work at various crafts whereas the "old old" grandmothers employ their creative skills, as health permits, in weaving and related activities. Some grandmothers continue to card, spin, dye, and weave wool into rugs. They may choose to weave traditional designs and techniques used in twills and double-sided rugs. We observed Jane Jim weaving a pine cone design with wool that she had spun. With a lot of strength in her ninety-four-year-old arms, her hands were skilled and deft as she wove.

One of the younger grandmothers, sixty-two-year-old June Kalleco, herded sheep and goats as well as carding, spinning, and dyeing wool to weave into rugs. When my aunt and uncle, Colleen and Zeron Bell, visited her to ask her to weave a rug for them, June described how she uses vegetal and mineral dyes for some wool and uses natural grey and white wool. She illustrated the process with her wool samples that had been dyed various colors using minerals and native plants. Her description of the weaving process, from shearing to weaving, instilled a profound appreciation for the final product.

Even weavers who weave traditional patterns and use vegetal dyes sometimes also use commercial yarns in their rugs. For example, in a rug I purchased from her, Mary Cayaditto highlighted the handspun natural and vegetal dyed yarns with a commercial turquoise yarn. The grey and white wool came from her grey and white sheep, and the gold was dyed with lichen. The black wool comes from her black sheep, but is darkened with mica rock. The commercial turquoise yarn substituted for a natural turquoise that is not readily available. Mary explained: "There is a form of a dye that almost gives a turquoise color from a stone, but it's really hard to get so I got a commercial dye. It is a rock," she continued, "a mineral, that you boil and use as a dye. They don't have it here. My boys took me out to get it" (11/22/96). Mary calls the design in the rug, the Navajo hair design, or *tsiiyéél*, the traditional women's hair knot tied with white wool.

During the time the grandmothers were raising their children, many wove traditional designs with handspun wool prepared with natural dyes and sold the rugs to help support their families. The traditional weavers among the grandmothers who carry on these centuries-old techniques incorporate spiritual elements of the Navajo worldview in their weavings (Willink and Zolbrod 1996).

Now grandmothers endeavor to pass on their skills to the younger generations. For example, Nellie Becenti, a grandmother who still weaves traditional-style rugs, was planning to encourage her granddaughters to learn to weave. She stated, "I have a plan for the summer. I am going to put up looms for my granddaughters and teach them to weave. They just come and play" (4/10/97).

Although weaving is by far the most common craft, grandmothers excel in others. Annie Burnside learned silversmithing from her father, but she also tans hides, weaves, and does beadwork. Loretta Benally weaves and in the past made baskets and moccasins.

Transmission of Cultural Traditions

Throughout their life course, Navajo grandmothers in Crownpoint and surrounding chapters practiced Navajo cultural traditions. Firmly rooted in a rural lifestyle that revolves around livestock and crops, they grew up herding sheep and had little or no schooling. After celebrating their transition to womanhood with a Kinaaldá following their first and second menses, the grandmothers later entered arranged marriages and began giving birth to numerous children. Major life events centered on their own and others' reproductive and ceremonial activities. Grandmothers carry on these traditions as they plan for Kinaaldás and wedding ceremonies, give advice about burying babies' umbilical cords, arrange babies' First Laugh ceremonies, and organize shoe games.

Besides their role as consultants for ceremonies and traditional customs, some grandmothers actually conduct the ceremonies. For example, Annie Mitchell, who learned many songs and prayers as well as a good portion of the Kinaaldá from her maternal grandmother, now helps others by conducting ceremonies. She recently guided her half brothers and half sisters and their families through several ceremonies. Annie stated, "I helped that family with a Kinaaldá two months ago. That was their first ceremony. I oversaw that ceremony. More recently they had an Evil Way Ceremony," she said, "and I helped. They had a ceremony to restore their medicine bundle. Before that, they were aimlessly wandering, and they had forgotten about tradition. Now they are restored to harmony" (6/13/96).

Burial of a Navajo infant's umbilical cord has implications for his or her future life. Burying the cord at home creates an enduring tie to home and land, encouraging the individual to return throughout life. A second purpose for burying the umbilical cord is gender specific; the location of burial affects the future interests of boy and girl infants. To assure that a baby girl will grow up to be a good weaver, the cord may be buried close to a loom. To assure that a boy will work with livestock, the cord will be buried near a corral. Alternatively, some grandmothers tied a baby boy's umbilical cord to a horse's tail and a baby girl's to a loom.

Navajos forced to relocate from Hopi Partitioned Lands grieved about their displacement from the site where their umbilical cord was buried, a personally meaningful event that marked their lifelong connection to home. In Maureen Schwarz's (1997b) analysis of the disruption brought about by relocation, she highlights the Navajo attachment to place, partially formed by the burial of the umbilical cord, which "anchors an individual to a particular place" (1997b, 43). Forced removal from home constitutes a slow death for a Navajo deprived of contact with one's source of connection to the earth within the four sacred mountains. Evidence of relocatees' pain and grief find expression in physical, psychological, and social problems such as depression, alcoholism, and family instability.

Mary Biggs, a fifty-nine-year-old grandmother of seven grandchildren, buried her four daughters' umbilical cords. "The mother would bury it near the hogan so they would stay around. A girl, they would bury it where she would weave. A boy, she would bury it where he would work with livestock. We did that for a grandson," Mary continued, "and he is interested in rodeo [pointing out a picture of her grandson wearing a white cowboy hat]. You really have to take care of the umbilical cord. I was taught that. I did that." Mary went on: "I disposed of it in a respectful way. I think that's why they all come visit me and don't leave me" (12/12/95).

Like Mary, Dorothy Martin buried her nine children's umbilical cords in appropriate places for boys and girls.

> Yes, there is a place for boys and girls. For boys it will usually be in the corral where the sheep are. They might take pieces of saddle leather and bury it with the umbilical cord. One of my sons, we tied the umbilical cord onto a horsetail bone with a piece of horse tail. He likes to ride horses a lot. For girls, it is near the corral, where the loom stand is. A long time ago, they dug posts near the corral, and it was permanent. My grandmother told me about that. . . .
>
> My daughter is married to a man from Many Farms. His father is a medicine man. Her child's umbilical cord was buried in Many Farms. Now my grandchild is into cattle and rodeo. He is in rodeo for children. My grandson rides a wether sheep that has a cinch on it like a bull. He wins a lot of first place ribbons. That's how I know it works. My grandson is into rodeo and livestock.
>
> My grandmother and other ladies would discuss in front of me that you have to save and store the umbilical cord and dispose of it properly. It is very important. If it is hidden he [the baby] will start taking things that don't belong to him. . . . He will be looking around for something, and it is the umbilical cord. (5/9/96)

Other grandmothers likewise cautioned that if the umbilical cord is not buried, the child will "be digging around" as if searching for something.

Nancy Pinto buried her children's cords to influence a proclivity toward either sheepherding or raising crops. She stated, "I saved my babies' umbilical cords, and later I buried them in the sheep corral and where we grow crops. My mother instructed me to do that," said Nancy. "If it was buried in the sheep corral, they would tend towards that; if it was buried where they grow crops, they would tend towards that" (2/12/96).

Sarah McCray, the mother of eleven children, tied her sons' umbilical cords inside a horse's tail and tied her daughters' cords to a rug loom. Like other grandmothers, she "heard that when you place the umbilical cord in a drawer, the child will be really looking around and may steal things" (8/7/97).

A Navajo infant's first laugh signifies a developmental milestone, showing that the baby has become a member of a social network of relatives, clan members, and friends. According to custom, the person who made the baby laugh must butcher a sheep to feed the guests who will come to the celebration. At the celebration, the baby, sitting on the mother's lap, gives out small gifts of salt or candy, symbolizing the child's future capacity to be a generous, responsible member of the family, kinship network, and community. Annie James had a First Laugh celebration for all of her eight children and for her grandchildren. She stated, "For all of my kids, I had it, and for all of my maternal and paternal grandchildren. It was stressed to me that it is very important so the baby will be generous and kind." Annie continued: "Navajo salt is always included to put on the baby's hand to be given out. A long time ago, it was boiled mutton and fry bread given out. I stress that. Also, it includes candy and pop given out now" (3/14/96).

Dorothy Martin associates a baby's excessive crying with not having had a First Laugh ceremony. She explained:

> When a baby is crying a lot it is because the baby has not had the gathering when a sheep is butchered and has given things away. We teach our children that.
>
> When my oldest son was a newborn when he had his first laugh, we took a trip to Jemez, and we got a big bag of rock salt [demonstrating with her hands held about eight inches apart]. My son is forty years old now, and I still have that piece of salt and that's what I give out to maternal and paternal grandchildren.
>
> For every one of my children, even though I was alone when

> Billy was away working, I had a baby laugh ceremony. I butchered a young goat.
>
> My kids had their babies, and some were born in Arizona. The one in Flagstaff, when their baby laughed, they called me and asked me what to do. I told them to fix the food and about the salt, too. (5/9/96)

Annie Mitchell, a grandmother who had First Laugh ceremonies for her three children, indicated that their purpose was to insure important values and the availability of food in the child's future. Annie stated, "I did that for all of my kids. The reason why we did that was to have a giveaway. We want the child to be generous, to be kind, to always have food, to be a good hostess when people come to their home. Even that is different now," said Annie. "There is so much that some is wasted now. It wasn't like that then" (3/13/96).

Besides the traditional mutton or lamb stew, a corn dish has a specific meaning when served at First Laugh celebrations. Mary Cayaditto declared, "My grandmother always said to make a dish with corn because that will give the child a clear head" (12/11/96).

Grandmothers animatedly explained the shoe game, a game played by two teams, representing animals of the night and animals of the day. The shoe game, played during the winter, the time for winter stories, divides players into two opposing teams. Each team has four shoes in which to hide a yucca ball. Teams take turns holding up a blanket while hiding the ball in one of the shoes. One team then sings songs in Navajo while a member of the opposing team guesses which shoe holds the ball. Points for each team are tallied with 102 yucca counters. When one team earns 102 points, the game is over.

In mythic times when animals spoke like humans, the nocturnal animals first played the shoe game against the diurnal animals. If the nocturnal animals won, the night would be endless; if the diurnal animals won, it would always be daytime. Because neither team won after four days of playing, there is both night and day.

Mary Biggs, who learned how to play the shoe game from her grandfather, hosted shoe games in her Crownpoint home. "My grandfather taught me and his other grandkids and instructed us to gather 102 yucca sticks. The yucca root was used to make a ball," said Mary. "He was careful to tell us not to use too high of a boot because it would snow too high. Use a shoe like I'm wearing [a low top tennis shoe]. He instructed us to give the dirt back to mother earth," Mary continued, "and not to throw the yucca sticks away, but to give them back to the greasewood or sagebrush and say a prayer" (12/12/95).

Grandmothers advocated getting up in the morning at sunrise to run and pray as they did when they were children. Nancy Pinto wants her children and grandchildren to continue the tradition of daily prayers. She emphasized, "Most important is prayer, in the morning at dawn and in the evening." Praying carries on old traditions since "Our ancestors from way back practiced the same prayers" (2/12/96). Loretta Benally remembers running every morning during her childhood toward the rising sun. "We got up at the white dawn and ran to the east" (12/5/95). Maureen Bitsuie tells her grandsons, "Always get up in the morning with the sun and be prepared for what you are going to do" (12/5/95).

Most grandmothers deplored the teachings of the "revival Christians," who insisted that adherents completely abandon Navajo ceremonial practices and destroy or get rid of "paraphernalia" or medicine bundles, *jish*. Rose Freeland blamed the lack of prayer to the Holy People and selling of jish as the cause of the windy and dry weather. She stated, "I'm thinking about when people forgot to pray to the Holy People. They forgot to offer precious stones and pray to the Holy People." Rose continued: "That's why we're having all the winds. . . . The explosion of the revival [Christians]. They want us to get rid of our jish; that's the reason for it" (4/21/96). The drought during the past winter had left the land parched, with little grass for the sheep to eat.

A top priority for the grandmothers was teaching children and grandchildren about their clan membership and clan relationships. Navajos identify with four clans: their own matrilineal clan; their "born for" clan, which is their father's clan; their maternal grandfather's clan; and their paternal grandfather's clan. Knowledge of clan membership is important in choosing a marriage partner, who must belong to different and unrelated clans. Clan relationships also guide respectful interactions with others according to clan membership. The nature of the relationship as well as the kinship term used derives from knowledge of these relationships. The grandmothers know the clans and the genealogies of individuals and thus address younger people by appropriate kin terms. Thus, Maureen Bitsuie addressed Bonnie, the interpreter, as *shideezhí*, my younger sister, because they share the same born for clan. Maureen stressed respect for elders, who must be addressed properly. She tells her grandchildren, "When you see your grandfather or grandmother walk by, be the first to greet them. Know how to greet your relatives" (12/5/95).

Conclusion

A paramount concern of the grandmothers was teaching younger generations about the traditional Navajo worldview, as well as their customs, beliefs, and ceremonies. For good reason, grandmothers worried that the Navajo way was dying out. Although younger generations learn some aspects of Navajo culture and language at home and in the classroom, grandparents' vast storehouses of experience and knowledge are essential not only to family history but also to cultural identity. As unique, irreplaceable sources of information in a time of monumental change, grandparents are the vital link between past and future.

Veneration for elders is readily apparent in the community and within families. For example, in Crownpoint, Navajo elders' requests for public housing often take precedence over those of others. Families respect the senior generation as trustees of valued knowledge, deferring to their opinions on many topics such as stewardship of the land, traditional crafts, and ceremonial activities. However, obstacles to the transfer of elders' knowledge and experience exist, with the language barrier perhaps being the greatest. Monolingual Navajo grandparents are often unable to communicate with their English-speaking grandchildren. Nuclear family residences and busy work and school schedules prevent opportunities that formerly existed in the context of extended families working together in the land-based economy. Also, conflicting ideologies associated with Western biomedicine and numerous Christian denominations create resistance to traditional ways.

In fulfilling their roles as respected members of Navajo society, Navajo grandmothers fully illustrate the four types of generativity. By raising and nurturing their large families, they demonstrate biological and parental generativity. With their knowledge of raising sheep, traditional foods, and crafts, grandmothers provide technical generativity. By instigating and planning such traditional activities as the disposal of the umbilical cord, the First Laugh ceremony, and the shoe game, grandmothers assure cultural generativity. Keenly aware of the implications of losing cultural knowledge and practices, grandmothers, as well as grandfathers, persist in efforts to transmit their Navajo cultural heritage to younger generations.

10

Themes in Crownpoint Area Navajo Women's Lives

The life histories of three generations of Crownpoint area Navajo women attest to the sweeping historical changes that affected the Navajo people during the twentieth century. When the grandmothers were girls and young women, their lives were altered but not transformed by the initial efforts to educate Navajo children, recruit Navajos into the work force, reduce sheep herds, institute political organization and leadership, convert Navajos to various Christian denominations, provide biomedical health care, and reshape the Navajo family to reflect Western ideals. However, as adults, most of them continued to sustain themselves and their families with their hard work in the land-based economy.

Not until midcentury did virtually all Navajo girls feel the pervasive impact of these changes. After attending school during their childhood years, they reached young adulthood with options, though limited, in the cash economy, fast eclipsing those that had existed in the land-based economy. The impact on the family was inescapable as well, affecting relationships with men and childbearing patterns. No longer did women expect to enter arranged marriages and begin having large numbers of children while living and working in a rural, extended family residence. Young Navajo women became adults in a world vastly different from that of their grandmothers, one that required Western education and employment for the full attainment of adulthood.

Persistent value systems endure across generations despite the vast historical changes. Just as the World Values Survey (Inglehart and Baker 2000) demonstrated, cultural values persist amidst invasive economic change. Representative of core cultural values, religion expresses traditional and sacred meanings. For Navajo women, the puberty ceremony, the Kinaaldá, carries on traditional religion while continuing the legacy of values that honor Navajo women for their reproductive capacity. As part of the Blessing Way Ceremony, the Kinaaldá enacts the legacy of Changing Woman, esteemed in her role as a nurturing mother.

The respected position of Navajo women endured after the federal government's devastating livestock reduction programs and recruiting of Navajo men for wage work. A powerful voice for her tribe, Jennifer Denetdale insists on understanding Navajo women as authoritative and autonomous individuals in their families and communities, undiminished by the ravages of colonialism. Denetdale states, "Women retained a measure of status and authority because they adapted traditional gender roles to new economic realities" (2001, 6). Whether in the labor force or informal economy, women found new ways to support their families. Women's weaving and commercial production of sandpaintings for the market illustrate this process of economic adaptation. Navajo women's vital economic contribution to their families fulfills the expectations for their role as women in a matrilineal, egalitarian society. With few exceptions, the midlife women in the Crownpoint sample worked while raising their children, either in the formal or the informal economy.

Navajo women's pursuit of higher education relates to their strategies of economic adaptation. In order to expand their employment opportunities, women seek more education to qualify for a limited number of jobs. Many women are "nontraditional students," who take college classes while raising their families, and for some, while working in the labor force. The local options for higher education in Crownpoint are Diné College or the Crownpoint Institute of Technology, which offer programs of study leading to an associate degree. To earn a bachelor's degree or higher, women commuted to the UNM Gallup branch or the New Mexico State University campus in Grants or left home for summer school in off-reservation colleges and universities. One midlife mother took correspondence courses from NMSU for a semester to earn credits toward her bachelor's degree. For the Crownpoint women who furthered their education, the effort paid off with local employment in schools, the IHS, tribal agencies, and even in research conducted by UNM.

Enduring cultural traditions place a high value on Navajo women and children. Although many changes have affected pregnancy, childbirth, family size, and family structure, pronatal values and the esteem for motherhood remain. Grandmothers had large families, giving birth to children throughout their reproductive years. In their view, the number of children they had was out of their control, a gift from the Holy People, and children were equated with wealth. Crownpoint grandmothers rejected birth control as an option and were opposed to abortion and adoption of Navajo children by non-Navajos. Midlife mothers in some respects differed from the grandmothers in their reproductive patterns by being receptive to the use of birth control and choosing to limit the size of their families. They questioned the maxim that children were wealth and were divided in their position on Navajo children being raised by non-Navajos. Similar to the grandmothers, midlife mothers remained steadfast in their opposition to abortion and welcomed children as blessings regardless of the circumstances of the parents. Among the group of young mothers, many had their first child during their adolescent years, often relying on the support of natal family members while assuming the responsibilities of motherhood and establishing stable relationships with the father of the child. Young mothers welcomed parenthood yet accepted the idea of using birth control.

Reflecting the high value placed on children and motherhood, the vast majority of Crownpoint women among all three generations opposed abortion, a practice they did not consider appropriate for Navajos. Also, children were welcome in both the mother's and father's natal and extended families, regardless of the strength of the relationship between the parents. Of great importance, at birth a mother bestows matrilineal clan membership on her child, thus assuring him or her a secure place in Navajo society.

Crownpoint women's relationships with men are characterized by complementarity and equality. A grandmother's description of her marriage as a team of horses, each one pulling his or her own weight, evokes this egalitarian principle. The pervasive view that all aspects of nature have male and female components applies to conjugal relationships, in which both the husband and wife are essential and equally valued. If women find themselves in the position of being the female head of the household, they readily carry on, drawing on their resilience and position of strength. One professional woman in Crownpoint, commenting on how the Kinaaldá prepares women to go through life, gave an example: "You don't crumble down into your problem." Instead, "If your husband leaves you, you stand up to it" (5/24/88).

Just as the legacy of Changing Woman and Navajo women's position in a matrilineal society have contributed to their complementary gender roles, so, too, has Navajo women's agency. Navajo women have adapted to the cash economy by entering the labor force or participating in the informal economy. In addition, women pursue higher education to qualify themselves for wage work. Another factor that supports complementary gender roles is Western society's designation of jobs as appropriate for females, thus making many reservation positions in schools, hospitals, and agencies available to women.

Eastern area Navajo women verify the importance of motherhood as the basis of their cultural identity. Denetdale asserts, "In Navajo, the definition of mother expands into economic, public, and political realms (2001, 13). In a matrilineal society, the role of mother strengthens rather than detracts, aligning motherhood with the foundations of social organization rather than a less-valued domestic realm. The ultimate source of Navajo women's perceptions of the ideal woman and mother is Changing Woman, the esteemed female deity.

Diné College campuses reinforce Navajo cultural identity by requiring courses in Navajo history, language, and culture. Not available to many of the women in the Crownpoint area while they were younger students, the "Navajo-ization" of Navajo schools (House 2002) currently promotes cultural identity by teaching Navajo language and culture. This trend is most pronounced in contract schools, which are run by local Navajo communities with funds from the federal government.

The desire to transmit valued cultural traditions to the younger generations is commonly attributed to elders. Among the Navajo grandmothers, cultural transmission is a major preoccupation. Grandmothers lament their own lack of education as well as the inability of children and grandchildren to speak Navajo. Navajo grandmothers devote much of their time and energy to traditional activities, sometimes for the benefit of their families and at other times because of their knowledge of specific events and ceremonies. Active, younger grandmothers continue to herd sheep and weave. With the exception of grandmothers who had converted to one of the Christian denominations that consider Navajo ceremonies sinful, most grandmothers participated in ceremonies held throughout the eastern Navajo area; they made arrangements for granddaughters' Kinaaldás, babies' First Laugh ceremonies, and ceremonies for sick children or grandchildren. In addition, grandmothers organized shoe games in the winter and instructed parents in how to save a baby's umbilical cord.

Cultural strategies survive despite the onslaught of repeated attempts by the U.S. government and missionaries to assimilate Navajos and other American Indians. The intent of a boarding school education, wage labor programs, and relocation was to transform Navajos into more acceptable citizens. Because the majority of Navajos were not affected by these changes until midcentury, a large proportion of grandmothers remained anchored in the land-based economy, herding sheep, preparing and weaving wool, and raising crops. The midlife mothers, born in the 1940s and 1950s, were the first generation of Navajo women to experience the full impact of Western innovations even though they worked in traditional pursuits during their early childhood years and the summers. Their childhood years spent in school prepared them to enter labor force positions defined as appropriate to women. The majority of the young mothers, however, grew up in households dependent on wage labor and attended local day schools.

Because the grandmothers were needed to help out in the land-based economy when they were young children, their parents and grandparents relied on a cultural strategy to preserve their way of life, and thus to resist efforts to send children away to boarding schools. Of course, children and parents also resisted because of the painful separation from home and family. As demonstrated by the many grandmothers who did not attend school at all or attended for only a few years, these are the Navajo speakers who carry on the lifestyle of their parents and grandparents. Currently, Crownpoint grandmothers regret their lack of education, acknowledging that their inability to speak, read, and write English limits them in today's world and often prevents their communication with grandchildren who don't speak Navajo.

Exposure to the outside world during World War II contributed to Navajo parents' change in attitudes toward children's education. As they recognized the value of an education to their children's future in the labor force, parents' strategies shifted to demand more schools and to make it possible for their children to attend school. At the same time, the growth of local public, BIA, contract, and Christian schools, as well as large fleets of buses, made it possible for children to attend day school from Headstart through high school graduation.

The twentieth-century federal programs designed to transform Navajo men and women into mainstream workers met with an opposing Navajo cultural strategy. Efforts to recruit Navajos for off-reservation jobs met with success, but rather than permanently relocating, Navajos adopted a cultural strategy that allowed them to adjust their wage work practices so that they could maintain their homes and fulfill their kin-based obligations. Until midcentury Navajo women's role in this cultural strategy was primary; they maintained rural reservation home, herds, and agricultural fields while raising their families.

With the passage of the Navajo-Hopi Long Range Rehabilitation Act in 1950, Congress funded the infrastructure that would support the on-reservation jobs at which Navajo women could work. In the labor force, Navajo women are carrying on a cultural strategy inherited from their own mothers and grandmothers. In the land-based economy, both boys and girls were given lambs earmarked as theirs to be the start of a future herd when they reached adulthood. When they married, the bride and groom united herds of sheep, and both contributed to the care of the herd. In addition, women helped care for crops and wove rugs to sell at nearby trading posts. Grandmothers were expected to make an economic contribution and experienced no conflict between their productive and reproductive roles. Similarly, midlife mothers and young mothers expect to work in the labor force whenever possible; in fact, they prefer to work in order to provide for their children. The jobs that are available on the reservation reinforce this cultural strategy by favoring women over men with more openings designated as women's jobs in schools, hospitals, stores, and agencies.

Although the on-reservation job structure favors Navajo women, high unemployment rates preclude employment for many women. Midlife women who have jobs in Crownpoint agencies, schools, and hospitals often work throughout their childbearing years, choosing to stay in positions that are hard to come by. Others work in the informal economy, supplementing other insufficient sources of income. For young mothers, often the most realistic option is to seek employment in border towns or more distant cities and return home for visits with relatives on days off or on weekends.

For Navajos, the predominant cultural strategy vis-à-vis the numerous Christian denominations on the reservation is to combine participation in traditional ceremonies and Native American Church meetings with church attendance. Crownpoint women, sometimes during different periods of their lives, and sometimes concurrently, attend traditional ceremonies, Native American Church meetings, and local churches. Except for those affiliated with the exclusive doctrines of fundamentalist churches, Navajo women prefer to maintain their culturally meaningful traditions while taking advantage of church membership.

As parents anticipate the economic and educational needs of their children in the contemporary world, they are deciding to have fewer children. The Crownpoint grandmothers had large families and followed a pattern of natural fertility. The midlife mothers gave birth to families approximately half the size of those of the grandmothers, in general, ending their childbearing years well before menopause. They stopped childbearing when they reached a desired family size, thus following a pattern of controlled fertility. In contrast to the grandmothers and midlife mothers, the young mothers were more likely to begin childbearing in their adolescent years and to have not yet married their boyfriends. Because of the obstacles to obtaining education, housing, and employment, marriage was deferred while young couples assumed the responsibility of parenthood as a more certain marker of adulthood.

One major goal of this study of eastern area Navajo women has been to let women's voices guide the interpretation of issues, values, and concerns. Although filtered through an Anglo, middle-class lens, this study has featured independent and forceful Navajo women who nevertheless spoke for themselves. As they told about their lives, their families, and their attitudes toward children, family, and motherhood, they revealed culturally based values to which they adhered in spite of the monumental social, economic, and political changes of the twentieth century. Fortified by a legacy of power originating in the Navajo worldview and social organization, women create cultural strategies to benefit themselves and their families and to pass on to future generations.

In their responses to contemporary challenges in their lives, Navajo women often react in ways similar to other American Indian women. In addition to the needs to pursue an education, to earn a living by working in the labor force or informal economy, and to raise children and maintain family relationships are the pressures to preserve and nurture a distinct cultural identity, cultural practices, and extended family and clan ties. In their shared history of domination, Indian women have also experienced the process of assimilation. The transformation in American Indian women's lives during the twentieth century testifies to the unrelenting power of the political, social, and economic interventions they have endured.

Countering the cumulative historical changes, both across the life spans of the three generations and within the life course of each woman, culturally informed values and attitudes shape identities and guide decisions and behaviors. Navajo women face multiple challenges as they proudly maintain their cultural identity at the same time that they confront the demands of the Bilagáana world. At the core of cultural strategies and identities are concepts that guide women's roles as mothers, daughters, and wives, which in turn influence their education and work. The Navajo Way is not limited to the reminiscences of the grandparents, but is a viable system of meanings, values, and traditions that shapes women's lives.

References

Aberle, David F.

1961 Navaho. In *Matrilineal Kinship*, David Schneider and Kathleen Gough, eds., 96–201. Berkeley: University of California Press.

1982 *The Peyote Religion among the Navaho*. 2d ed. Chicago: University of Chicago Press.

1983 Navajo Economic Development. In *Handbook of North American Indians*, vol. 10: *Southwest*, Alfonso Ortiz, ed., 641–58. Washington, D.C.: Smithsonian Institution.

1989 Education, Work, Gender, and Residence: Black Mesa Navajos in the 1960s. *Journal of Anthropological Research* 45 (4): 405–30.

Ackerman, Lillian A.

2003 *A Necessary Balance: Gender and Power among Indians of the Columbia Plateau*. Norman: University of Oklahoma Press.

Adair, John

1947 The Navajo and Pueblo Veteran: A Force for Culture Change. *American Indian* 4 (1): 5–11.

Adams, William

1993 Growing Up in Colonial Navajoland. In *Papers from the Third, Fourth, and Sixth Navajo Studies Conferences*, June-el Piper, ed., 305–10. Window Rock, Ariz.: Navajo Nation Historic Preservation Department.

Albers, Patricia C.

1989 From Illusion to Illumination: Anthropological Studies of American Indian Women. In *Gender and Anthropology: Critical Reviews for Research and Teaching*, Sandra Morgen, ed., 132–70. Washington, D.C.: American Anthropological Association.

Alvord, Lori Arviso, and Elizabeth Cohen Van Pelt

1999 *The Scalpel and the Silver Bear: The First Navajo Woman Surgeon Combines Western Medicine and Traditional Healing*. New York: Bantam Books.

Amott, Teresa, and Julie Matthaei

1996 *Race, Gender, and Work: A Multi-cultural Economic History of Women in the United States*. Rev. ed. Boston: South End Press.

Austin, Martha, and Regina Lynch

1983 *Saad Ahąąh Sinil: Dual Language, a Navajo-English Dictionary*. Rough Rock, Ariz.: Rough Rock Demonstration School.

Bahr, Howard M.

1994 Multiplying Glimpses, Gleaning Genres: A Multidisciplinary Approach to the Study of Change among Navajo Peoples. *Human Organization* 53 (1): 55–73.

Bailey, Flora L.

1948 Suggested Techniques for Inducing Navaho Women to Accept Hospitalization during Childbirth and for Implementing Health Education. *American Journal of Public Health* 38 (10): 1418–23.

1950 *Some Sex Beliefs and Practices in a Navaho Community*. Papers of the Peabody Museum of American Archaeology and Ethnology, vol. 40. Cambridge, Mass.: Peabody Museum of American Archaeology and Ethnology, Harvard University.

Bailey, Garrick, and Roberta Glenn Bailey

1986 *A History of the Navajos: The Reservation Years*. Santa Fe: School of American Research Press.

Begay, Rita Weyrauch

1985 Navajo Childbirth. Ph.D. dissertation, Public Health. University of California, Berkeley.

Bell, Duran

1997 Defining Marriage and Legitimacy. *Current Anthropology* 38 (2): 237–44, 250–53.

Benally, Karen Ritts

1999 Thinking Good: The Teachings of Navajo Grandmothers. In *American Indian Grandmothers: Traditions and Transitions*, Marjorie M. Schweitzer, ed., 25–52. Albuquerque: University of New Mexico Press.

Berman, Tressa

2003 *Circle of Goods: Women, Work, and Welfare in a Reservation Community*. Albany: State University of New York Press.

Billson, Janet Mancini

1995 *Keepers of the Culture: The Power of Tradition in Women's Lives*. New York: Lexington Books.

Bingham, Sam, and Janet Bingham

1987 *Navajo Chapters*. Rev. ed. Tsaile, Ariz.: Navajo Community College Press.

Bledsoe, Caroline

1990 School Fees and the Marriage Process for Mende Girls in Sierra Leone. In *Beyond the Second Sex: New Directions in the Anthropology of Gender*, Peggy Reeves Sanday and Ruth Gallagher Goodenough, eds., 281–309. Philadelphia: University of Pennsylvania Press.

Bowman, Shirley

2002 Personal communication with author. April 2.

Boyce, W. Thomas, Catherine Schaefer, H. Robert Harrison, William H. J. Haffner, Marguerite Lewis, and Anne L. Wright

1986 Social and Cultural Factors in Pregnancy Complications among Navajo Women. *American Journal of Epidemiology* 124 (3): 242–53.

Brim, Orville G., Jr., and Carol D. Ryff

1980 On the Properties of Life Events. In *Life-Span Development and Behavior,* Paul B. Baltes and Orville G. Brim Jr., eds., 3:367–88. New York: Academic Press.

Brugge, David

1980 *A History of the Chaco Navajos.* Reports of the Chaco Center, No. 4. Division of Chaco Research, National Park Service, U.S. Department of the Interior. Washington, D.C.: U.S. Government Printing Office.

Burton, Michael L.

1997 Comments on Defining Marriage and Legitimacy. *Current Anthropology* 38 (2): 244–46.

Caffrey, Margaret M.

2000 Complementary Power: Men and Women of the Lenni Lenape. *American Indian Quarterly* 24 (1): 44–63.

Caldwell, John C., and Pat Caldwell

1997 What Do We Now Know about Fertility Transition? In *The Continuing Demographic Transition,* G. W. Jones, R. M. Douglas, J. C. Caldwell, and R. M. D'Souza, eds., 15–25. Oxford: Clarendon Press.

Carrese, Joseph A., and Lorna A. Rhodes

1995 Western Bioethics on the Navajo Reservation: Benefit or Harm? *Journal of the American Medical Association* 274 (10): 826–29.

Chadwick, Bruce A., Stan L. Albrecht, and Howard M. Bahr

1986 Evaluation of an Indian Student Placement Program. *Social Casework: Journal of Contemporary Social Work* 67 (9): 515–24.

Chisholm, James

1986 Social and Economic Change among the Navajo: Residence Patterns and the Pickup Truck. *Journal of Anthropological Research* 42 (3): 289–98.

Choudhary, Trib

1997 Unemployment Rate on the Navajo Nation, 12/31/96. Table No. 5. Window Rock, Ariz.: Support Services Department, Division of Economic Development, Navajo Nation. Mimeographed.

1998 Unemployment Rate on the Navajo Nation, 12/31/97. Table No. 5. Window Rock, Ariz.: Support Services Department, Division of Economic Development, Navajo Nation. Mimeographed.

2001 *2000–2001 Comprehensive Economic Development Strategy.* Window Rock, Ariz.: Support Services Department, Division of Economic Development.

2003 *Data from Census 2000.* Window Rock, Ariz.: Navajo Nation, Support Services Department, Division of Economic Development.

Coley, Rebekah Levine, and P. Lindsay Chase-Lansdale

1998 Adolescent Pregnancy and Parenthood: Recent Evidence and Future Directions. *American Psychologist* 53 (2): 152–66.

Collins, Patricia Hill

1994 Shifting the Center: Race, Class, and Feminist Theorizing about Motherhood. In *Representations of Motherhood,* Donna Bassin, Margaret Honey, and Meryle Mahrer Kaplan, eds., 57–74. New Haven, Conn.: Yale University Press.

Comaroff, John L.

1980 Bridewealth and the Control of Ambiguity in a Tswana Chiefdom. In *The Meaning of Marriage Payments,* John L. Comaroff, ed., 161–95. London: Academic Press.

Csordas, Thomas J.

1999 Ritual Healing and the Politics of Identity in Contemporary Navajo Society. *American Ethnologist* 26 (1): 3–23.

Dalla, Rochelle L., and Wendy C. Gamble

1997 Exploring Factors Related to Parenting Competence among Navajo Teenage Mothers: Dual Techniques of Inquiry. *Family Relations* 46 (2): 113–21.

1998 Social Networks and Systems of Support among American Indian Navajo Adolescent Mothers. In *Resiliency in Native American and Immigrant Families,* Hamilton I. McCubbin, Elizabeth A. Thompson, Anne Thompson, and Julie E. Fromer, eds., 183–98. Resiliency in Families Series. Thousand Oaks, Calif.: Sage Publications.

2000 Mother, Daughter, Teenager—Who Am I? Perceptions of Adolescent Maternity in a Navajo Reservation Community. *Journal of Family Issues* 21 (2): 225–45.

2001 Teenage Mothering on the Navajo Reservation: An Examination of Intergenerational Perceptions and Beliefs. *American Indian Culture and Research Journal* 25 (1): 1–19.

Davis, Jim

2001 Personal communication with author. Division of Government Research, University of New Mexico, Albuquerque, New Mexico. November 16.

Dehoyos, Genevieve

1992 Indian Student Placement Services. In *Encyclopedia of Mormonism: The History, Scripture, Doctrine, and Procedure of the Church of Jesus Christ of Latter-day Saints,* Daniel H. Ludlow, ed., 2:679–80. New York: Macmillan.

Dempsey, Patricia, and Theresa Gesse

1995 Beliefs, Values, and Practices of Navajo Childbearing Women. *Western Journal of Nursing Research* 17 (6): 591–604.

Denetdale, Jennifer

2001 Representing Changing Woman: A Review Essay on Navajo Women. *American Indian Culture and Research Journal* 25 (3): 1–26.

Deyhle, Donna

1998 From Break Dancing to Heavy Metal: Navajo Youth, Resistance, and Identity. *Youth and Society* 30 (1): 3–31.

Deyhle, Donna, and Frank Margonis

1995 Navajo Mothers and Daughters: Schools, Jobs, and the Family. *Anthropology and Education Quarterly: Journal of the Council on Anthropology and Education* 26 (2): 135–67.

Dirks, Nicholas B., Geoff Eley, and Sherry B. Ortner, eds.

1994 Introduction. In *Culture/Power/History: A Reader in Contemporary Social Theory*, Nicholas B. Dirks, Geoff Eley, Sherry B. Ortner, eds., 3–45. Princeton, N.J.: Princeton University Press.

Donovan, Bill

1989 Chairman Admits Receiving Gifts from Contractors. MacDonald: "So Yes. I Have Accepted Gifts. But That Is Not a Crime." *Navajo Times*, February 9, 1989.

Edin, Kathryn, and Laura Lein

1997 *Making Ends Meet: How Single Mothers Survive Welfare and Low-Wage Work*. New York: Russell Sage Foundation.

Ellis, Bernard H., Jr.

2003 Mobilizing Communities to Reduce Substance Abuse in Indian Country. *Journal of Psychoactive Drugs* 35 (1): 89–96.

Ellis, Bernard H., Jr., Barbara B. Heilman, and Jeanne K. Miner

1999 The Latest View: An Updated Report on Substance Abuse-Related Indicators, McKinley County, New Mexico, April, 1999. Prepared for Northwest New Mexico Fighting Back.

Elmore, Francis H.

1943 *Ethnobotany of the Navajo*. University of New Mexico Bulletin with the School of American Research. Monograph Series, vol. 1, no. 7. Albuquerque: University of New Mexico Press.

Emerson, Gloria J.

1983 Navajo Education. In *Handbook of North American Indians*, vol. 10: *Southwest*, Alfonso Ortiz, ed., 659–71. Washington, D.C.: Smithsonian Institution.

Erickson, Erik H.

1963 *Childhood and Society*. 2d ed. New York: W.W. Norton.

Etsitty, Duane

1994 *NN Fax 93: A Statistical Abstract of the Navajo Nation*. Window Rock, Ariz.: Support Services Department, Division of Economic Development.

Evans, Palmer C., and Juanita Fike

1975 The Navajo Way: As Related to Pregnancy, Childbearing, and Childrearing. *Arizona Medicine* 32 (2): 97–99.

Fast, Phyllis Ann

2002 *Northern Athabascan Survival: Women, Community, and the Future*. Lincoln: University of Nebraska Press.

Frisbie, Charlotte Johnson

1982 Traditional Navajo Women: Ethnographic and Life History Portrayals. *American Indian Quarterly* 6 (1 and 2): 11–33.

1993 [1967] *Kinaaldá: A Study of the Navaho Girl's Puberty Ceremony*. Salt Lake City: University of Utah Press.

Fuermann, Lee

1990 Personal communication with author. February 12.

Gallup (N.M.) Independent

1989 25 Chapters Ask for Resignation of MacDonald. February 14.

Geronimus, Arline T.

1997 Teenage Childbearing and Personal Responsibility: An Alternative View. *Political Science Quarterly* 112 (3): 405–30.

Geronimus, Arline T., and Sanders Korenman

1992 The Socioeconomic Consequences of Teen Childbearing Reconsidered. *Quarterly Journal of Economics* 107 (4): 1187–214.

Ginsburg, Faye, and Rayna Rapp

1991 The Politics of Reproduction. *Annual Review of Anthropology*, Bernard J. Siegel, Alan R. Beals, and Stephen A. Tyler, eds., 20:311–43. Palo Alto, Calif.: Annual Reviews.

Gough, E. Kathleen

1959 The Nayars and the Definition of Marriage. *Journal of the Royal Anthropological Institute of Great Britain and Ireland* 89 (1): 23–34.

Grantham-Campbell, Mary

1998 It's Okay to Be Native: Alaska Native Cultural Strategies in Urban and School Settings. *American Indian Culture and Research Journal* 22 (4): 385–405.

Hardeen, George

1988 Families Find Ailing Alyssa. *Gallup (N.M.) Independent*, April 18.

Hareven, Tamara K.

2000 *Families, History, and Social Change: Life-Course and Cross-Cultural Perspectives*. Boulder, Colo.: Westview Press.

Hartle-Schutte, Maureen

1988 Contemporary Usage of the Blessingway Ceremony for Navajo Births. Master's thesis, University of Arizona, Tucson.

Hedlund, Ann Lane

1999 Give-and-Take: Navajo Grandmothers and the Role of Craftswomen. In *American Indian Grandmothers: Traditions and Transitions*, Marjorie M. Schweitzer, ed., 53–78. Albuquerque: University of New Mexico Press.

Henry, Louis

1982 [1961] Some Data on Natural Fertility. *Social Biology* 29 (1–2): 145–59.

Hofferth, Sandra L., Lori Reid, and Frank L. Mott

2001 The Effects of Early Childbearing on Schooling over Time. *Family Planning Perspectives* 33 (6): 259–67.

Hoffman, Saul D.

1998 Teenage Childbearing Is Not So Bad After All. Or Is It? A Review of the New Literature. *Family Planning Perspectives* 30 (5): 236–43.

House, Deborah

2002 *Language Shift among the Navajos: Identity Politics and Cultural Continuity*. Tucson: University of Arizona Press.

Howard, Cheryl

1993 *Navajo Tribal Demography, 1983–1986 in Comparative and Historical Perspective*. New York: Garland.

Hua, Cai

2001 *A Society without Fathers or Husbands: The Na of China*. New York: Zone Books.

Inglehart, Ronald, and Wayne E. Baker

2000 Modernization, Cultural Change, and the Persistence of Traditional Values. *American Sociological Review* 65 (1): 19–51.

Iverson, Peter

2002 *Diné: A History of the Navajos*. Albuquerque: University of New Mexico Press.

Johnston, Denis Foster

1966 *An Analysis of Sources of Information on the Population of the Navajo*. Bulletin 197, Bureau of American Ethnology, Smithsonian Institution. Washington, D.C.: U.S. Government Printing Office.

Juan, Wanda

2002 Personal communication with author. April 23.

Kelley, Clara B., and Peter M. Whitely

1989 *Navajoland: Family and Settlement and Land Use*. Tsaile, Ariz.: Navajo Community College Press.

Klein, Laura F., and Lillian A. Ackerman

1995 Introduction. In *Women and Power in Native North America*, Laura F. Klein and Lillian A. Ackerman, eds., 3–16. Norman: University of Oklahoma Press.

Kluckhohn, Clyde

1944 *Navaho Witchcraft*. Boston: Beacon Press.

1966 The Ramah Navaho. *Bureau of American Ethnology Bulletin*, no. 19, 327–470. Washington, D.C: U.S. Government Printing Office.

Kluckhohn, Clyde, and Dorothea Leighton

1974 [1946] *The Navaho*. Cambridge, Mass.: Harvard University Press.

Knack, Martha C., and Alice Littlefield

1996 Native American Labor: Retrieving History, Rethinking Theory. In *Native Americans and Wage Labor: Ethnohistorical Perspectives*, Alice Littlefield and Martha C. Knack, eds., 3–44. Norman: University of Oklahoma Press.

Konner, Melvin, and Marjorie Shostak

1986 Adolescent Pregnancy and Childbearing: An Anthropological Perspective. In *School-Age Pregnancy and Parenthood: Biosocial Dimensions*, Jane B. Lancaster and Beatrix A. Hamburg, eds., 325–45. New York: Aldine De Gruyter.

Kotre, John

1984 *Outliving the Self: Generativity and the Interpretation of Lives.* Baltimore: The Johns Hopkins University Press.

Kunitz, Stephen J.

1989 *Disease Change and the Role of Medicine: The Navajo Experience.* Berkeley: University of California Press.

Kunitz, Stephen J., and Jerrold E. Levy

2000 *Drinking, Conduct Disorder, and Social Change: Navajo Experiences.* New York: Oxford University Press.

Kunitz, Stephen J., and Michael C. Tsianco

1981 Kinship Dependence and Contraceptive Use among Navajo Women. *Human Biology* 53 (3): 439–52.

Lamphere, Louise

1974 Strategies, Cooperation, and Conflict among Women in Domestic Groups. In *Women, Culture, and Society,* Michelle Zimbalist Rosaldo and Louise Lamphere, eds., 97–112. Stanford, Calif.: Stanford University Press.

1977 *To Run after Them: Cultural and Social Bases of Cooperation in a Navajo Community.* Tucson: University of Arizona Press.

1989 Historical and Regional Variability in Navajo Women's Roles. *Journal of Anthropological Research* 45 (4): 432–56.

Landon, Susan

1989 Tribal Court Kills Order Reinstating MacDonald: Navajo Chairman Out of Office Again. *Albuquerque Tribune,* February 25.

Laslett, Peter

1996 What Is Old Age? Variation over Time and between Cultures. In *Health and Mortality among Elderly Populations,* Graziella Caselli and Alan D. Lopez, eds., 21–38. Oxford: Clarendon Press.

Leighton, Dorothea, and Clyde Kluckhohn

1947 *Children of the People.* Cambridge, Mass.: Harvard University Press.

Lewis, Judith A., and Judith Bernstein

1996 *Women's Health: A Relational Perspective across the Life Cycle.* Sudbury, Mass.: Jones and Bartlett.

Litson, Louise

2001 Personal communication with author. Diné College Registrar's Office, Tsaile, Ariz.

Lock, Margaret

1993 *Encounters with Aging: Mythologies of Menopause in Japan and North America.* Berkeley: University of California Press.

Locke, Patrice

1989 Gallup's Desire for Sobriety Moved Marchers, United City. *Albuquerque Journal,* March 5.

Lockett, Clay

1939 Midwives and Childbirth among the Navajo. *Plateau* 12 (1): 15–17.

Maltz, Daniel, and JoAllyn Archambault

1995 Gender and Power in Native North America: Concluding Remarks. In *Women and Power in Native North America*, Laura F. Klein and Lillian A. Ackerman, eds., 230–49. Norman: University of Oklahoma Press.

Manuelito, Brenda

1999 Personal communication with author. October 29.

Markstrom, Carol A., and Alejandro Iborra

2003 Adolescent Identity Formation and Rites of Passage: The Navajo Kinaaldá Ceremony for Girls. *Journal of Research on Adolescence* 13 (4): 399–425.

Massey, Barry

2001 State Alcohol-Linked Road-Death Rate Falls: N.M. Still Fourth in Nation in 2000. *Albuquerque Journal*, October 10.

May, Philip A., and Matthew B. Smith

1988 Some Navajo Indian Opinions about Alcohol Abuse and Prohibition: A Survey and Recommendations for Policy. *Journal of Studies on Alcohol* 49 (4): 324–34.

Mayes, Vernon O., and Barbara Bayless Lacy

1989 *Nanise': A Navajo Herbal: One Hundred Plants from the Navajo Reservation*. Tsaile, Ariz.: Navajo Community College Press.

McAdams, Dan P., and Ed de St. Aubin

1992 A Theory of Generativity and Its Assessment through Self-Report, Behavioral Acts, and Narrative Themes in Autobiography. *Journal of Personality and Social Psychology* 62 (6): 1003–15.

McCloskey, Joanne

1993 Changing Fertility Patterns of Three Generations of Navajo Women. Ph.D. dissertation, Department of Anthropology, University of New Mexico.

1998 Three Generations of Navajo Women: Negotiating Life Course Strategies in the Eastern Navajo Agency. *American Indian Culture and Research Journal* 22 (2): 103–29.

McDonald, Terrence J., ed.

1996 *The Historic Turn in the Human Sciences*. Ann Arbor: University of Michigan Press.

McReynolds, Mary Jane

1997 "Hitting the Mountain": Educational Success among Native American Women in Albuquerque, New Mexico. Ph.D. dissertation, Department of Anthropology, University of New Mexico.

Medicine, Beatrice

2001 *Learning to Be an Anthropologist and Remaining "Native": Selected Writings*. Edited with Sue Ellen Jacobs. Urbana: University of Illinois Press.

Meriam, Lewis

1928 *The Problem of Indian Administration: A Summary of the Meriam Report*. Bulletin No. 16. New York: Eastern Association on Indian Affairs.

Milligan, Carol B.

1984 Nursing Care and Beliefs of Expectant Navajo Women (Part I). *American Indian Quarterly* 7 (2): 83–101.

Mingo, Clo, Carla J. Herman, and Marla Jasperse

2000 Women's Stories: Ethnic Variations in Women's Attitudes and Experiences of Menopause, Hysterectomy, and Hormone Replacement Therapy. *Journal of Women's Health and Gender-Based Medicine* 9, Supplement 2:S27–S38.

Mitchell, Rose

2001 *Tall Woman: The Life Story of Rose Mitchell, A Navajo Woman, c. 1874–1977*. Charlotte Frisbie, ed. Albuquerque: University of New Mexico Press.

Moore, Henrietta L.

1988 *Feminism and Anthropology*. Cambridge, Eng.: Polity Press.

Navajo Area Indian Health Service (NAIHS).

1988 Outpatient Visits by Method of Contraception, Fiscal Year 1988 in Navajo Area Service Sites. Window Rock, Ariz.: Navajo Area Indian Health Service. Mimeographed.

2002 *Health Profile*. Window Rock, Ariz.: Office of Program Planning and Evaluation.

Navajo Times

1988 Tribal Council Wants to Hear about "Baby K" Case. April 28.

1989 Crownpoint Opens Shopping Center. February 9.

New Mexico Vital Records and Health Statistics

1995 *1993 New Mexico Selected Health Statistics: Annual Report*. Santa Fe: New Mexico Department of Health, Public Health Division.

1997 *1995 New Mexico Selected Health Statistics: Annual Report*. Santa Fe: New Mexico Department of Health, Public Health Division.

2002 *New Mexico Selected Health Statistics: Annual Report for 2000*. Santa Fe: New Mexico Department of Health, Public Health Division, State Center for Health Statistics.

Niethammer, Carolyn

1974 *American Indian Food and Lore*. New York: Collier Books.

2001 *I'll Go and Do More: Annie Dodge Wauneka, Navajo Leader and Activist*. Lincoln: University of Nebraska Press.

O'Neill, Colleen

1999 The "Making" of the Navajo Worker: Navajo Households, the Bureau of Indian Affairs, and Off-Reservation Wage Work, 1948–1960. *New Mexico Historical Review* 74 (4): 375–405.

O'Nell, Theresa DeLeane

1996 *Disciplined Hearts: History, Identity, and Depression in an American Indian Community*. Berkeley: University of California Press.

Ortner, Sherry B.

1999 Introduction. In *The Fate of "Culture:" Geertz and Beyond*, Sherry B. Ortner, ed., 1–13. Berkeley: University of California Press.

Patton, Michael Quinn

2002 *Qualitative Research and Evaluation Methods*. 3d ed. Thousand Oaks: Sage Publications.

Pavlik, Steve

1997 Navajo Christianity: Historical Origins and Modern Trends. *Wicazo Sa Review* 12 (2): 43–58.

Pesman, M. Walter

1967 *Meet the Natives: An Easy Way to Recognize Rocky Mountain Wildflowers, Trees and Shrubs*. 7th ed., rev. Denver: Denver Botanic Gardens.

Platero, Paul R., Elizabeth A. Brandt, Gary Witherspoon, and Paul Wong

1986 *Navajo Students at Risk: Navajo Area Student Dropout Study*. Window Rock, Ariz.: Navajo Division of Education, Navajo Tribe.

Powers, Marla N.

1986 *Oglala Women: Myth, Ritual, and Reality*. Chicago: University of Chicago Press.

Rank, Mark Robert

1994 *Living on the Edge: The Realities of Welfare in America*. New York: Columbia University Press.

Reichard, Gladys A.

1928 *Social Life of the Navajo Indians with Some Attention to Minor Ceremonies*. New York: AMS Press.

Richards, Audrey

1956 *Chisungu: A Girls' Initiation Ceremony among the Bemba of Zambia*. New York: Tavistock.

Roessel, Robert A., Jr.

1979 *Navajo Education, 1948–1978: Its Progress and Problems. Navajo History*, vol. 3, pt. A. Rough Rock, Ariz.: Navajo Curriculum Center, Rough Rock Demonstration School.

Roessel, Ruth

1981 *Women in Navajo Society*. Rough Rock, Ariz.: Navajo Resource Center, Rough Rock Demonstration School.

1991 Keynote address. Eastern Navajo Agency Women's Conference. Crownpoint, N.M.

Rushforth, Scott, and James S. Chisholm

1991 *Cultural Persistence: Continuity in Meaning and Moral Responsibility among the Bearlake Athapaskans*. Tucson: University of Arizona Press.

Russell, Scott C., and Mark B. McDonald

1982 The Economic Contributions of Women in a Rural Western Navajo Community. *American Indian Quarterly* 6 (3–4): 262–82.

Sanday, Peggy Reeves

1981 *Female Power and Male Dominance: On the Origins of Sexual Inequality*. New York: Cambridge University Press.

Schulz, Amy J.

1998 Navajo Women and the Politics of Identity. *Social Problems* 45 (3): 336–55.

Schwarz, Maureen Trudelle

1997a *Molded in the Image of Changing Woman: Navajo Views on the Human Body and Personhood*. Tucson: University of Arizona Press.

1997b Unraveling the Anchoring Cord: Navajo Relocation, 1974–1996. *American Anthropologist* 99 (1): 43–55.

2001 *Navajo Lifeways: Contemporary Issues, Ancient Knowledge*. Norman: University of Oklahoma Press.

2003 *Blood and Voice: Navajo Women Ceremonial Practitioners*. Tucson: University of Arizona Press.

Schweitzer, Marjorie M., ed.

1999 *American Indian Grandmothers: Traditions and Transitions*. Albuquerque: University of New Mexico Press.

Seccombe, Karen, Delores James, and Kimberly Battle Walters

1998 "They Think You Ain't Much of Nothing": The Social Construction of the Welfare Mother. *Journal of Marriage and the Family* 60 (4): 849–65.

Seltzer, Judith A.

2000 Families Formed Outside of Marriage. *Journal of Marriage and the Family* 62 (4): 1247–68.

Shepardson, Mary

1982 The Status of Navajo Women. *American Indian Quarterly* 6 (1–2): 149–69.

1995 The Gender Status of Navajo Women. In *Women and Power in Native North America*, Laura F. Klein and Lillian A. Ackerman, eds., 159–76. Norman: University of Oklahoma Press.

Shepardson, Mary, and Blodwen Hammond

1964 Change and Persistence in an Isolated Navajo Community. *American Anthropologist* 66 (5): 1029–50.

Smith-Battle, Lee

2000 The Vulnerabilities of Teenage Mothers: Challenging Prevailing Assumptions. *Advances in Nursing Science* 23 (1): 29–40.

Spicer, Edward H.

1980 *The Yaquis: A Cultural History*. Tucson: University of Arizona Press.

Szasz, Margaret Connell

1999 *Education and the American Indian: The Road to Self-Determination Since 1928*. 3d ed. Albuquerque: University of New Mexico Press.

Technical Support Department, Navajo Nation

1988 Navajo Nation Fax 88. Window Rock, Ariz.: Technical Support Department, Commission for Accelerating Navajo Development, Navajo Nation.

Thompson, Hildegard

1975 *The Navajos' Long Walk for Education: A History of Navajo Education*. Tsaile, Ariz.: Navajo Community College Press.

Topper, Martin D.

1979 "Mormon Placement": The Effects of Missionary Foster Families on Navajo Adolescents. *Ethos: Journal of the Society for Psychological Anthropology* 7 (2): 142–60.

Tsosie, Rebecca

1988 Changing Women: The Cross-Currents of American Indian Feminine Identity. *American Indian Culture and Research Journal* 12 (1): 1–37.

Uchendu, Victor Chikezie

1976 Seasonal Agricultural Labor among the Navaho Indians: A Study in Socio-Economic Transition. Ph.D. dissertation, Department of Anthropology, Northwestern University.

Upchurch, Dawn M., and James McCarthy

1990 The Timing of a First Birth and High School Completion. *American Sociological Review* 55 (2): 224–34.

Vestal, Paul A.

1952 *Ethnobotany of the Ramah Navaho*. Papers of the Peabody Museum of American Archaeology and Ethnology, vol. 11, no. 4. Cambridge, Mass.: Harvard University Press.

Waller, Margaret A., and Shirley Patterson

2002 Natural Helping and Resilience in a Diné (Navajo) Community. *Families in Society* 83 (1): 73–84.

Watson-Franke, Maria-Barbara

1993 The Lycian Heritage and the Making of Men: Matrilineal Models for Parenting. *Women's Studies International Forum* 16 (6): 569–79.

Waxman, Alan G.

1990 Navajo Childbirth in Transition. *Medical Anthropology* 12 (2): 187–206.

Weaver, Hilary N.

2001 Indigenous Identity: What Is It, and Who Really Has It? *American Indian Quarterly* 25 (2): 241–55.

Weiss, Gillian, ed.

2000 *Trying to Get It Back: Indigenous Women, Education and Culture*. Waterloo, Ont.: Wilfrid Laurier University Press.

Whitehorse, Emmi

1995 In My Family, the Women Ran Everything. In *Messengers of the Wind: Native American Women Tell Their Life Stories*, Jane Katz, ed., 55–65. New York: One World Ballantine Books.

Willeto, Angela A. A.

1999 Navajo Culture and Family Influences on Academic Success: Traditionalism Is Not a Significant Predictor of Achievement Among Young Navajos. *Journal of American Indian Education* 38 (2): 1–24.

Williams, Robert

1987 Meningitis and Unpaved Roads. *Social Science and Medicine* 24 (2): 109–15.

Willink, Roseanne S., and Paul G. Zolbrod

1996 *Weaving a World: Textiles and the Navajo Way of Seeing*. Santa Fe: Museum of New Mexico Press.

Witherspoon, Gary

1975 *Navajo Kinship and Marriage*. Chicago: University of Chicago Press.

1983 Language and Reality in Navajo World View. In *Handbook of North American Indians*, vol. 10: *Southwest*, Alfonso Ortiz, ed., 570–78. Washington, D.C.: Smithsonian Institution.

Wright, Anne

1982a An Ethnography of the Navajo Reproductive Cycle. *American Indian Quarterly* 6 (1–2): 52–70.

1982b Attitudes toward Childbearing and Menstruation among the Navajo. In *Anthropology of Human Birth*, Margarita Artschwager Kay, ed., 377–94. Philadelphia: F.A. Davis.

Wyman, Leland

1983 Navajo Ceremonial System. In *Handbook of North American Indians*, vol. 10: *Southwest*, Alfonso Ortiz, ed., 536–57. Washington, D.C.: Smithsonian Institution.

Wyman, Leland C., and Stuart K. Harris

1941 *Navajo Indian Medical Ethnobotany*. University of New Mexico Bulletin, Anthropological Series, vol. 3, no. 5. Albuquerque: University of New Mexico.

Young, Robert W.

1961 *The Navajo Yearbook: 1951–1961, A Decade of Progress*. Report no. 3, Bureau of Indian Affairs, Department of the Interior. Window Rock, Ariz.

Index

Note: Page numbers in italics indicate figures.

About the Author

Joanne McCloskey has studied Navajo cultural and health-related issues since 1983. These include studies of mother-infant interaction, women's roles, and childbearing patterns, alcohol abuse, and diabetes. Between 1998 and 2005, she taught social science and history classes at the Crownpoint campus of Diné College. She is currently conducting a study of the impact of the Women, Infant, and Children's program on the nutritional status of Navajo women and their children. She is a research assistant professor with the Department of Family and Community Medicine at the University of New Mexico.